BOMB
POWER

ALSO BY GARRY WILLS

BOMB
POWER

THE MODERN PRESIDENCY AND
THE NATIONAL SECURITY STATE

GARRY WILLS

THE PENGUIN PRESS

New York

2010

THE PENGUIN PRESS
Published by the Penguin Group
Penguin Group (USA) Inc., 375 Hudson Street, New York, New York 10014, U.S.A. •
Penguin Group (Canada), 90 Eglinton Avenue East, Suite 700, Toronto, Ontario,
Canada M4P 2Y3 (a division of Pearson Penguin Canada Inc.) • Penguin Books Ltd,
80 Strand, London WC2R 0RL, England • Penguin Ireland, 25 St. Stephen's Green,
Dublin 2, Ireland (a division of Penguin Books Ltd) • Penguin Books Australia Ltd,
250 Camberwell Road, Camberwell, Victoria 3124, Australia (a division of Pearson
Australia Group Pty Ltd) • Penguin Books India Pvt Ltd, 11 Community Centre,
Panchsheel Park, New Delhi–110 017, India • Penguin Group (NZ), 67 Apollo Drive,
Rosedale, North Shore 0632, New Zealand (a division of Pearson New Zealand Ltd) •
Penguin Books (South Africa) (Pty) Ltd, 24 Sturdee Avenue,
Rosebank, Johannesburg 2196, South Africa

Penguin Books Ltd, Registered Offices:
80 Strand, London WC2R 0RL, England

First published in 2010 by The Penguin Press,
a member of Penguin Group (USA) Inc.

Library of Congress Cataloging-in-Publication Data

Wills, Garry, 1934–
Bomb power : the modern presidency and the national security state / by Garry Wills.
p. cm.
Includes bibliographical references and index.
ISBN 978-1-59420-240-7
1. National security—United States—History—20th century.   2. National security—
United States—History—21st century.   3. Atomic bomb—Political aspects—United
States—History.   4. Presidents—United States—History—20th century.   5. Presidents—
United States—History—21st century.   6. Executive power—United States—History.
7. Secrecy—Political aspects—United States—History.   8. United States—Military
policy.   9. United States—Politics and government—1945–1989.   10. United States—
Politics and government—1989–   I. Title.
UA23.W4596   2010
355'.033073—dc22
2009030182

Printed in the United States of America

1   3   5   7   9   10   8   6   4   2

DESIGNED BY MEIGHAN CAVANAUGH

CONTENTS

IV. INFORMATION POWER

V. EXECUTIVE USURPATIONS

INTRODUCTION:
WAR IN PEACE

American society in peacetime began to experience wartime regulation. The awful dilemma was that in order to preserve an open society, the U.S. government took measures that in significant ways closed it down.

—SENATOR DANIEL PATRICK MOYNIHAN[1]

This book has a basic thesis, that the Bomb altered our subsequent history down to its deepest constitutional roots. It redefined the presidency, as in all respects America's "Commander in Chief" (a term that took on a new and unconstitutional meaning in this period). It fostered an anxiety of continuing crisis, so that society was pervasively militarized. It redefined the government as a National Security State, with an apparatus of secrecy and executive control. It redefined Congress, as an executor of the executive. And it redefined the Supreme Court, as a follower of the follower of the executive. Only one part of the government had the supreme power, the Bomb, and all else must defer to it, for the good of the nation, for the good of the world, for the custody of the future, in a world of perpetual emergency superseding ordinary constitutional restrictions.

All this grew out of the Manhattan Project, out of its product, and even more out of its process. The project's secret work, secretly funded at the behest of the President, was a model for the covert activities and overt authority of the government we now experience. Congress was kept in the dark about the Manhattan Project. Even Vice President

Harry Truman was kept in the dark—until he became President. Control over the mystery of Los Alamos presaged control over "the button" and "the football," which made the presidency a lone eminence above constitutional scrutiny. The care and keeping of the Bomb ramified across a worldwide network of military bases for supply, refueling areas, radar installments, radiation monitoring, and launch sites. The round-the-clock Strategic Air Command—which kept in the air nuclear-armed planes able to respond to orders anywhere in the world—set the pattern for later nuclear submarine deployment, satellite intelligence, and anti-ballistic space programs. The National Security State articulated itself in various intelligence agencies, the Central Intelligence Agency, the National Security Agency, the programs of classification and clearance, the new doctrines of executive power (the unitary executive without check from the other branches, or presidential signing statements that nullified laws passed by Congress). State secrets multiplied far beyond the power to clear them for release or for courts to demand their production.

In the past, wartime had led to suspension of various parts of the Constitution. Loyalists were rounded up in the Revolution. Suspected aliens were imprisoned in the Quasi-War of the 1790s. Lincoln canceled habeas corpus in the Civil War. Roosevelt interned Japanese-American citizens in World War II. These were seen as temporary measures, and the Constitution was generally restored to integrity after the crisis was over. But since the inception of World War II we have had a continuous state of impending or partial war, with retained constitutional restrictions. World War II faded into the Cold War, and the Cold War into the war on terror, giving us over two-thirds of a century of war in peace, with growing security measures, increased governmental secrecy, broad classification of information, procedural clearances of those citizens able to know what rulers were doing in secret. The requirements became more stringent, not less, after World War II and then again after the Cold War. Normality never returned, and the executive power increased decade by decade, reaching a new high in the twenty-first century—a continuous story of unidirectional increase in the executive power.

At the bottom of it all has been the Bomb. For the first time in our history, the President was given sole and unconstrained authority over all possible uses of the Bomb. All the preparations, protections, and auxiliary requirements for the Bomb's use, including secrecy about the whole matter and a worldwide deployment of various means of delivery, launching by land, sea, air, or space—a vast network for the study, development, creation, storage, guarding, and updating of nuclear arsenals, along with an immense intelligence apparatus to ascertain conditions for the weapons' maintenance and employment—all these were concentrated in the executive branch, immune from interference by the legislative or judicial branches. Every executive encroachment or abuse was liable to justification from this one supreme power.

If the President has the sole authority to launch nation-destroying weapons, he has license to use every other power at his disposal that might safeguard that supreme necessity. If he says he needs other and lesser powers, how can Congress or the courts discern whether he needs them when they have no supervisory role over the basis of the claim he is making? To challenge his authority anywhere is to threaten the one great authority. If he is weakened by criticism, how can other nations be sure he maintains the political ability to use his ultimate sanction? Every citizen is conscripted into the service of the Commander in Chief. As Vice President Dick Cheney put it on Fox News, in a December 21, 2008, interview with Chris Wallace:

The President of the United States now for fifty years is followed at all times, twenty-four hours a day, by a military aide carrying a football that contains the nuclear codes that he would use, and be authorized to use, in the event of a nuclear attack on the United States. He could launch the kind of devastating attack the world has never seen. *He doesn't have to check with anybody, he doesn't have to call the Congress, he doesn't have to check with the courts.* (Emphasis added)

The Vice President was using these facts precisely to justify the policies of the Bush administration on a whole range of issues—warrantless surveillance of American citizens, indefinite detention of suspects without legal representation or habeas corpus, kidnappings across the world by "rendition," imprisonment of those kidnapped in secret "black sites" outside the United States, "enhanced interrogation" of the accused by techniques like waterboarding. Cheney was right to say that the real logic for all these things is the President's solitary control of the Bomb. He was also right to say that something like what the Bush administration did was tried, adumbrated, or justified by other Presidents, going all the way back to the creation of the Manhattan Project, without any authorization, funding, or checks by the Congress. That was the seed of all the growing powers that followed. Every President since has found ways to leverage concessions on the basis of the great mystery of his power over the very continuance of the world. Executive power has basically been, since World War II, Bomb Power.

I.

THE MAKING OF
BOMB POWER

1

FATAL MIRACLE

At the end of his presidency, Dwight Eisenhower warned his countrymen against a "military-industrial complex." That might seem, at one level, historically ungrateful on Eisenhower's part, since a military-industrial complex won the war that made him famous. Without an incredible explosion of industrial productivity, put to military use, the armed forces of the United States could never have prevailed over the industrial might of Germany (and, to a lesser extent, Japan). The United States was drawn into World War II in a state of inadequate military preparation. The army (with its air force) and navy were not in full readiness. Their weaponry was meager and partly obsolete. The fleet was badly damaged in the first surprise of the war, at Pearl Harbor. The nation's capacity to produce was still lagging after a decade of the Depression. Yet in a mere four years—a shorter time than the span of either the Vietnam War or the Iraq War—mobilization on fronts all around the world was supplied with overwhelming resources. How did this miracle occur?

The lack of manpower was made up by a military draft far more inclusive than had occurred before or would occur after. Not to be in

uniform made any man of military age suspect. To be (or to be thought)
a "draft dodger" was a source of deep shame. Years later, in 1960, that
charge would be used in John Kennedy's presidential primary campaign against Hubert Humphrey. Factories and offices, drained of men
by the draft, filled the void with women, immigrants, and others previously unemployed. A heave of effort rearranged the national demo-
graphics for decades to come.

For material production, "conversion" from a peacetime economy
to a war economy both changed the focus and expanded the capacity
of American industry. Automobile companies stopped making cars to
build tanks and jeeps and supply vehicles. The Willow Run plant in
Michigan adapted Ford's assembly line to the mass manufacture of
B-24 bombers. Shipyards stopped building cruise ships and pleasure
boats to make aircraft carriers and landing vessels. Laboratories in corporations and universities turned their attention to military inventions
and technology—for radar, bomb sights, the proximity fuse (on anti-
aircraft shells), other new ordnance, new metals, synthetics. All this was
fueled by a massive injection of government money and the imposition
of government regulation and rationing. Businessmen who had resented and resisted government activism in the peaceful days of the
New Deal were forced at first, and glad afterward, to accept federal
intervention on a scale never before dreamed of in America.

They accepted the new rules gladly since they prospered under
them. The nation's gross domestic product doubled during the war and
real wages rose dramatically, so that the United States "was producing
an astonishing 50 percent of the world's goods and services at war's
end."[1] Not surprisingly, the conflict that leveled cities and displaced
whole populations all around the globe became known, in America, as
"the Good War." The government made it good. Federal power could
compel suppliers to give manufacturers new resources, requisition the
means for building new facilities, and commandeer the technology to
forge new products. All these resources, put into corporate hands dur-

ing the war, would still be available for use after victory. That is why conversion after the war—back to a peacetime economy—was as swift and rewarding as conversion had been during hostilities. Legal advantages given to "big business" were immense. And, human nature being what it is, ways were found to take even more illegal advantages, as Senator Harry Truman's investigation of war profiteering began to reveal.

What Truman found was only a small part of the profits made off the war. The rush of emergency, the willingness of the people to grant short-cuts if this produced goods so desperately needed, the difficulty of investigating procedures under the stress of deadlines for war production—all these led to the abuses described in a neglected but telling book by a man who, after the war, became a Civil War historian, Bruce Catton's *The War Lords of Washington* (1948).[2]

The war revealed what might be called "the dirty little secret" of American capitalism. The myth of capitalism is that the free market is the most efficient economic system. But it is not. Governmentally sponsored and regulated production is far more efficient. It was the war, not the New Deal, that finally reversed the Great Depression. In wartime, the government can compel the collection of raw material, channel research, subsidize new production methods without taking time for them to prove profitable, redistribute labor pools, eliminate distracting competition by the incompetent. All these things happened during the military-industrial explosion of the 1940s, without which there would have been no American victory. That is why, in wartime, governmental interference with business competition is always, in some measure, adopted. When it is important to get things done, and done fast, the government must be relied on.[3] War, which by a superficial logic destroys so many assets, is often good for the economy—at least for the economy of the winner. Sometimes even the economy of the loser gains—as when England lost its war with the nascent United States. The results of the Good War were in this way comforting.

Of course, people are not going to submit to war's regimentation unless there is an emergency which makes them willing to submit. Men will not be drafted in peacetime. Competitors will not give up their efforts if the war does not make them willing to stop making cars and other commercial products. Consumers will not give up luxuries unless a greater need supervenes. Scientists will not give up pure research for applied invention unless military technology becomes an overriding priority. There is a real argument for the free market—but it is not an argument based on its being efficient. The argument for the free market is that it is *free*. But freedom becomes superfluous if an enemy is threatening the very basis of all freedoms.

MANHATTAN PROJECT

All these points were made most persuasively by a miracle within the larger miracle of wartime productivity—the invention, production, testing, and deployment of a brand-new thing on earth, the atom bomb. Which occurred in a mere two and a half years. The triumph of secrecy, of vast tax moneys unaccounted for, of research compelled, of resources commandeered, of human tasks assigned, of huge sites built or expanded—only the combination of all these things led to an achievement that some of the most knowledgeable experts considered impossible. The project would not have succeeded, certainly not in the constricted time available, without strict governmental supervision—and, more to the point, without *military* control. After President Franklin Roosevelt secretly authorized the effort to produce a bomb, it was his decision, and that of his advisers, that the project must not be trusted to civilian management. Private individuals could not coordinate the scattered efforts of laboratories and universities, keep the project secret, pre-empt funds and resources, draw on engineering and manufacturing firms, and evade congressional oversight. All these things called for the cover of a military operation.

One of the main reasons for putting the operation under military discipline was to hide the funding. In a time of war, when vast sums were being poured out for military purposes, the discretionary spending of the Pentagon could hide even the two billion dollars (in 1940s money) that the Bomb finally cost. General Leslie Richard "Dick" Groves, who was put in charge of the project, had clashed with Congress over military spending when he was a chief engineer in the Quartermaster General's office. Senator Truman questioned expenditures on the Pentagon building when Groves was completing that project early in the war. To avoid such oversight, Groves wanted Congress to know nothing about the Bomb until it was not only completed but used on the enemy.

Groves was competing with many other war urgencies. When he looked for a secret site for the Bomb's final assembly, he needed an isolated place inland from both coasts, at the very time when army training spots and ordnance testing areas were shouldering their way toward such prime locales. On every bid for labor and materials, he found competitors flocking around him. He made sure that he was granted a AAA priority for war needs, but there were many other programs with that rating. He had powerful men running interference for him—Secretary of War Henry Stimson, Chief of Staff George C. Marshall, Chairman of the National Defense Research Committee Vannevar Bush, and Army Chief of Supply Brehon B. Somervell—but they all labored under the difficulty that they could not explain why their demands outranked requests for more obviously useful and immediate military needs. Colonel Groves was promoted to Brigadier General to protect his back against military men who outranked him, but even so it took all his abrasive aggressiveness to overcome the obstacles in his way.

He succeeded so well that Senator Truman left the project alone while still presiding over his investigating committee, and remained unaware of it when he became Vice President in 1944. He was not informed about it until he succeeded Roosevelt in 1945, just as construction of the Bomb was about to be completed. Of course, as Senator he learned something about an expenditure on the scale of the Manhattan Project, but Secretary of War Stimson warned him off, saying it was "a very important secret development," one that only "two or three men in the whole world . . . know about." Truman assured him, "You won't have to say another word to me. Whenever you say that to me that's all I want to hear." When new suspicions arose about money spent at Hanford in Washington State (where plutonium was secretly being processed), Truman did send a man to ask what was going on; but that envoy was told that the Senator was breaking an agreement with the Secretary of War, and Stimson dressed Truman down.[4] This was a harbinger of later developments, when the mere mention of "national security" would take a subject out of the purview of Congress, the courts, the press, and the public. Even when Roosevelt died, though Stimson told Truman on his first day as President that he must inform him about a new weapon, he waited twelve more days before letting him know that the weapon was an atomic bomb.[5]

Keeping all the secrets involved in the project was a massive achievement. The main goal—that the Germans and Japanese should not learn of it—was accomplished to perfection. It is true that some of America's allies knew of the program. British scientists at the Cavendish Laboratory had done pioneer work, and were included in the project from the beginning. The Soviets became aware of the effort through espionage, but how close the project was to success remained unknown until the Bomb was actually used on Hiroshima. The degree of silence is astonishing, given the scale of the operation. It involved many dozens of sites, hundreds of thousands of workers, and billions of dollars. When Groves took over the project, he knit together research that was already going on at Cavendish, the University of Chicago, the University of California at Berkeley, Harvard (whose president, James B. Conant, was a scientific organizer for the program), MIT (Groves's alma mater), and Columbia. At Berkeley, a physics professor, J. Robert Oppenheimer, ran an international (but secret) conference of physicists in the summer of 1942 to consider the feasibility of atomic weaponry. In December of that year scientists working with Enrico Fermi at the University of Chicago achieved the first atomic chain reaction.[6]

The drain of physicists from all the best universities was noticed, of course—but as men were being drawn from all classes by the draft, or for work on other scientific projects (like radar research), this did not seem extraordinary. Nonetheless, physicists who left from the same university were asked to go to other cities to book their tickets for New Mexico, so it would not be apparent that a number of them had the same out-of-the-way destination.[7] Various cover stories were used according to different circumstances. It was said that some were working on developments in ordnance, including military rockets. The scientists at the principal undisclosed location (Los Alamos, New Mexico) were technically paid with checks from the University of California at Berkeley, as if their work were still academic. The university was a conduit for government funds unknown to Congress. Well-known scientists took assumed names during their travel and residence. New Mexican authorities issued driver's licenses with "Name on File" where the names would normally be. When it came time to vote in 1944, some Los Alamos personnel could not register because they would have had to reveal their true names.[8]

Groves built up three main industrial sites that were cloaked in secrecy: Hanford in Washington State to collect, extract, and purify plutonium; Oak Ridge in Tennessee for enrichment of uranium; and Los Alamos in New Mexico for the construction of the Bomb itself. He also developed the test site at Alamogordo, New Mexico, secret air bases in America to test the delivery planes, and the Tinian Island staging area in the Pacific for the Bomb's delivery. The three main sites were extensive complexes, with many buildings, large installations of equipment calling for heavy technical maintenance, extensive energy needs (Oak Ridge drew electricity from the Tennessee Valley Authority), and large workforces. Most of the public's attention would later be given to the final place of assembly, Los Alamos. But many industrial and academic laboratories, testing sites and staging areas, and construction and shipping firms were involved in the huge effort.

Work eventually went on at over eighty places under Groves's supervision. His earlier commissions for military construction in the 1930s, culminating in his great feat of raising the Pentagon building, had made him familiar with industrial firms and their research and development departments; and he was able to enlist, on secret terms, the highest officials at Du Pont, General Electric, Westinghouse, Eastman Kodak, Allis-Chalmers, and other companies. These firms did not know what larger project they were working on—Groves gave them limited assignments, keeping their ultimate use mysterious.

Groves had been given an interim assignment between completion of the Pentagon and work on the Manhattan Project: construction of the Holston Ordnance Works in Tennessee, to develop and manufacture the super-explosive RDX (ten times more powerful than TNT). This project alone ended up with 242 buildings, 141 magazines, and hundreds of miles of roads and train tracks, set in 6,500 acres of secluded land.[9] Groves would have to build on an even greater scale at the various atomic sites. Hanford alone employed 132,000 people in the course of its work, almost as many as had been employed in building the Panama Canal.[10] Just one of the electromagnetic plants at Oak Ridge had 200 buildings, raised on 825 acres.[11] At Los Alamos, by 1945, there were 3,500 people—scientists, soldiers, construction workers, staff, and families—living inside a triple ring of fences, with sentries on horseback or in jeeps patrolling the circuit twenty-four hours a day.

The tech area, inside the inmost ring of fencing, had 37 buildings, and the support structures totaled 350 buildings and 200 trailers.[12]

The scientists involved in the Manhattan Project were, most of them, no great admirers of the military. They had to give up their deepest professional instincts to submit to Groves's dictates. They were accustomed to the free exchange of ideas, to following their curiosity into intriguing questions, to discussing openly any uses that might be made of their discoveries. All these freedoms would be curtailed if not canceled once they were dragooned into the Manhattan Project, where they were censored, surveilled, policed, told what research they must engage in, what part of the project each must work on, what they were excluded from. Groves originally meant to confine the scientists to limited assignments, performed in ignorance of other parts of the effort—the discipline he imposed on outside corporations working for him.

But the director of the scientific work, chosen by Groves personally, was J. Robert Oppenheimer, who persuaded the General that scientists had to explore problems together, criticizing one another's work and developing one another's insights. Oppenheimer suggested that a total isolation of the working team from the outside world would meet the security requirements while allowing for free play of ideas within the compound. But even within this area the scientists were not supposed to use certain words—"Bomb," for instance (it was "Gadget"), or "physicist." Papers were locked up after their use, blackboards immediately erased.

Groves gave in reluctantly to the idea of free discussion, then tried to make the resulting center into an army camp. He wanted to draft the scientists, put them in uniform, lodge them in barracks, exclude wives and children. Oppenheimer said that he would never be able to recruit top scientists for confinement away from their families for several years. Even army camps allowed men passes to visit their wives— and these scientists would not be permitted free travel away from their work. Again Groves had to give in. Wives and children were admitted, so long as they, too, were isolated from the outside world. This meant that the compound had to have schools, churches, health services for women and children. The isolation of the company set the young couples there to energetic baby making, which kept the resident obstetrician extremely busy and General Groves uneasy. The baby boom led to sly limericks and other naughty poems, the politest of which, says historian Jennet Conant, ran like this:

> *The General's in a stew,*
> *He trusted you and you.*
> *He thought you'd be scientific,*
> *Instead you're just prolific,*
> *And what is he to do?*[13]

Oppenheimer was able to recruit the superstars and coming stars of physics, including famous men driven from Europe by repression—the Hungarians Leo Szilard, Edward Teller, and John von Neumann; the Germans Hans Bethe, Rudolf Peierls, and (the spy) Klaus Fuchs; the Austrian Victor Weisskopf, the Ukrainian George Kistiakowsky, the Pole Stanislaw Ulam, the Dane Niels Bohr, the Briton James Chadwick; and the Italians Enrico Fermi, Emilio Segrè, and Bruno Rossi. This immigrant talent was joined by brilliant Americans—Luis Alvarez, Robert Bacher, Kenneth Bainbridge, Richard Feynman, Philip Morrison, I. I. Rabi, Robert Serber, Robert R. Wilson, and others, along with Oppenheimer himself.[14] Groves had a team of security men spying on the scientists even in their isolated community, and he resented the use of foreign languages his security team could not understand and report on. One day Groves himself overheard Fermi speaking Italian with Segrè and he told them to stop talking Hungarian.[15]

Though the superstars were important for guidance and inspiration, most of the work was done by young explorers in the comparatively new field of atomic-particle physics, many of them future Nobel Prize winners. The average age of the scientific community was twenty-four. Theoretical physicists tend to do their best work when they are very young—seven of the younger men at Los Alamos had Nobel Prizes in their future. A symbol of this was the greatly gifted Richard Feynman, who came to Los Alamos with his freshly earned doctorate from Princeton. He was twenty-four and already showed the brilliance that would make him a Nobel winner. He was also a world-class cutup, whose clowning covered deep concern for his young wife being treated for tuberculosis at a hospital in nearby Albuquerque.

Feynman was occasionally let out of the compound, trailed by spies, to visit his wife, but he kept in touch with her through constant correspondence, through which he tweaked the censors. He amused himself by having his wife make up a new code for him to decipher with each letter. The censors eventually demanded that she send them the key to the code, which they would turn over to Feynman only after he had puzzled it out. Few problems evaded him. He picked the locks in the compound and cracked the safes where classified documents were stored, to show he could enter them at will. He found a hole in the security fence made by local workers wanting a shortcut home, then circled through it to check back in repeatedly at the entry gate, with no evidence he had ever left the premises.[16] Younger children tunneled under the intermediate fence, while older ones climbed over it, to play in the mesa's caves—they used lookouts to go undetected by the jeep patrols.

General Groves did not think such antics were amusing, but Oppenheimer convinced him that the inhabitants of his pressure cooker were under great stress and needed ways to blow off steam, some of the ways silly. The company indulged in amateur theatricals, Oppenheimer playing a corpse in a hastily rehearsed *Arsenic and Old Lace*.[17] Theoreticians, cooped up, bent their great minds to different uses—Fermi to square dancing, Kistiakowsky to poker, Bethe to skiing, Teller to the piano,

Feynman to bongo drums.[18] Many hiked, picnicked, and fished. There was a lot of drinking—the thin desert air on the mesa, eight thousand feet above sea level, made booze take quick effect.[19] Oppenheimer's wife was an alcoholic.[20] Oppenheimer himself mixed famously potent vodka martinis. With so many temperamental stars pent up together, anger flared at times. Groves hated Szilard; Teller resented Oppenheimer. Prima donnas who were crowded together in primitive housing, on a site alternately muddy and dusty according to season, working under great pressure, found it hard to maintain control of themselves. It is astonishing that Oppenheimer generally kept the peace, easing resentments against the military guards, the censors, the tapped phones, the opened letters.

Some scientists refused to join the mysterious program they were sounded out for—which is why it was kept mysterious in the first approaches to them. The military authorities debated what to do with people who knew what was going on at Los Alamos but either refused to join in or left the confines. Groves wanted to draft them into the army and either reassign them to Los Alamos or send them to some distant military outpost, to be watched over for the duration of the war. One of his more fanatical security officers—a Russian-American anti-Communist zealot named Boris Pash—seems to have had more drastic measures in mind. An FBI agent reported on one of Pash's plans for dealing with men who knew too much about the research:

> Pash has been negotiating for authority from Washington for the purpose of Shanghaiing various Communists employed in the [radiation] laboratory and taking them out to sea where they would be thoroughly questioned after the Russian manner. [Deleted] states that he realized that any statement so obtained could not be used in prosecution, but apparently Pash did not intend to have anyone available for prosecuting after questioning.[21]

Pash was convinced that Oppenheimer was a Communist. Groves knew he could not succeed without Oppenheimer's essential contribution as leader of the scientific team—but he put Pash in the compound to spy continually on Oppenheimer.

The elegant Oppenheimer and the dumpy Groves made a visual contrast that called to mind, according to the age of the beholder, Mutt and Jeff, Stan and Ollie, or even Quixote and Sancho. But in both men's cases, appearance was misleading. Oppenheimer resembled a medieval ascetic, a monk like Houdon's brooding *Saint Bruno,* a giant mind inside a skeleton. But there was a dog-whistle signaling of sensuality, too. It showed in his eyes, so intensely blue they might as well have been radioactive for their impact on women. The accountant who became the guardian of clearances at Los Alamos said she went to meet him expecting to turn down his offer of a job, but took one look at him and instantly accepted. She wrote: "I never met a person with a magnetism that hit you so fast and so completely."[22] Another of Oppenheimer's secretaries said, "Part of his legend was that all women fell on their faces in front of him."[23] Everyone noticed the eyes.[24] Even the gruff soldier Groves said, "He has the bluest eyes I've ever seen."[25]

Groves, by contrast, was as charismatic as a bulldozer. A body inflated by his love of chocolate belied the fact that he had been a good athlete, a football player and wrestler at West Point who still played a strategic game of tennis. He had a more than rudimentary scientific training, at MIT, West Point, the army engineering school, and the War College, and in the field as a construction chief. But that worked against him when he tried to claim to the scientists working under him that he understood what they were doing—which is like a man who played schoolyard basketball telling Michael Jordan that he was acquainted with his skills. Groves's defensive boasting exacerbated the contempt some of the physicists had for military minds in general. What Groves had was organizational genius, a shrewd assessment of men, and driving will. It was a tribute to the judgment of Vannevar Bush and James Conant that they saw he was just the man to perform an almost impossible task. It is, moreover, a tribute to the characters of Oppenheimer and Groves that they sensed how their styles might mesh—one of them seductive, the other bullying—in order to make the whole thing work. Oppenheimer was not so foolish as to underestimate Groves. And Groves was sensible enough not to resent Oppenheimer for his brilliance—as he did some of the other scientists.

It surprised many that Groves put Oppenheimer in charge of the physicists. The eminent I. I. Rabi questioned Oppenheimer's dabbling in mystical writings, and considered him an improbable leader for a scientific project.[26] Edward Teller thought Hans Bethe, who was more popular in the scientific community, should have been put in charge—but Groves, who knew he would ultimately have to give an account of his work to Congress, realized that Senators and Representatives, with an eye on their constituents, would not be happy having a German national in charge of an American weapon. Oppenheimer's Berkeley colleague Ernest O. Lawrence might have made a more obvious choice, but Groves did not want to take him away from his vital work on the cyclotron he was perfecting for creating the high-energy beams needed to bombard atoms and split them.

Jennet Conant, the granddaughter of James Conant, the presidential adviser on the Bomb, has an interesting thesis. She thinks that Groves saw some of his own qualities in Oppenheimer. Both men were stalled below the peak of their own professions. Groves had graduated early from West Point, rushed through because World War I was being waged, then stranded in the flood of lieutenants created by that conflict. Despite solid work in the 1920s and 1930s, he was only a colonel at age forty-four, until he got a boost to hold his own in this project.[27] Oppenheimer was about to turn forty in 1942, and he would be placed over a number of distinguished holders of the Nobel Prize in Physics, though he had never won that honor. Nor was he likely to. Theoretical physicists, it has already been noted, usually do their breakthrough work early on. Oppenheimer, for all his brilliance, had not focused on one problem and made it his signature achievement. He had broader cultural interests than many scientists, which made some think him a dilettante.

I. I. Rabi, who understood that Oppenheimer was on a spiritual journey (away, among other things, from his Jewishness), confirms Conant's insight. Rabi's wife had been a high-school student with Oppenheimer at the Ethical Culture School in New York, and Rabi had known him from Leipzig in the 1920s. He thought Oppenheimer dazzled people by mingling the halos of an Einstein and a Gandhi. But that very combination hampered his purely scientific career.

> With the vast intellectual arsenal at his disposal, there were important questions in physics in which Oppenheimer worked diligently, where he was very often on the track of the solutions, and where his taste in the selection of the questions was impeccable, and yet—as in the case of quantum electrodynamics—the definitive solution came from others. In pondering this subject, it seems to me that in some respects Oppenheimer was overeducated in those fields which lie outside the scientific tradition, such as his interest in religion, in the Hindu religion in particular, which resulted in a feeling for the mystery of the universe that surrounded him almost like a fog. He saw physics clearly, looking toward what had already been done, but at the border he tended to feel that there was much more of the mysterious and novel than there actually was. He was insufficiently confident of the power of the intellectual tools he already possessed, and did not drive his thought to the very end because he felt instinctively that new ideas and new methods were necessary to go further than he and his students had already gone. Some may call it a lack of faith, but in my opinion it was more a turning away from the hard, crude methods of theoretical physics into a mystical realm of broad intuition.[28]

Teller was more hostile to Oppenheimer (and envious of him). He would later tell an FBI agent, "He also had great ambitions in science and realizes that he is not as great a physicist as he would like to be."[29]

A brilliant synthesizer and teacher, Oppenheimer had shown no gift, before Los Alamos, for organization and administration, the skills that would be most needed there. But Groves, with his eye for sizing up people who could get things done, saw the deep ambition Oppenheimer covered with his surface charm. Groves, Rabi says, had "an eccentric administrative genius."[30] Oppenheimer and Groves guessed that they could use each other to make history. Once committed, each drove himself and others unremittingly. Groves was the iron fist, Oppenheimer the velvet glove. The very deficiencies in each one, taken singly, interlocked—two defective parts making a perfect whole.

When the Bomb was successfully exploded on July 16, 1945, in a test code-named Trinity, it proved more powerful than the scientists had expected, the equal of fifteen thousand to twenty thousand tons of dynamite. Oppenheimer returned to Los Alamos to cheers. His team had won. Even before the Bomb was dropped, the team savored victory from this desert test. Later, the publicist of the program whom Groves had recruited said of Trinity: "One felt as though one were present at the moment of creation when God said, 'Let there be light.'"[31] President Truman would call the Bomb "the greatest thing in history," and his revelation of it to the nation "the happiest announcement I ever made."[32] There was, at first, a proud and proprietary feeling among the Bomb's makers. Richard Feynman did a kind of victory dance with his bongo drums after the Trinity explosion.[33] When the Los Alamos gatekeeper, Dorothy McKibbin, heard of the explosion at Hiroshima, she turned proudly to her son and said, "That's our bomb."[34]

The great seal of the United States was to be redesigned three weeks after Hiroshima, and President Truman suggested that lightning bolts be substituted for the arrows in the eagle's claw, as a symbol of the Bomb's sudden and obliterative might.[35] He was accused of wearing the Bomb like a gun on his hip, and he boasted of America's atomic monopoly. Oppenheimer reported this exchange with the President:

"When will the Russians be able to build the bomb?" asked Truman.

"I don't know," said Oppenheimer.

"I know."

"When?"

"Never."[36]

Initially, at least, Truman thought that the secrecy around the Bomb could be maintained forever. His Secretary of War, Henry Stimson—like the President, a poker player—told him that the Bomb gave America "a royal straight flush" in world power.[37]

Some would have different feelings about the Manhattan Project—that it was a *fatal* miracle because of its awesome product. But it was also a fatal miracle because of its process. The military-industrial complex, with a poisonous admixture of government and secrecy, had scored a triumph that would show the way to many other governmental activities. It offered a seductive model for dealing with Russians as well as Germans, Communists as well as Nazis, terrorists as well as totalitarians. The secrecy that had enveloped Los Alamos would steal quietly across the entire American landscape in the years to come.

2

ATOMIC POLITICS

Two months before the Trinity test proved that the Bomb worked, Germany surrendered. Many of the scientists involved in the Manhattan Project were under the impression that German scientists had been racing toward their own creation of an atom bomb. But even before VE (Victory in Europe) Day, May 8, that fear was undermined. It was part of General Groves's extraordinary grant of power that he could send spies into Europe trying to pick up evidence of German progress in atomic research. He had other personnel tracking German collection of uranium samples. He even sent an agent, the intellectual baseball star Moe Berg, to explore the possibility of kidnapping or killing the leading physicist, Werner Heisenberg, to drain off German expertise.[1] As American forces took parts of Europe, Groves had his old stalker of Oppenheimer, Boris Pash, race through the liberated areas rounding up German physicists who might know anything about atomic research.[2]

As it became clear that the Germans had not been building an atomic weapon, many of the scientists in the Manhattan Project began to lose their desire to unleash such a weapon on human targets. Germany, not

Japan, had been on their minds when they began their work. Leo
Szilard, who had originally urged Roosevelt to develop the Bomb,
tried to reach the President before he died on April 12, 1945—three
months before the Trinity test—to protest a first use on humans. The
terrifying results of the Trinity test made others even more uneasy.

But the decision to use the Bomb had been reached and conveyed
to the new President, Harry Truman, even before the Trinity explosion.
There would have been no debate over use of the Bomb if Germany
had still been at war. It had been designed expressly for that purpose.
But after VE Day Secretary of War Stimson, with President Truman's
approval, set up the neutrally named Interim Committee to decide
whether to use the Bomb on Japan. The presidents of Harvard and
MIT were members of the committee, which unanimously recommended on June 1 "that the bomb should be used against Japan as soon
as possible; that it be used on a war plant surrounded by workers'
homes; and that it be used without prior warning."[3] None of the official
advisers to Truman, military or civilian, disagreed with this recommendation, though one member of the Interim Committee, Undersecretary of the Navy Ralph Bard, three weeks later changed his mind on
one point, the phrase "without prior warning."[4]

Two other committees confirmed the decision by the Interim Committee. The Scientific Panel of four physicists (Oppenheimer, Fermi,
Ernest Lawrence of Berkeley, and Karl Compton, the president of
MIT) rejected the idea of a demonstration of the Bomb away from
populated areas, and concluded "we see no acceptable alternative to
direct military use." The Target Committee convened by General Groves
made a list of Japanese cities for use of the Bomb, deliberately choosing ones not yet damaged by the firebomb raids (which could make it
hard to see the extent of the Bomb's own devastation) and ones with
dense populations.[5] Stimson wrote in his diary how he explained the
choice of previously unbombed cities to President Truman: "[I said] I
was a little fearful that before we could get ready, the Air Force might

have Japan so thoroughly bombed out that the new weapon would not have a fair background to show its strength. He laughed and said he understood."[6]

Given Japanese endurance of the firebombings (which had killed hundreds of thousands) and the suicidal holdouts on Okinawa, it was felt that only an immense shock could break Japanese resistance. That is why Groves never considered dropping just one bomb. It would later be asked why Nagasaki was bombed only three days after Hiroshima—why not wait for a Japanese response? But the attacks were always seen as a one-two punch, with the second (plutonium-implosion) bomb more powerful than the first (uranium-explosion) one, to suggest an endless escalation in the power of this new weapon. Oppenheimer argued forcibly that only a supreme proof of the Bomb's terrifying power could guarantee that it would never be used again.[7] Oppenheimer had even suggested that several bombs should be dropped on the same day, to end the agony at once—though Groves said that would not let the first drop be a guide or corrective to the use of later ones.[8]

Leo Szilard and seventy other scientists tried unsuccessfully to get a protest to Truman before he left for the Potsdam Conference with other Allied leaders (July 17–August 2).[9] But news of the successful Trinity test reached Truman in Potsdam, and he never considered reversing the recommendations of the three panels that had already sealed Japan's fate. Szilard and others felt the Bomb should be demonstrated in some unpopulated place, with full publication of its powers. But Oppenheimer's Scientific Panel had already rejected this idea. There was no assurance that the Bomb would show its potential aside from a military target, and there was a lingering suspicion that it might not work at all outside the controlled conditions, long preparations, and stationary placement of the Trinity explosion.

The Bomb tested at Trinity was a plutonium-implosion one, and the first scheduled for Japan was a uranium-explosion one, not yet fully tested. Oppenheimer and his fellow panelists feared that if the United

States announced that a terrible new weapon was being demonstrated and it somehow did not work, or work as effectively as was trumpeted, the war effort would be set back. For that matter, there were uncertainties even in a military use, which is why the Interim Committee decided against giving the Japanese a warning. Could the Bomb be properly triggered from a moving plane, coping with weather conditions, with the possibility of anti-aircraft fire, with the timing of the trigger mechanisms and the functioning of the plane and its bombsight? In fact, the second target had not been Nagasaki, but Kokura. When the plane could not get through cloud cover at Kokura, after three runs that brought up artillery flak, the pilot went on to a backup city, Nagasaki, but found it also clouded over. Working to a twenty-second break in the clouds, the plane dropped its bomb off-target, so its greater power caused fewer casualties (forty thousand killed, forty thousand injured) than the bomb at Hiroshima (seventy thousand killed, fifty thousand injured).[10] After the detour to a different target, there was not enough fuel left to get the B-29 back to its base at Tinian. It barely reached an American strip on Okinawa.

The difficulties of delivering an atom bomb from the air, very much on the minds of the men commissioned by Groves to do it in 1945, were confirmed in the first test of a bomb after the war, at Bikini Island, on July 1, 1946. The point of that exercise was to prove that the Bomb could be effective against navies. More than ninety vessels (captured, obsolete, or surplus ships) were stationed like sitting ducks in Bikini Lagoon. The plane, sent out under chosen conditions, with no enemy opposition or adverse weather, dropped the Bomb half a mile wide of the target, so only five ships were sunk.[11] This confirmed what risks were entailed in the drops on Japan.

The later justification of the atomic attacks, offered to the American people, was that use of the Bomb was necessary to prevent massive American casualties during an invasion of Japan. Secretary of War Stimson claimed that there would be a million American casualties in such an invasion. Some people, on the other hand—including Generals Douglas MacArthur and Dwight Eisenhower, and Admirals William Leahy and William Halsey—believed that Japan would have surrendered under continued firebombing and blockade, without the need for an invasion.[12] The best judgment on this was reached by the United States Strategic Bombing Survey of 1946. After employing 1,150 investigators, and writing two hundred detailed reports, the survey found that the people of Japan were starving and displaced, the naval and air defenses were crippled, the will to resist was broken: "Sixty-four percent of the population stated that they had reached a point prior to surrender where they felt personally unable to go on with the war."[13] The Summary Report, under the supervision of Paul Nitze and others, concluded:

> It seems clear that, even without the atomic bombing attacks, air supremacy over Japan could have exerted sufficient pressure to bring about unconditional surrender and obviate the need for invasion. Based on a detailed investigation of all the facts, and supported by the testimony of the surviving Japanese leaders involved, it is the Survey's opinion that certainly prior to 31 December 1945, and in all probability prior to 1 November 1945, Japan would have surrendered even if the atomic bombs had not been dropped, even if Russia had not entered the war, and even if no invasion had been planned or contemplated.[14]

But the mood at the end of the war was not to wait one more day, not to risk one more life, if the war could be ended with a quick knockout blow. There was exasperation that the Japanese did not recognize the end of their hopes with the fall of Italy and Germany. There was residual anger over Pearl Harbor, inflamed racism at reports of Japanese war atrocities, and that hate (*Hass*) that Clausewitz calls the real fuel of war. President Truman, when he officially announced the dropping of the Bomb on Hiroshima, said, "The Japanese began the war from the air at Pearl Harbor. They have been repaid manyfold."[15] General Groves, when he was asked to consider the innocent Japanese civilians who would die from the Bomb, said he was thinking, instead, of the thousands of Americans who died on the Bataan Death March in the Philippines. General Henry "Hap" Arnold thanked him for expressing his own feeling with those words.[16] It was time to avenge the fallen, life for life.

Whether an invasion of Japan occurred or not, the mere possibility of its happening without use of the Bomb was a nightmare prospect to Groves and other officials. If it became known that the United States had a knockout weapon it did not use, the families of any Americans killed after the development of the Bomb would be furious. The public, the press, and Congress would turn on the President and his advisers. There would have been a cry to impeach President Truman and court-martial General Groves. The administration would be convicted of spending billions of dollars and draining massive amounts of brainpower and manpower from other war projects, and all for nothing. This was the truly terrifying prospect that made use of the Bomb an easy, if not inevitable, choice for those who had harbored their secret project so long and wanted to reveal it with a supreme vindication. Groves even suggested that Truman would be betraying the memory of President Roosevelt, who authorized the Bomb's development, if he rejected its use.[17] The Bomb's tenders had put themselves in a position where they could not *not* use it. They were now the prisoners of their own creation.

Groves was always concerned about the way the Manhattan Project would be revealed—to Congress and to the nation. Early on he had gone to the *New York Times* and put its science writer, William L. Laurence, on his own payroll, taking him secretly to Los Alamos to write the first statements, after the drops on Japan, about the Bomb's creation, and to present the project as a triumph of humanity, as the way to end not only this war but all future wars. Laurence said that the

Bomb gave America a literally godlike power—"a sense, you might say, of divinity"—over life.[18] Laurence became so associated with glorification of the Bomb that he became known at the *New York Times* as "Atomic Bill."

At Los Alamos, the main concern was not with dropping or not dropping the two bombs available but with producing more, as soon as possible, in case those did not do the trick. The directors already planned to create a stockpile of bombs, to discourage other nations from trying to equal America's lead. Groves was so aware of the difficulties he had overcome—the lavish outlay of funds, the processing of plutonium and uranium, the dragooning of expertise from many nations, the disciplines of secrecy—that he doubted any other country could equal such a feat in the foreseeable future. But just to make sure, Groves was taking measures to counter any Soviet attempt at making the Bomb. Even before the Germans had surrendered, General Groves circumvented the State Department to send squads into Europe to take objectives before the Soviet army could. He asked General Marshall to have the Army Air Corps destroy a plant at Oranienburg that might be producing uranium, and to do it before the Soviets could reach it. Marshall turned the job over to General Carl "Tooey" Spaatz, who performed as Groves desired.[19]

After Japan surrendered, Groves wanted to keep the Bomb in military custody and continue the work at Los Alamos. The Interim Committee wrote a recommendation, with Groves helping to craft it, that would keep control of atomic energy in the War Department. The bill was reported to Congress, sponsored by Representative Andrew May and Senator Edwin Johnson. President Truman wanted quick action on the May-Johnson Bill.[20] But without the justification of the war, such freedom from accountability was rightly seen as a threat to ordinary democratic procedures. Herbert Marks, a close aide to Undersecretary of State Dean Acheson, made an inspection tour of Los Alamos and was appalled by what he saw:

[Los Alamos] bore no relation to the industrial or social life of the country; it was a separate state, with its own airplanes and its own factories and its thousands of secrets. It had a peculiar sovereignty, one that could bring about the end, peacefully or violently, of all other sovereignties.[21]

Custody of the Bomb had to be brought back under civilian control. This was accomplished when Congress shelved the May-Johnson Bill and passed the McMahon Act in 1946, establishing the Atomic Energy Commission, a civilian body to control all domestic uses of atomic energy.

Most of the Manhattan Project's scientists, like Oppenheimer, planned to get away from their war work and go back to their universities or institutes. But Groves wanted to keep making bombs, to create an arsenal that would absorb all the available uranium and plutonium and make any challenge by others (read: the Soviet Union) unthinkable. Norris Bradbury, who replaced Groves as the director of the Los Alamos laboratory under AEC supervision, thought rather in terms of more elegant solutions to bomb construction. The Hiroshima Bomb had weighed nine thousand pounds, the Nagasaki one ten thousand— unwieldy things to handle and deliver. Bradbury would pursue his own dream of more usable bombs for the next quarter century (1945–1970) as he directed work at Los Alamos:

We had only scratched the surface of atomic bombs. We had, to put it bluntly, lousy bombs. We had a set of bombs which were totally wrongly matched to the production empire. . . . [We needed] a new weapon whose aims should be . . . increased reliability, ease of assembly, safety, and performance; in short, a better weapon. . . . Possibly in six months, possibly in a year—maybe in a few years—weaponeering will stop, but our present lead is our chief weapon in procuring a peace—we must not lose it until that peace and that cooperation is established.[22]

Bradbury thought that the next big step might be a fusion bomb, which had been the dream of Edward Teller at Los Alamos, instead of a fission one. (A fusion bomb releases energy by fusing hydrogen's atomic nuclei together, a fission one by exploding a uranium nucleus.) Teller was so insistent in calling for this development, from early on in the Manhattan Project, that Oppenheimer had shunted him aside to work on it while the rest of the team concentrated on the more immediately achievable fission process. Oppenheimer put Hans Bethe in charge of the theoretical team to accomplish this, a decision that Teller deeply resented. After the war, Teller went back to the University of Chicago, but he kept urging production of the fusion bomb, and he would return to Los Alamos after the Soviets tested their first atomic bomb in 1949.

Emphasis on atomic supremacy was driven by fear of the Soviet Union, as were all aspects of American foreign policy. After George Kennan sent his famous "Long Telegram" from Moscow in 1946, arguing that the Soviet Union was expansionist and had to be contained, the Secretary of State appointed by President Truman, James F. Byrnes, set up a committee to control international use of atomic energy. Byrnes made his undersecretary, Dean Acheson, the chairman of the committee, and Acheson recruited as his co-chairman the head of the Tennessee Valley Authority, David Lilienthal. Acheson later wrote: "All the participants would, I think, agree that the most stimulating and creative mind among us was Robert Oppenheimer's."[23] This distinguished panel decided that policing the atomic research of all nations would not be acceptable to suspicious regimes like the Soviet one, so it proposed setting up an international agency to monopolize possession and distribution of uranium and plutonium.

Presenting this proposal to the UN was an assignment President Truman gave to the aging financier Bernard Baruch, a purported "wise man." Baruch, who distrusted the members of Acheson's committee, recast its proposal to his own liking, reintroducing the idea of policing other nations, with the certain result that the Soviet Union scuttled this plan with a counter-proposal. The original committee members were furious. Acheson had fought Baruch's appointment from the outset, claiming that Baruch's "reputation was without foundation in fact and entirely self-propagated." But he was overruled by his superior, the Secretary of State: "Mr. Byrnes, like his successor, General Marshall, had fallen victim to Mr. Baruch's spell."[24] When Oppenheimer heard of Baruch's appointment, he turned to a friend and said, "We're lost"—like Acheson, he thought that Baruch was an old fool.[25] That, he said later, "was the day I gave up hope" for controls on nuclear weaponry.[26]

The U.S. government began stockpiling atom bombs, securing bases where they could be deployed, and creating a delivery system called the Strategic Air Command to fly them toward future targets. Secretary Byrnes, like his President, thought that America could preserve its unique custody of the Bomb. Scientists like Oppenheimer knew that knowledge cannot be kept private. It was only a matter of time before the Russians had their own bomb. That time came far earlier than most had expected—after only four years—which led to American panic and to internal recriminations. It was felt that the Soviets could not have done this on their own. They must have "stolen" the secret through various spies. There had been spies at Los Alamos, most famously Klaus Fuchs; but any help they gave to the Soviet Union only speeded what was inevitable in any case. Stimson, who had consulted the scientists, told Truman in 1946 what the President did not want to hear: "It is as certain as any future pronouncement can be that the method of manufacture of these bombs, as now known by the United States, cannot be preserved as a secret from other nations beyond a relatively short time."[27]

The main response to the Soviets' discovery was a renewed determination to build a more powerful bomb. Edward Teller at Los Alamos, in conjunction with Ernest Lawrence at UC-Berkeley, promoted development of the fusion (or hydrogen) bomb, which would be a thousand times more powerful than the Hiroshima weapon—so powerful that it needed an atom bomb to generate enough heat for its own detonation. They mounted a campaign to get President Truman's approval of this project (Truman had, till this point, never heard of a hydrogen bomb).[28] This was what had always been referred to at Los Alamos as the Super (as opposed to the Gadget, the fission bombs of Hiroshima and Nagasaki).

Most of the leading scientists who had created the first bombs felt that a weapon on the Super's apocalyptic scale was unusably destructive. To possess it was intrinsically immoral. To contemplate its use was unthinkable. To make it available would be an evil temptation, subject to accidental use or proliferation into irresponsible hands. A formidable lineup of all-star scientists opposed developing the Super: Oppenheimer, Conant, Lilienthal, Bethe, Morrison, Rabi, Fermi, Segrè, Weisskopf. The General Advisory Committee that Truman set up to give the Atomic Energy Commission technical advice was opposed to development of the Super. Its majority report, signed by Oppenheimer among others, rejected any rapid plunge into work on the Super, warning that it "might become a weapon of genocide." Its minority report, written by Fermi and Rabi, was even more emphatic:

> Necessarily such a weapon goes far beyond any military objective and enters the range of very great natural catastrophes. By its very nature it cannot be confined to a military objective but becomes a weapon which in practical effect is almost one of genocide.
>
> It is clear that the use of such a weapon cannot be justified on any ethical ground which gives a human being a certain individuality and dignity even if he happens to be a resident of an enemy country. It is evident to us that this would be the view of peoples in other countries. Its use would put the United States in a bad moral position relative to the peoples of the world.
>
> Any postwar situation resulting from such a weapon would leave

unresolvable enmities for generations. A desirable peace cannot come
from such an inhuman application of force. The postwar problems
would dwarf the problems which confront us at present.

The fact that no limits exist to the destructiveness of this weapon
makes its very existence and the knowledge of its construction a danger to humanity as a whole. It is necessarily an evil thing considered
in any light.[29]

The author Thomas Powers would write, of the combined majority
and minority reports: "It is probable that no other official American
document, on a subject of such consequence, was ever argued so lucidly
and seriously on moral grounds; it is certain that there has been none
since."[30] Historian Priscilla McMillan notes: "Of the president's fourteen atomic energy advisers, ten had opposed an accelerated H-bomb
program and one had abstained, and it had been the two non-scientists
who had been most eager to go ahead."[31]

Teller and Lawrence had some scientists on their side, too—Luis
Alvarez, John von Neumann, Stanislaw Ulam, and Arthur Compton—
and they had political and military support. Lewis Strauss, the financier
who played an important role on the Atomic Energy Commission from
1947 and became its chairman in 1953, was an ardent proponent of
the Super. So were Dean Acheson, who was now Secretary of State,
and Secretary of Defense Louis A. Johnson. The military Joint Chiefs
of Staff, of course, never turn down an addition to their tools. They
told the President that it was "necessary to have within the arsenal of
the United States a weapon of the greatest capability, in this case the
super bomb." Reflecting the charge that would be leveled against
Oppenheimer—that opposition to the Super was a (possibly treason-
ous) gift to the Soviets—they claimed that refusal to build the Bomb
"might be interpreted as the first step in unilateral renunciation of the
use of all atomic weapons."[32]

President Truman was under great pressure to prove his anti-

Communist credentials at this time (a matter to be considered later), and he appointed a special committee to study the development of the Super. It was a three-man committee, made up of Secretary of State Acheson, AEC Chairman Lilienthal, and Secretary of Defense Johnson. Acheson was the driving force supporting the Bomb's development. He had just replaced Kennan as the head of the State Department's Policy Planning Staff with Paul Nitze. Kennan opposed the Super, while Nitze was an enthusiast for it. Acheson later explained his own position:

> Nitze was doubtful of the line of argument George Kennan had taken . . . that if we wished to secure nuclear disarmament we should renounce first use of atomic weapons; rely on other weaponry for deterrence and defense against all threats short of atomic attack . . . and make every effort to reach international agreement on control, even at a certain risk. I could only join Nitze in measuring the risks on a different scale, the one on which NSC 68 was to be based.[33]

Lilienthal reluctantly signed the committee report, which recommended going forward with the H-bomb, but asked to voice his objections directly to the President. When he began to voice these, Truman brushed him aside. Truman, who boasted that he never lost a night's sleep over dropping the first Bomb, was just as cavalier about pushing the Super forward. When, in October of 1945, Oppenheimer had expressed his own agonizing over the Bomb, adding that "I feel I have blood on my hands," Truman brushed that aside, too, and told Dean Acheson, "I don't want to see that son of a bitch ever in this office again."[34] To his staff Truman said, "There actually was no decision to make on the H-bomb. . . . We have got to have it if only for bargaining purposes with the Russians."[35] Now the Bomb's handlers were prisoners to a *prospective* bomb. Once again, they could not *not* develop it.

The advocates of the Super were grieved that the scientific community continued to oppose its development. Oppenheimer himself, once the President decided to go forward, gave up his public opposition to the Super and in no way impeded its development. But this was not enough for Teller and Strauss. They said that he was insufficiently enthusiastic over the Super. They resented the moral onus thrown on the project by his former criticisms of it. Oppenheimer was resented for his technical and moral authority. In the eyes of Teller and Strauss, he had not merely upheld a policy different from theirs but was undermining their authority to make such policy.

It was imperative that they destroy his moral sway, and the way to do this was to remove his security clearance, so he could not stay abreast of information in classified documents. He could be refuted by people who spoke from documents he could not read and they could not quote, which made him unqualified to express an opinion. (Many are the political uses of government secrecy.) Teller made the real aim of this move clear to Strauss's emissary. He said it was necessary to "unfrock" Oppenheimer in the church of science, which would dismantle what Teller called "the Oppie machine." The AEC emissary sent to interview Teller reported:

> Teller feels deeply that [this] "unfrocking" must be done or else—regardless of the outcome of the current hearings—scientists may lose their enthusiasm for the [fusion bomb] program. . . . Teller talked at length about "the Oppie machine," running through many names, some of which he listed as "Oppie men" and others as not being "on his team" but under his influence.[36]

That influence was what must be destroyed. Strauss, like Teller, felt his own importance was under siege from Oppenheimer. He described the security hearing of the Atomic Energy Commission, to decide whether Oppenheimer should be denied clearance, in doomsday terms: "If this case is lost, the atomic energy program . . . will fall into the hands of left-wingers. If this occurs, it will mean another Pearl Harbor."[37]

Strauss shepherded the "unfrocking" of Oppenheimer through the commission's special procedures. His ally in this was William Borden, an aide to Brien McMahon, the Democratic Senator from Connecticut who had sponsored the McMahon Act establishing civilian control over atomic policy. Borden had conceived the idea that Oppenheimer was a conscious Soviet agent throughout the whole creation of the Bomb, an idea nurtured in meetings and correspondence with Edward Teller.[38] Though Borden left Congress when the Republicans won a majority with the election of Eisenhower in 1952, he fired a Parthian poisoned dart after his departure. Using access to the AEC's security file that Strauss procured for him, he wrote a letter to J. Edgar Hoover at the FBI making his case that Oppenheimer was a spy and traitor.[39] Strauss took this letter to President Eisenhower in 1953 and asked that Oppenheimer's security clearance be taken from him without a hearing (since a hearing would give Oppenheimer a platform for his own defense). The President did not think much of the letter's case, but he told Strauss quietly to build a "blank wall" around Oppenheimer, denying him access to classified material.[40] That settled the security matter. Oppenheimer could not give away information he was not privy to. But it was far from satisfying Strauss. Security was not the issue. The public discrediting of Oppenheimer was.

Next, Strauss gave Oppenheimer the material against him and asked him to surrender his clearance without a struggle. When Oppenheimer refused, Strauss rigged an AEC hearing on the matter in 1954. He handpicked a three-man Personnel Security Board and appointed a hard-charging prosecutor against Oppenheimer. Though Strauss would be, in effect, the presiding judge over the final court in this matter, as head of the five-member AEC board that would act on the panel's recommendation, he acted as lead prosecutor as well. He denied Oppenheimer's lawyer advance notice of material to be used against him. In the resulting hearing, eminent physicists who had worked with Oppenheimer testified for him—with the notable exception of Edward Teller. Called as a prosecution witness, Teller answered a question about Oppenheimer's security clearance with these words: "I would feel personally more secure if public matters would rest in other hands."

That answer played perfectly to the new rules under which the panel was operating. President Truman's loyalty ruling—Executive Order 9835 (1947)—denied government employment where "reasonable grounds exist for belief that the person involved is disloyal to the Government" (Part V). The Oppenheimer panel would "find no evidence of disloyalty" (General Considerations), but expressed regret that "we were not allowed to exercise mature practical judgment without the rigid circumscription of regulations and criteria established for us." The panelists were referring to Eisenhower's Executive Order 10450 (1953), which went beyond disloyalty and banned those under any allegations of "behavior, activities, or associations which tend to show that the individual is not reliable or trustworthy" (Section 8a). Since Oppenheimer had ties with friends and lovers that he misrepresented, he fell victim to this "Caesar's wife" rule.[41] (Julius Caesar divorced his wife on the basis of mere rumor and suspicion, saying Caesar's wife must be above suspicion.)

Only because of the rigid rule preventing a "mature practical judgment" did two of the three panelists fail to "recommend reinstatement of clearance." But the panel showed that it was concerned with what bothered Teller and Strauss—that Oppenheimer had shown insufficient enthusiasm for the Super. It found no grounds for the most serious allegations brought forward by the prosecution—that Oppenheimer continued to oppose the Super *after* President Truman ordered it, that he *continued* to circulate the majority and minority reports that initially criticized it, that he discouraged others from working on it.

But even the fact that he had opposed the Super in the past was considered reprehensible:

> The Board further concludes that after it was determined, as a matter of national policy (January 31, 1950) to proceed with development of a hydrogen bomb, Dr. Oppenheimer did not oppose the project in a positive or open manner, nor did he decline to cooperate in the project . . . [but] his views in opposition to the development of the H-bomb as expressed in 1949 became widely known among scientists, and since he did not make it known that he had abandoned these views, his attitude undoubtedly had an adverse effect on recruitment of scientists and the progress of the scientific effort in this field. In other words, the board finds that if Dr. Oppenheimer had *enthusiastically* supported the thermonuclear program either before or after the determination of national policy, the H-bomb project would have been pursued with considerably more vigor, thus *increasing* the possibility of earlier success in this field. . . . The Board does not find that Dr. Oppenheimer urged other scientists not to work on the program. However, *enthusiastic* support on his part would perhaps have encouraged other leading scientists to work on the program. (Emphasis added)

The government did not want an independent view of the Super, given by an expert. It wanted cheerleading; and it punished an enthusiasm-deficit by discrediting any form of dissent. Most other physicists had also opposed the Super. Oppenheimer was to be punished because he had *too much respect,* the thing that rankled with Teller and Strauss. His defrocking was accomplished by denying him access to secrets. Secrecy had become a way of punishing, not protecting.

3

THE CARE AND KEEPING
OF THE BOMB

onversion" after a war never means reversion to the status quo
ante. Conditions have been altered by the progress of the war.
Going off a war footing involves incorporating some of the new possibilities opened up by the war itself. After the Revolutionary War, closer
ties among the former colonies, modeled on the cooperation made
necessary by General Washington's integrated fighting troops, led at
first to the Articles of Confederation and then to the Constitution.
After the War of 1812, engineering feats of the military led to advanced
techniques for harbors, canals, roads, and manufacturing in general.
After the Civil War, use of the railroads and telegraph was entrenched
and extended and the drive westward was accelerated. But no conversion
was so continuingly military as that after the Second World War. The
Bomb ensured that. This was a peace to be based on a weapon, and the
care and keeping of that weapon began a whole series of security
measures that made it impossible to put the nation back on a truly
peacetime basis.

We have seen, in the Manhattan Project, what an extensive apparatus General Groves spread secretly across the nation, and outside the

nation. But that network was the dimmest harbinger of what lay ahead in the nuclear future. According to Richard Rhodes,

> The Atomic Energy Commission's eight sites and 55,000 employees in 1950 expanded to twenty sites and 142,000 employees by 1953, and the expansion continued. By the mid-1950s, the nuclear production complex consumed 6.2 percent of total U.S. electrical power and exceeded in capital investment the combined capitalization of Bethlehem Steel, U.S. Steel, Alcoa, Du Pont, Goodyear, and General Motors. Between 1953 and 1955, the U.S. strategic stockpile doubled, from 878 weapons to 1,756, while its total yield increased almost forty times, from seventy-three megatons (4,867 Hiroshimas) to 2,880 megatons (192,000 Hiroshimas).[1]

The actual making of the bombs was not an important part of the nation's expenditure on this arsenal—in fact, that would become relatively cheap in time. "Nuclear warheads cost the United States about $250,000 each; less than a fighter bomber, less than a missile, less than a patrol boat, less than a tank."[2] The immense costs of the nuclear establishment, social costs as well as financial ones, would be in the maintenance of the vast security system around it, and—even more—in the delivery systems needed to deploy the Bomb. This would eventually expand from a new military concept, the Strategic Air Command, to tactical missiles, to nuclear submarines, to intercontinental ballistic missiles (ICBMs), and (in Ronald Reagan's costly dream) to plans for missile stations in space, each component of this far-flung system cocooned with secrecy and with expensive security safeguards.

In the Manhattan Project, a delivery system had been almost as great a concern of General Groves as development of the Bomb itself. The Bomb would be useless without a way of getting it to Germany (the imagined first objective) or to Japan. Well before he had a bomb to send off, Groves was assembling teams, sites, and equipment to carry the weapon. With his AAA priority rating and secret contacts, he was able to commandeer dozens of the army's newest and best bombers (B-29s), and to set up three secret bases for their testing and alteration. He was exploring with Admiral Chester Nimitz what islands taken from the Japanese could become bases close enough for the heavily loaded planes to begin their runs on Japan. Special crews were secretly being trained, with only their top officers told what they would be doing. Planes were rebuilt and retested, over and over. Their multiple bomb bays had to be combined, with a wide new drop area, to accommodate the five-ton Little Boy and Fat Man. A special large bomb ("the Pumpkin") was created, using the contours of the atomic weapons but with conventional explosives inside, and four practice bombing raids on Japan dropped such Pumpkins, using the equipment and crews that would fly the atomic versions.

Tinian Island in the Marianas was finally chosen as the principal base for launching the nuclear attacks. Radioactive material and components of the Bomb were sent there by plane and boat. Other islands—including Guam and Okinawa—were used as staging areas. General Curtis LeMay ran the military preparations, under Groves's direction. Robert Norris does not much exaggerate when he says that Groves formed his very own air force for atomic purposes.[3]

After the war, arrangements of this sort would be multiplied a thousand times as the Strategic Air Command set up bases in foreign countries for the servicing of its nuclear-cargoed planes, which operated on a twenty-four-hour basis every day. Besides strategically located bases, a steady supply of oil had to be secured to keep our air empire running at peak efficiency. Then, when the arsenal was expanded to include tactical nuclear forces, bases for them had to be secured around the world. With the advent of ICBMs, observation and guidance satellites had to be launched and kept in space. All this apparatus was directly descended from General Groves's private air force, the first nuclear delivery system.

Foreign governments that granted us territory and protection were to be supported, even if they were not very good at recognizing the rights of their citizens. Thus began a long history of friendly relations with dictators. Obtaining and securely maintaining our bases was considered more important than the moral legitimacy of the regimes granting us such access. Being the champion of "the free world" meant maintaining nuclear superiority, not actually advancing freedom in the countries that cooperated with us. Later we would need similar access to ports for our nuclear subs, and launch sites for our intermediate missiles. Our anxiety over nations "going Communist" was in large part prompted by a fear that this would shrink the area for such bases. Maintaining this vast network also required radar bases—and, later, satellite orbits. The care and keeping of the Bomb was a continually expanding set of tasks. It was not enough to secure the actual bases themselves, their equipment, and their personnel—the politics of the host countries would have to be continually checked, to make sure our secrets as well as our weapons were safe. This meant spying on other countries, propping up those that gave us what we needed, and undermining those that did not.

The centrality of the Bomb to American military policy can be seen in the reorganization of the military that President Truman effected in 1947. The air force, as the Bomb's first deliverer, would at first take pride of place. The planes that had struck Japan were still part of the *Army* Air Corps, the air arm that had fought World War II. But in 1947, President Truman split off the air branch from the army and made it a separate service, the United States Air Force. This took the lion's share of technological experiment, government contracts, and the military budget, as jet fighters and bombers replaced the propeller-driven aircraft of the world war. The trend became clear as the air force gobbled up resources and talent. In the mid-1950s, the air force received 47 percent of the annual defense budget, as opposed to 29 percent for the navy (also a Bomb deliverer, for carriers with tactical nukes and—shortly—for nuclear subs), and a mere 22 percent for the army, the previous budget leader.[4]

The wide dispersal of so many "assets," with the added burden of secrecy, meant that tight control and narrow responsibility were needed to hold it all together. That was clear in the prototype of the operation, the Manhattan Project, where General Groves carried the whole enterprise in his head. One man had to be given extraordinary powers, outside the normal systems, to bring off the creation and delivery of the bombs. Though President Roosevelt gave the highest approval for development of the bombs, and President Truman authorized delivery of them, Groves had a free hand in the actual creation and practical delivery of them. He was so much outside the rules that the official army report on the air war cannot trace a clear line of responsibility for the nuclear bombing of the Japanese cities. Groves, the key figure, was outside the military chain of command.[5] Groves himself, musing over the muddled official account, noticed that it made him subordinate to General Hap Arnold. That was only nominally true, he said, "in the sense that if Arnold had not *done what I wanted* I could have asked for Marshall to order him to do so" (emphasis added). Actually, he claimed, "I was controlling the situation."[6] The lack of accountability to others was a key to the whole operation, as Congress—and even the President, until the last minute—remained shut out.

The need for concentrated personal authority, outside democratic procedure, would continue in the postwar era. This time the sole responsibility would be lodged in the President. The Atomic Energy Act of 1946 created "a system that made atomic weapons a separate part of the nation's arsenal, with the President of the United States the *sole authority* over their use."[7] That act ruled that the Atomic Energy Commission must develop atomic bombs "only to the extent that the express consent and direction of the President of the United States has been obtained," and the bombs are to be readied "for such use as he deems necessary in the interest of national defense."[8]

President Truman did not know anything about the first atom bomb until he became President, and though he appointed the Interim Committee to advise him on its use, he had little independent information or preparation for assessing the committee's recommendation. The situation of later Presidents has been different. They know about the Bomb even as they run for office, and promise responsible use of it. They present themselves as capable of assuming control over what became known as "the button" that would launch atomic weapons. They travel with the codes for such a move in what has been called "the football." Now, when Presidents enter office, they are extensively briefed on the procedure for authorizing use of nuclear weapons. They are regularly invited to attend Pentagon war games that simulate nuclear attack, though few attend them. (Jimmy Carter was an exception—his time on a nuclear submarine had made him especially aware of the problems.)[9]

Lodging "the fate of the world" in one man, with no constitutional check on his actions, caused a violent break in our whole governmental system. General Groves had a mere simulacrum of that authority, and only for a single project. Presidents now have it as part of their permanent assignment. This was in effect a quiet revolution. It was accepted under the impression that technology imposed it as a harsh necessity. In case of nuclear attack on the United States, the President would not have time to consult Congress or instruct the public. He must respond instantly—which means that he must have the whole scientific apparatus for response on constant alert, accountable only to him. If, on the other hand, a danger to our allies or our necessary assets is posed, calling for a nuclear initiative on his part, he cannot issue a warning ahead of time without alerting the enemy. Like President Truman, who was told he could not forewarn Japan, he must act with a lone authority.

The nature of the presidency was irrevocably altered by this grant of a unique power. The President's permanent alert meant our permanent submission. He became, mainly, the Commander in Chief, since he could loose the whole military force of the nation at any moment. Elections became fateful because we were choosing a Commander in Chief, a custodian of the football, a person whose hand was on the button. We were told that we must honor and protect "our Commander in Chief"— the "our" referring to the entire citizenry. In 1973, the White House Chief of Staff, Al Haig, acting for President Nixon, ordered a civilian— Deputy Attorney General William Ruckelshaus—to fire an independent prosecutor, and when Ruckelshaus refused, Haig thundered at him: "Your Commander in Chief has given you an order."[10]

The President was not Ruckelshaus's Commander in Chief. Nor is he ours. The Constitution severely limits the President's function as Commander in Chief. Article II, Section 2, Clause 1, says:

> The President shall be Commander in Chief *of the Army and Navy* of the United States; *and of the Militia* of the several states, *when called into the actual service of the United States.* (Emphasis added)

The President is not even the Commander in Chief of the National Guard, except when it is nationalized—and the Constitution gave the power to call up the militias to Congress, not the President. Article I, Section 8, of the Constitution decrees:

> The Congress shall have power . . . to provide for calling forth the militia to execute the laws of the Union, suppress insurrections, and repel invasions [and] to provide for organizing, arming, and disciplining the militia, and for governing such part of them as may be employed in the service of the United States.

The President has no power, as Commander in Chief, over any civilian. Yet so common is the assumption that he does that when I wrote an op-ed piece in the *New York Times* saying that the President is not my Commander in Chief, I received abusive mail saying I was clearly not a citizen of the United States and I should leave the country. Loyalty to the Commander in Chief is now equated with loyalty to the country, though it is clearly a form of disloyalty to the Constitution.

This emphasis on the Commander in Chief's role is recent in our history. For most of the past, the Commander in Chief clause was known as "the forgotten clause"—and with good reason. It was not heavily debated in the drafting convention or the ratifying conventions, since it had been clarified by Washington's appointment when he was serving the Continental Congress. The title does not refer to an office, but to a function. Its history is clear. It was used in British military operations to designate an officer in some theater of war, or some campaign, to obviate any dispute over which admiral or general should be in charge of the coordinated forces being deployed. Where, for instance, several of His Majesty's ships or formations were operating in the same seas, one or other captain would be named commander in chief of all those in the area. For that reason, there could be as many commanders in chief as there were different theaters of conflict. The office of admiral or general, or even of lower rank, was not changed during the period when a man functioned as leader of the joint forces. Sometimes a lower rank can overrule one of higher rank while he is functioning as commander in chief. That happened in the War of 1812 when federal officers of lower rank than militia officers were named commander in chief for the campaign they engaged in.

When Washington was sent to Boston to take charge of the revolutionary forces, the command situation was muddied. Officers of different colonies' militias were gathering there. Congress had sent troops earlier without clarifying the command situation—they were dispatched simply to "the army near Boston," to serve "under the command of the chief officer of that army."[11] The unified effort of the whole continent was made clear when Congress appointed Washington to both his office and his function, making him both "general *and* Commander in

Chief to take the supreme command of the forces raised, and to be raised, in defense of American liberty" (emphasis added).[12]

In just this way, the Republic's chief executive is both President (his civilian office) and Commander in Chief (his military function). He acts as Commander in Chief only when directing the army and navy in military operations, and is superior to all officers in the various services. If there are no military operations occurring, his function is not exercised. He does not himself hold military office or rank. A New York court ruled that Franklin Roosevelt's estate could not benefit from a tax break given *to military personnel* for his property in Dutchess County, New York:

> The President receives his compensation for his services rendered as Chief Executive of the Nation, not for the individual parts of his duties. No part of his compensation is paid from sums appropriated for the military or naval forces; and it is equally clear under the Constitution that the President's duties as Commander in Chief represent only a part of duties *ex officio* as Chief Executive. . . . The President does not enlist in, and he is not inducted or drafted into, the armed forces. Nor is he subject to court martial or military discipline.[13]

Despite the importance of civilian rule in our Republic—Washington flaunted no military symbols at Mount Vernon—modern presidents have assumed military airs. Since Ronald Reagan's time they have taken to being saluted and answering the salute, though salutes are supposed to be only to military superiors recognized by their rank *in uniform*, and those standing in file are to salute only when ordered to.

In the atomic era, the President as Commander in Chief has taken on a mystique that makes him a power apart. Those around him are ready to cultivate that aura. The power over the atom is outside the constitutional order of succession under the Twenty-fifth Amendment, and outside the military chain of command. We see that in the delegation of his atomic responsibility. If the President is removed from action by a surprise attack, which is presumed to be nuclear, his power over the Bomb does not move to the prescribed civilian or military authority. The line of succession in case of disablement is, according to the Presidential Succession Act of 1947, from the President to the Vice President, to the Speaker of the House, to the President Pro Tem of the Senate, to the Secretary of State, to the Secretary of the Treasury, to the Secretary of Defense, to the Attorney General, and then to the Secretary of the Interior, to the Secretary of Agriculture, and then to the next nine members of the cabinet, in the chronological order of their office's being instituted.[14]

This provision for succession so far down the line was enacted in 1947 because the idea of nuclear attack made it important to establish elaborate procedures in case of massive and sudden casualties in government. Yet the actual passing of authority over the Bomb, as provided for by the White House, does not follow this public order. It is secret, classified, and outside the legal pattern. In practice it is assumed that people like the Speaker of the House or the President Pro Tem of the Senate will not know how to activate the technology of nuclear response. That will be entrusted to a secret few trained to handle the assignment. If these procedures fail, the responsibility for launching a nuclear attack could devolve upon the "Looking Glass" command center kept aloft, away from the first-strike capability of an enemy.[15] The problem of control is how to identify those with knowledgeable access to the weapon systems, without having too many "loose cannons in the field."[16] This system is another descendant of General Groves's authority. He, too, identified one or two men to step into his shoes if he should drop dead or be killed before completing his mission, and these were men of his own choosing, outside the military chain of command or political instruction. In fact, Groves's role made him a kind of commander in chief of the nuclear project, a function in which he directed those of higher rank or different authority.

The prospects for a secret transfer of power over the Bomb in the postwar world can be observed in a procedure established during the Reagan presidency. Former White House chiefs of staff—primarily Donald Rumsfeld and Dick Cheney—were told to leave their homes in the middle of the night, telling no one (including their wives) where they were going. They were flown to "undisclosed locations," where they worked with White House national security people to set up emergency governments, working on the assumption that the President and Vice President had been killed by nuclear attack. Using a cabinet member as their interim "President," they spent days with sophisticated communication equipment managing a response to war. All this was done outside the constitutional and statutory provisions for succession of presidential authority. The groups, like Groves in his headiest days, were a law to themselves. Their plan would not work if Congress or the public knew about it—that would ensure that a future enemy would know about it.[17] This was not about power as the law provided for it. This was Bomb Power, a thing new and absolute.

It is not surprising that, when a real attack against New York and the Pentagon occurred on September 11, 2001, Mr. Cheney—who was now the Vice President, and in actual line of succession—assumed the powers of the presidency, even though George Bush was still alive (if absent from Washington). After taking up his position in the White House bunker, Cheney ordered jet fighters to shoot down the last airliner that terrorists had seized. He claims that he cleared this instruction with the President; but the findings of the 9/11 commission indicate that President Bush was informed only after Cheney gave the instruction. Cheney's Chief of Staff, Lewis "Scooter" Libby, who was standing next to him in the bunker, and who did not hear a preceding phone call with the President, said that Cheney hesitated in giving the order to shoot down the airliner only "about the time it takes a batter to decide to swing."[18] Obviously the emergency drills during the Reagan administration had made Cheney fast on the trigger.

The military chain of command was never considered here. As the 9/11 commission noted: "In most cases, the chain of command authorizing the use of force runs from the president to the secretary of defense and from the secretary to the combatant commander"—yet Secretary of Defense Rumsfeld had no part in the decision to shoot down the airliner.[19] Cheney's early impression was that his order had been carried out—in fact, that "a couple of aircraft" had been "taken out."[20] He did not know that the plane had crashed before the air interceptors could reach it. After the President returned to Washington, Cheney disappeared to "an undisclosed location," presumably to continue his atomic-attack drills from the 1980s, this time against an anticipated second terrorist attack.

Cheney would in later days make the most extreme claims for executive authority without oversight or check of any kind. Among other things, he was defending his own action on September 11, 2001. Nor should this be considered a personal idiosyncrasy. The concentration of emergency authority in the executive branch, and more specifically in the White House, makes many officials say they can speak for the President, even when they are giving him "plausible deniability." The aura rubs off on those around the Commander in Chief. Al Haig not only gave orders to William Ruckelshaus in the name of "your Commander in Chief"—he took on himself presidential powers when Ronald Reagan was shot in 1981. Haig, by now the Secretary of State, went before reporters to say:

Constitutionally, gentlemen, you have the President, the Vice President, and the Secretary of State [himself], in that order, and should the President decide he wants to transfer the helm to the Vice President, he will do so. He has not done that. As of now, I am in control here in the White House, pending return of the Vice President and in close touch with him. If something came up, I would check with him, of course.

Haig should not have brought up the Constitution, since the Twenty-fifth Amendment on succession does not mention the Secretary of State, and the amended Succession Act put him at number four in sequence, not number two. But what mattered to him were the words "I am in control here *in the White House.*" That is what matters in the Commander in Chief era.

Those in the modern executive office—that of the Commander in Chief—often act without letting Congress or the people know. These surrogates can be Republicans like Oliver North illegally funding guerrilla fighters in Nicaragua, or Democrats like Robert Kennedy plotting the assassination of Fidel Castro. They have the means of acting this way because of the vast and secret apparatus of the National Security State, which was set up in the era of Bomb Power and the newly empowered Commander in Chief. An elaborately constructed set of institutions enforces the idea that anything executive agencies do is justified in the name of national security. The Bomb instilled a structure of fear.

II.

THE NATIONAL
SECURITY STATE

4

BEGINNINGS
(1945–1946)

For the first time in history, the United States [after 1945] had to maintain a large peacetime national security establishment, perhaps on a permanent basis.[1]

—MICHAEL J. HOGAN, *A Cross of Iron*

General Groves was planning to counter Russian access to nuclear materials even before the war ended in Europe. Other parts of the government had the same thing in mind, but their fear was at first diffuse, and the means of response had not yet been articulated. The country had no tradition of peacetime war measures, or of a permanent agency for spying abroad. These had to be created from scratch in the era of the Bomb. Prewar isolationist instincts and some lingering regard for the wartime ally status of the Soviets made for a halting start to the National Security State. But the instruments were being assembled, piece by piece, for permanent war in peace. I give here a time line of the step-by-step creation of the structure, not just as a convenient overview but to suggest how the whole was put together in its interlocking parts. I will spell out in this and the next chapters how each later step contributed to the force of the others.

(1) 1945 (October 1)	Strategic Services Unit (SSU) organized
(2) 1946 (January 22)	Central Intelligence Group (CIG) inaugurated
(3) 1946 (February 22)	Long Telegram (from George Kennan in Moscow)
(4) 1946 (September 24)	Clifford memorandum for Truman
(5) 1946 (October 7)	Kennan critique of Willett paper
(6) 1947 (January 7)	Kennan speech to Council on Foreign Relations
(7) 1947 (January 31)	Kennan memo to Forrestal
(8) 1947 (March 12)	Truman Doctrine speech
(9) 1947 (March 21)	Loyalty order
(10) 1947 (April 3)	Attorney General's list of subversive organizations
(11) 1947 (May 5)	Policy Planning Staff created (State Department)
(12) 1947 (May 8)	Delta Council speech (Acheson)
(13) 1947 (June 5)	Marshall Plan announced
(14) 1947 (July)	"X" article in *Foreign Affairs* (Kennan)
(15) 1947 (July 16)	National Security Act (CIA)
(16) 1947 (December 17)	NSC 4/A (covert psywar)
(17) 1948 (March 30)	NSC 7 (counteroffensive)
(18) 1948 (June 18)	NSC 10/2 (Office of Policy Coordination)
(19) 1948 (August 18)	NSC 20/1 (rollback)
(20) 1948 (November 24)	NSC 20/4 (war aims)
(21) 1949 (April 4)	North Atlantic Treaty
(22) 1949 (September 14)	NSC 58 (freeing satellite countries)
(23) 1950 (April 14)	NSC 68 (war mobilization)
(24) 1951 (April 4)	Psychological Strategy Board
(25) 1952 (November 4)	National Security Agency inaugurated

These parts, cobbled together over time, would interlock to concentrate power in the executive branch, in its most secretive operations, and (nominally) in the Commander in Chief. Congressional oversight was minimized when not evaded by most of the functioning parts of this assemblage. Taken separately, they are:

(1) STRATEGIC SERVICES UNIT ORGANIZED (OCTOBER 1, 1945)

The SSU was a rump organization in the Pentagon meant to salvage remaining parts of the Office of Strategic Services, the wartime intelligence agency that President Truman had just disbanded. The OSS was a legendary (in all senses) unit organized by William Joseph Donovan. As a football player at Columbia University in the first years of the twentieth century, Donovan acquired the nickname "Wild Bill" from baseball player William *Edward* Donovan, who was starring at the same time in Brooklyn. After a successful Wall Street career, Donovan organized a team of daredevil risk takers to engage in espionage and sabotage during World War II. He had wanted to set up an intelligence agency even before the war broke out, suspecting that there were subversives and saboteurs in peacetime America. In answer to Henry L. Stimson's famous 1929 criticism of spying, on the grounds that "gentlemen do not open each other's mail," Donovan said that a nation should not be "crippled by civilized inhibitions."[2]

During the war, Donovan wanted panache to be shown by his "cowboys" at the OSS, and he usually got more panache than results. President Roosevelt was suspicious of the self-glorifying tales coming out of the OSS, and he commissioned his chief White House military aide, Colonel Richard Park, to make a secret investigation of the agency's record. The report, devastating in its explosion of OSS myths, was classified until much later; but President Truman was able to read it at the war's end, and he disbanded the OSS, despite heavy lobbying from Donovan and others to maintain it for postwar service.[3]

Truman's departing Secretary of War, Henry Stimson, the protector of "gentlemen's mail," agreed that the OSS must be abolished. Other intelligence units had been more productive (and law-abiding) than the OSS during the war: G-2 (army intelligence), the State Department intelligence analysts, the army and navy signal corps. (The latter was responsible for breaking Japan's secret PURPLE cipher and running America's decryption of it called MAGIC.) The Park Report said that the one part of the OSS worth retaining was its Research and Analysis Branch (R and A), which should be saved but lodged in the State Department. The other remains of the OSS, including what was left of European and Asian operations, should be turned over to the Pentagon for "salvage and liquidation." Donovan was angry at the disbanding of his dream team.

The newly appointed Assistant Secretary of War, John J. Mc-Cloy, was an old friend of Donovan's. A Donovan deputy from the OSS, Brigadier General John Magruder, went to McCloy with the message that "the holy cause of Central Intelligence" could not be allowed to lapse. An interim agency, the Strategic Services Unit, was quickly set up to give a home in the Pentagon to OSS personnel and resources. It was called a separate "unit" to prevent its dispersal into unconnected resources. Its mission, to continue covert operations (which Truman said he did not desire), was disguised as "services of common concern" to all intelligence agencies.[4] The State Department went forward with Truman's plan for an intelligence agency concerned with the collation of all available information, but the Joint Chiefs of Staff promoted its SSU as capable of collecting as well as collating information, and of using it to counter foreign activities, overtly or covertly.

(2) CENTRAL INTELLIGENCE GROUP
INAUGURATED (JANUARY 22, 1946)

Truman was convinced that he needed an agency responsible to the President directly, not to the State Department or the Pentagon. He would later write, "There were a large number of people in the State Department when I took over who were certain I did not know what was going on in the world, and they tried to keep me from finding out."[5] He wanted his own source of intelligence, but when he set up the CIG, out of suspicion of the State Department, he used the core of men and ideas put together by McCloy and Magruder in the Pentagon. Re-infiltration of the CIG by old OSS hands would make the spy agency revert to the kinds of activity engaged in, fecklessly, during the world war.

Truman set up the CIG in January of 1946. It was called a "group," not an institution, to give it a function. The President called on naval intelligence, distinguished during the war, for its first director—Rear Admiral Sidney W. Souers. But Souers had a vague mandate he only vaguely fumbled at before retiring after five and a half months. He was replaced by Army Air Corps General Hoyt Vandenberg, best known for his command of the air war in Europe, though he had briefly served during the war as Chief of Military Intelligence.

Vandenberg meant to build up an aggressive intelligence agency, but the dubious status of the CIG left him few resources. Truman had not procured congressional authorization for this new entity, so regular appropriations could not be relied on. Vandenberg followed the precedent of General Groves and got a secret fund from compliant congressmen of fifteen million dollars. Then he used the Washington old-boy network to get another ten million dollars of unauthorized funds from Secretary of State James Byrnes and Secretary of War Robert Patterson. At the same time he informed the President's Chief Counsel, Clark Clifford, that the CIG would engage in covert activities, which Truman had not previously authorized, and which Congress was not informed of. Postwar intelligence activities, like the wartime Manhattan Project, would operate outside the law.[6] Vandenberg, using old OSS agents, promptly in 1946 set up an underground resistance operation in Romania.

(3) LONG TELEGRAM (FEBRUARY 22, 1946)

A rationale for large operations against the USSR was unexpectedly supplied by a diplomatic undersecretary who had been neglected theretofore and was considering resignation from the service. Lying on a sickbed in Moscow, George Kennan was infuriated by what he took to be a dunderheaded expression of surprise by U.S. Treasury officials that Moscow was refusing to join the World Bank or the International Monetary Fund. He felt that America was slipping back into its isolationist know-nothingism about foreign affairs. Did Treasury not get it? How could he convince them that Stalin was not in the cooperating business? He fired off a five-thousand-word telegram to his superiors at State which became a secret sensation in Washington.[7] Probably no other document of diplomatic advice had more influence in twentieth-century America. Kennan says that Truman read it, the State Department rewarded him with honors, and "my official loneliness came in fact to an end. . . . My reputation was made. My voice now carried."[8]

What first readers of the telegram took from it was a trumpet blast that opened its last section:

> We have here [in Moscow] a political force committed fanatically to the belief that with the US there can be no permanent modus vivendi, that it is desirable and *necessary that the internal harmony of our society be disrupted, our traditional way of life be destroyed, the international authority of our state be broken. . . .* (V, emphasis added)

Kennan claimed that he later read his own words with horror—they sounded, he said, as if written "by the Daughters of the American Revolution" in one of their seizures of anti-communism.[9] He had wanted to shake some silly people out of their naive views of Stalin, but—as with others who would find it necessary to "scare the hell out of people" for political purposes—he spent many years professing regret at his success in this effort.

Kennan later argued that the telegram, despite its intemperate lapses, was not as extreme as some (like Secretary of the Navy James Forrestal) instantly made it out to be. "The Secretary of the Navy, Mr. James Forrestal, had it reproduced and evidently made it required reading for hundreds, if not thousands, of higher officers in the armed services"—an odd treatment of a classified document.[10] Admittedly, there were different facets to the telegram, each capable of different emphases. For one thing, Kennan made a sharp distinction between the Soviet state and the Russian people, who were well disposed to Americans, "friendly to [the] outside world, eager for experience of it" (II). Ordinary Russians were tired, he said, depleted by the grinding war with Hitler, and in no mood for conflict—so their rulers had to be cautious, not "adventuristic" (V 1). These authorities "feared direct contact between [the] Western world and their own [people]" (II). They could afford to let history do their work for them, since they believed Marx's teaching that capitalism would die of its own inner contradictions (I b). To foster that implosion, progressive forces friendly to Russia should be encouraged, but "false friends of the people," wanting to ameliorate conditions in the capitalist countries, would just slow history down—so "relentless battle must be waged against socialist and social-democratic leaders abroad" (I g, d).

The logical conclusion from this line of thought works entirely against a later strategy of isolating the USSR, refusing to deal with it. Russia's rulers were paranoid about "capitalist encirclement" of their country, afraid of an invasion—which, Kennan said, was "sheerest nonsense" (II). Kennan wrote that dealing with Russia was "undoubtedly [the] greatest task our *diplomacy* has ever faced" (V, emphasis added). He would later complain that people thought more about military than about diplomatic action, despite the fact that he said clearing up internal problems in our own society was the effective way to oppose communism. "We must have the courage and self-confidence to cling to our own methods and conceptions of human society. After all, the greatest danger that can befall us in coping with this problem of Soviet communism is that we shall allow ourselves to become like those with whom we are coping" (V 5).

Yet, despite what might be called civil-libertarian counsel, Kennan did say that the United States must be on guard against internal subversion.

> [The Soviet Union] has an elaborate and far-flung apparatus for exertion of its influence *in other countries,* an apparatus of amazing flexibility and versatility, managed by people whose experience and skill in *underground* methods are presumably without parallel in history. (V, emphasis added)

This apparatus penetrated "organizations less likely to be suspected of being tools of Soviet government," preferring them to outright Communist organizations. Thus it targeted "labor unions, youth leagues, women's organizations, racial societies, religious societies, social organizations, cultural groups, liberal magazines, publishing houses, etc." International organizations offered similar targets. "Particular, almost vital importance is attached in this connection to [the] international labor movement" (IV 2–4).

Given this picture of a worldwide and secret force "without parallel in history," used by a fanatical foe hating our "way of life," it is no wonder that some at the highest levels in government reacted to the Long Telegram with sheer panic. It has been argued that the final recommendation, that we should fight the foe by being our best selves, looked almost comically anticlimactic. Kennan had also said, after all, that the Soviets responded only to "[the] logic of force" (V 7), that they would back off only if "strong resistance is encountered *at any point.* Thus, if the adversary has sufficient *force* and makes clear his *readiness to use* it, he rarely has to do so" (V 1, emphasis added). Some would take that readiness to meet the Soviets at *any* point to mean that we should confront them at *every* point. And the President would adopt that as American policy in the month immediately after this telegram was sent. But Truman himself was responding less to Kennan's telegram than to a memorandum it had prompted his Counsel, Clark Clifford, to write.

(4) CLIFFORD MEMORANDUM
(SEPTEMBER 24, 1946)

In the six months after the Long Telegram, all of official Washington was quietly buzzing with its message. Kennan, once on the verge of quitting the diplomatic corps, was the greatest celebrity the public had still not heard of. He quickly acquired patrons in high places—James Forrestal, John McCloy, George Marshall, Clark Clifford, and Dean Acheson (who later became a critic). To be considered an expert on the Soviet threat, one had to show that he was communicating with Kennan. President Truman, wondering what all the fuss was about, asked his trusted Counsel, Clark Clifford, to write him a report on the matter. Clifford consulted Kennan and his growing circle of powerful advocates, along with his own aide George Elsey, and wrote a long memorandum that called for aid to countries that might fall under Soviet influence (which became the Truman Doctrine), for an economic buildup of potential U.S. allies (which became the Marshall Plan), and for safeguards against internal subversion (which became the Truman loyalty program). The well-connected journalist Arthur Krock

of the *New York Times* thought the Clifford memorandum so important
to the formation of Truman's policy toward the USSR that he devoted
a chapter of his 1968 *Memoirs* to its impact, and provided the first
public airing of the text as an appendix to his book.[11]

Clifford began by quoting several paragraphs from Kennan's Long
Telegram (428–30), but he soon went beyond it, reflecting the air of
crisis that was spreading through Washington's upper echelons. Kennan
had said that the Soviets, following Marxist dogma, expected the cap-
italistic world to commit suicide from its internal contradictions. But
Clifford concluded that the Soviet Union was planning the "ultimate
destruction of capitalist states *by communist states,*" and "the Kremlin
acknowledges no limit to the eventual power of the Soviet Union"
(431, emphasis added). Kennan laid much of his emphasis on diplomatic means, but Clifford was interested in military power, even that
of biological weaponry. *No limits* must be placed on U.S. development
of atomic *and biological* weapons and the means of delivering them, over
long distances, by air. This document is important enough to be quoted
at length.

> The language of military power is the only language which disciples
> of power politics understand. The United States must use that language
> in order that Soviet leaders will realize that our government is deter-
> mined to uphold the interests of its citizens and the rights of small
> nations. Compromise and concessions are considered, by the Soviets,
> to be evidences of weakness. . . . It must be made apparent to the Soviet
> government that our strength will be sufficient to repel any attack and
> sufficient to defeat the USSR decisively if a war should start. The
> prospect of defeat is the only sure means of deterring the Soviet
> Union.
>
> The Soviet Union's vulnerability is limited due to the vast area over
> which its key industrial and natural resources are widely dispersed, but it
> is vulnerable to atomic weapons, biological weapons, and long-range air

power. Therefore, in order to maintain our strength at a level which will be effective in restraining the Soviet Union, the United States must be prepared to wage atomic *and biological warfare*. . . . The United States, with a military potential composed primarily of highly effective technical weapons, should entertain no proposal for disarmament or limitation of armament as long as the possibility of Soviet aggression exists. (477–78, emphasis added)

On the threat of internal subversion, about which Clifford would later sing a very different tune, he was acutely apprehensive in 1946.

The Soviet government is actively directing espionage and subversive movements in the United States. Two major intelligence organizations are engaged in large-scale espionage in this country. They are the groups controlled by the Soviet Ministry of Internal Affairs and the Intelligence Department of the Red Army, and they operate in this country under the cover and protection of diplomatic and consular establishments. . . . In this regard it must be remembered that *every American Communist* is potentially an espionage agent of the Soviet government, requiring only the direct instruction of a Soviet superior to make the potentiality a reality. . . . One of the objectives of the American Communist Party is the subversion of the armed forces of the United States. . . . There is continuous Communist propaganda, within the United States Army and from without, to promote left-wing sentiment among soldiers. . . . A definite campaign, in the making at present, is being sponsored by the Communist Party to indoctrinate soldiers to refuse to act in the event the United States Army is called on to suppress domestic disturbances, to take over essential industries, or to operate public utilities. (472–75, emphasis added)

Did that last sentence stick in Truman's mind for use six years later, when he tried to use the army to seize the steel industry during the

Korean War? Then it was the Supreme Court, not Communist propaganda, that stopped him.

Clifford was taking the hardest of hard lines, and the President knew
it. He asked Clifford, "How many copies of the report do you have?"
Clifford answered, "Ten." Truman was urgent: "I want them all. Go to
your office and get them." The report must be kept secret or there
would be an end to all dealings with the Soviet Union, and widespread
panic in the United States. "If this got out, it would blow the roof off
the White House; it would blow the roof off the Kremlin."[12] Though
Clifford went beyond Kennan's written statements thus far, Kennan saw
a draft of Clifford's memo and said, "I think the tone is excellent." He
especially commended the call for urgent development of nuclear and
biological weapons, saying it was "important this country be *prepared*
to use them if need be, for the mere fact of such preparedness may
prove to be the only deterrent to Russian aggressive actions and in this
sense the only sure guarantee of peace" (emphasis in the original).[13]

(5) KENNAN CRITIQUE OF WILLETT PAPER
(OCTOBER 7, 1946)

Kennan's career took off like a rocket after the Long Telegram. James
Forrestal, it has already been noted, had circulated the telegram to all
kinds of important people in Washington, and he soon brought Kennan in on one of his favorite causes at the time, the National War
College. As diplomatic historian David Mayers writes:

> In Forrestal, Kennan also had a powerful sponsor whose friendly inter-
> vention resulted in Kennan's transfer [from the State Department] in
> April 1946 to the National War College, where he served as deputy
> commandant in charge of instruction in foreign relations. The presti-
> gious college, based in Washington and owing its existence primarily

to Forrestal, was charged with teaching geopolitics and strategy to senior military and Foreign Service officers.[14]

Though he was appointed to the college in April, he would not start teaching until the beginning of the academic year in September, so he could perform a service to the State Department through the summer. He was asked to tour the country lecturing on Soviet hostility. He found the audiences less receptive to his message than his charges at the War College would be.[15] His post let him be a principal link between the Defense and State departments, between James Forrestal and George Marshall.

Later, after Forrestal's growing instability led him to suicide, Kennan would try to play down his close relationship with the man. But initially Forrestal was his principal promoter, the one who indirectly inspired the *Foreign Affairs* article that made Kennan famous with the general public. Forrestal was using every means he could think of to brand the Soviet Union as a deadly threat to America. As part of this effort, he distributed to various officials a paper written by a Smith College professor, Edward Willett: "Dialectical Materialism and Russian Objectives." Kennan got the paper shortly after beginning his term at the college. He wrote a critique of Willett's paper, arguing that its main recommendation—a massive military buildup—was not the most effective way of countering Soviet influence. Forrestal asked Kennan to supply a more nuanced analysis. Early in October, Kennan drafted a memo recommending that pressure on the Soviets be mainly diplomatic. Forrestal thought this too "soft," and asked Kennan to rewrite his memo.[16] Kennan worked on this version into 1947, which proved a fateful year.[17]

5

ANNUS MIRABILIS
(1947)

In 1945 and 1946, the rudiments of the National Security State were being gestated in secret, in unauthorized efforts at a peacetime intelligence agency, in bureaucratic scurrying, in internal documents. But in 1947 this backstage activity became a visible surge. That was the year when the instruments of war in peace were locked into place. As before, the intellectual leadership came mainly from George Kennan.

(6) KENNAN SPEECH TO THE COUNCIL ON FOREIGN RELATIONS (JANUARY 7, 1947)

While his Long Telegram was being passed around in Washington, secretly but busily, George Kennan was giddied with offers and invitations. Speaking at Yale in October 1946, he joined Forrestal and others in condemning Henry Wallace's claim that the Soviets were weak and could be dealt with by diplomacy. Then, at the beginning of 1947, he gave a speech to the Council on Foreign Relations, "The Soviet Way of Thought and Its Effect on Soviet Foreign Policy." This speech is important because it incorporates items Kennan was working up in his revised memo for Forrestal, and it prompted the council to ask for a version of it to be published in its journal, *Foreign Affairs*. This became the famous "X" article, which put "containment" in the foreign-policy vocabulary of the period.

In the CFR speech Kennan argued that "the Soviet ideology of today flows with iron logic and with irresistible force from the inner necessities of Soviet power."[1] The Soviets, he said, had an internal compulsion to demonize external foes, making them hostile in principle to the West. The speech analyzed the Russian mentality with a mixture of the psychological and the ideological that especially appealed to Forrestal. Offices and honors were being pushed on Kennan. He was assured that President Truman had read the Long Telegram.[2] Truman had Clark Clifford consult Kennan for his own memo to Truman, which went beyond Kennan's recommendations and led to the Truman Doctrine.

(7) KENNAN MEMO TO FORRESTAL (JANUARY 31, 1947)

Kennan's second version of his comments on the Willett paper was tougher than the first. He recommended that the U.S. "confront the Russians with unalterable counterforce at every point where they show signs of encroaching upon the interests of a peaceful and stable world." Forrestal was highly pleased with this.[3] He circulated it through officialdom, as he had the Long Telegram—he even showed it to the journalist Arthur Krock, whom he cultivated.[4] This made it possible for Krock to blow Kennan's cover when the memo reappeared as the "X" article in *Foreign Affairs*.

(8) TRUMAN DOCTRINE SPEECH
(MARCH 12, 1947)

After the war, the British government supported the rather question-
able regimes in Greece and Turkey, to keep Communist insurgents from
toppling them. The British, still reeling from the siege of their island,
wanted to hand this task off to America, but Americans found it hard
to believe that Communists so far away could be a threat to them, or
that the governments of Greece and Turkey deserved protection. The
Greek foes of communism had been collaborators with Hitler. Even
Kennan had misgivings about supporting the Greek "colonels." President Truman called in a former isolationist, Michigan's Republican
Senator Arthur Vandenberg, who had sponsored bipartisan support for
the Democratic administration during the war, and asked if Republicans could be persuaded to support a large commitment to aid for
Greece and Turkey. Loy Henderson, who was present at this meeting,
representing the State Department, said Vandenberg responded: "Mr.
President, the only way you are ever going to get this is to make a
speech and scare the hell out of the country."

The President gave just that speech, and people were appropriately
scared. A World War II veteran going to school in Oklahoma said, "I
told my wife to dust off my uniform."[5] Columnist Walter Lippmann
denounced this "tocsin of an ideological crusade."[6] What astounded
people was the "doctrine" used to justify the intervention in Greece
and Turkey—that America must oppose any Communist threat to freedom anywhere in the world. Truman told the Congress: "Totalitarian
regimes imposed on free people, by direct or indirect aggression, undermine the foundation of international peace *and hence the security of
the United States*" (emphasis added).

There is a main pillar of the National Security State. *Any* Communist gain anywhere undermines the very security of the United

States. Kennan objected to the language of the speech when he saw a draft of it, but he was unable to get it changed. He thought some targeted aid to Greece made sense, but not to Turkey; and he objected to "the sweeping nature of the commitments . . . [in] the framework of a universal policy rather than in that of a specific decision addressed to a specific set of circumstances."[7] Kennan's doubts were expressed at the time, but in a classified document, his first as director of the Policy Planning Staff. He thought Truman's language was a blank check, and that the doctrine did not distinguish vital threats from peripheral ones.[8]

These would be the concerns of later historians, like the diplomatic scholar Robert McMahon:

> What is particularly significant about the Truman Doctrine . . . is less that basic fact of power politics [that America was filling a void left by the British] than the manner in which the American president chose to present his aid proposal. Using hyperbolic language, Manichean imagery, and deliberate simplification to strengthen his public appeal, Truman was trying to build a public and Congressional consensus not just behind this particular commitment but behind a more activist American foreign policy—a policy that would be at once anti-Soviet and anti-communist. The Truman Doctrine thus amounted to a declaration of ideological Cold War along with a declaration of geopolitical Cold War.[9]

(9) LOYALTY ORDER (EXECUTIVE ORDER 9835, MARCH 21, 1947)

The Communist menace was not only everywhere else in the world, but in the vitals of America itself. Keeping security secrets had been a concern during the war, but President Truman would exact a series of loyalty oaths in 1947 that went beyond anything in the war. General Groves had spied on everyone involved in the Manhattan Project. Truman ordered a spying apparatus for everyone employed by the executive branch of the federal government. All must be subject to investigation, must open their records to the government, and must swear loyalty to the United States. Was this necessary? The man who helped draft and implement the program later told a reporter that it was not. Clark Clifford recalled that at the time there was a challenge to President Truman from a third party on the left, headed by Henry Wallace, and a series of attacks from the right, by superpatriots calling the Democratic administration soft on communism. This latter criticism was abetted by J. Edgar Hoover at the FBI. Here is what Clifford said in an interview with Carl Bernstein in December 1978:

> My own feeling was there was not a serious loyalty threat. I felt the whole thing was being manufactured. . . . I have the sensation that the President didn't attach fundamental importance to the so-called Communist scare. He thought it was a lot of baloney. But political pressures were such that he had to recognize it. We used to comment on the fact that so far as J. Edgar and the Congress were concerned, there was a problem. . . . It was a political problem. We did not believe there was a real problem. A problem was being manufactured. There was a certain element of hysteria.[10]

Truman had "scared the hell out of the country," and now he had to live with the fears he had loosed. Clifford's self-serving later comments to Bernstein are contradicted, as we have seen, by his own memorandum of September 24, 1946, which was as panicky as any anti-Communist fulminations by J. Edgar Hoover. Clifford, like Kennan, like Truman himself, would try afterward to say that he had never succumbed to panic. But his memo to Truman disproves his later claim, as do documents he helped shape at the National Security Council.

(10) ATTORNEY GENERAL'S LIST OF SUBVERSIVE ORGANIZATIONS (APRIL 3, 1947)

Attorney General Tom Clark, in order to enforce the President's Executive Order 9835, assembled a list of subversive organizations as a tool for testing loyalty. Membership in any of the listed bodies supplied prima facie grounds for dismissal of executive employees. Clark turned to the investigative staff of the House Committee on Un-American Activities to help draw up his list. This was done partly in response to unofficial "blacklists" compiled by entrepreneurial anti-Communists—but, by a circular process, it stimulated new lists to amplify or correct the official one. That the Attorney General felt compelled to make such a list was an informal ratification of the process as it was being carried out by others.

(11) POLICY PLANNING STAFF CREATED (MAY 5, 1947)

George Marshall, as Secretary of State, wanted to formulate policies to meet the escalating security problems around the world. He did not want to rely on the Central Intelligence Group, which was more an arm of the Pentagon. Marshall captured Forrestal's prize intellectual, George Kennan, took him from the post Forrestal had created for him at the National War College, and created a department for him in the State Department, as head of the Policy Planning Staff. Marshall relied on him in many areas, including the drafting of the Marshall Plan for Europe's economic recovery.

Kennan continued to advise Forrestal, as when he asked him (on September 27, 1947) to form a "guerrilla warfare corps" in the Pentagon and to put OSS veteran Frank Wisner in control of it. Kennan admitted this was not something Americans had done before, but he thought the times demanded that we "fight fire with fire," countering Communist subversion with our own counter-subversives.[11] Kennan said that security trumped democracy in places where we needed assets, urging Forrestal to call off opposition to the dictatorship of Francisco Franco in Spain.[12]

(12) DELTA COUNCIL SPEECH BY ACHESON (MAY 8, 1947)

In a book highly praised by Kennan and Dean Acheson, *The Fifteen Weeks,* Joseph M. Jones says that one short period in 1947 was marked by three speeches that set American policy for the postwar world— Truman's "Doctrine" speech in March, Acheson's Delta Council speech in May, and Marshall's "Plan" speech in June.[13] The first and last of these are rightly famous. But the Acheson speech has faded from memory. Why does Jones place such emphasis on it? One reason is that he had a hand in writing all three. From his place in the State Department's Office of Public Affairs, he served as the leading speechwriter for high officials in the Truman administration.[14] But Acheson makes strong claims for his own speech's importance, calling it a "reveille" or wake-up call on the need to rebuild Europe. President Truman called the speech a preparation for the Marshall Plan.[15]

The speech was supposed to have been given by President Truman himself, to the agricultural growers and exporters of the Delta region of Mississippi; but the Democratic Party in that state was deeply divided over who should succeed the gravely ill Senator Theodore Bilbo. Truman did not want to step into that crossfire himself, so he sent Acheson, still only an Undersecretary of State, to deliver the desired message in his own name. The speech said that faltering economies in Europe had to be assisted by import and export policies which would require governmental production and trade controls. The speech was meant to forestall attack from free-market advocates by presenting economic regulation as an anti-Communist measure. The fact that it is so little remembered or resented is a mark of its success.

(13) MARSHALL PLAN SPEECH
(HARVARD, JUNE 5, 1947)

In one of the most influential college commencement speeches ever given, Secretary of State Marshall proposed what would be passed as the European Recovery Program (ERP). The economic aid given to European countries, including recent enemies, has been celebrated widely as an act of practical altruism—we helped others and, at the same time, stabilized the world situation and guaranteed our future markets. It cost Americans about thirteen billion dollars. The United States was even so generous as to offer the same assistance to the Soviet Union as to its European allies. But George Kennan, with his views on the Soviet psychology, knew that the USSR was bound to turn down the offer—it was ideologically unacceptable for Marxists to cooperate in restoring capitalist markets, and administration of the program would bring American officials behind the Iron Curtain. Kennan, remember, had written in the Long Telegram that the Soviets feared and resented any ameliorative measures that would put off what Marx had taught was the inevitable implosion of the capitalist system.

Sure enough, when the Americans invited all the European countries to a summer conference in Paris to plan the distribution of resources, the Soviet Union refused to attend, and persuaded its dependents, Czechoslovakia, Poland, and Hungary, to absent themselves as well. Kennan and others were pleased by this—opposing aid to war-torn countries undercut Soviet attempts to woo those countries. This was just one of the national security advantages provided by the Marshall Plan, beyond its overt purpose of stabilizing Europe. American administrators of the fund were now placed throughout Europe, in what proved to be useful listening posts for political developments. These administrators looked more benign than an occupying force.

These distribution posts were also infiltrated with covert operators of the sort Kennan was promoting with such vigor at the time. The plan provided these agents with funds not accounted for, that necessary condition of secret activities. Ten percent of the aid money went to administrative costs (5 percent from the American grants and 5 percent from the participating countries' matching funds). Much of this was diverted into covert activities. Richard Bissell, who dispensed the funds, said most of the ERP administrators did not know how much was being spent this way, and why. The funds were quietly tapped, country by country. At first they went mainly to the Office of Policy Coordination, the mild name for the first covert action team, and later they went to the CIA. Even the overall supervisor of the European operation, Paul Hoffman, was either unaware of this large diversion of sums, or chose to be ignorant of it. Hoffman "didn't want to know," Bissell said in a 1983 interview.[16]

The anti-Soviet dynamics of the Marshall Plan were spelled out by the National Security Council in the first year of its operation. Describing ways to place maximum strain on the Iron Curtain, the council included the European Recovery Program as one of these means:

> The most striking step in this direction was the original proposal for the ERP, as stated in Secretary Marshall's Harvard speech on June 5, 1947. By forcing the Russians either to permit the satellite countries to enter into a relationship of economic collaboration with the west of Europe, which would inevitably have strengthened east-west bonds and weakened the exclusive orientation of these countries toward Russia, or to force them to remain outside the structure of collaboration, at heavy economic sacrifice to themselves, we placed a severe

strain on the relations between Moscow and the satellite countries, and undoubtedly made more awkward and difficult [the] maintenance by Moscow of its exclusive authority in the satellite capitals. . . . The disaffection of Tito [in the Soviet satellite Yugoslavia], to which the strain caused by the ERP problem undoubtedly contributed in some measure, has clearly demonstrated that it is possible for stresses in the Soviet-satellite relations to lead to a real weakening and disruption of the Russian domination.[17]

(14) "X" ARTICLE IN *FOREIGN AFFAIRS* (JULY 1947)

Just as Kennan's Long Telegram was one of the most influential diplomatic dispatches sent in the twentieth century, his *Foreign Affairs* article was perhaps the most influential diplomatic article published in that time. Hamilton Fish Armstrong, the editor of *Foreign Affairs,* the journal of the Council on Foreign Relations, had not been at Kennan's CFR lecture, but he heard good things of it and asked Kennan to publish it.[18] Kennan told him he had spoken from notes, but shortly after the talk he finished his revised memo for Forrestal. It is often said that the *Foreign Affairs* article was just a public version of the Long Telegram, but in fact it was taken from the Forrestal memo. When Kennan asked permission of the State Department to publish it, he was advised that it would be best to use a pseudonym (Kennan chose "X"), so it would not be taken as an official policy statement—an effort quickly made futile when Forrestal leaked the identity of the author to Arthur Krock. Secretary of State Marshall was upset that Kennan had gone public, but he could do nothing about the fact that a midlevel official had given a prior approval.

The emphasis of the article is psychological, reflecting the original memo's direction to Forrestal. The "X" paper is a period piece, strongly marked by its time. Kennan says that diagnosing the "political personality" of the Soviets is one of the most testing "tasks of psychological analysis." He speaks of the Russian leaders' "compulsion" and "insecurity" and "frustration" and "self-delusion," as well as of "the oriental mind." We are in the era of Alfred Hitchcock's *Spellbound*. Dating the piece more obviously, Kennan describes Soviet responses to the Communist line in terms not of Pavlov's dog, but of the dog in the Victor Records commercial of the time: "Like the white dog before the phonograph, they hear only 'the master's voice.'"

Kennan at one point chooses a more historical comparison to describe Communist delusions, but it is a strange one—the religion of Socrates! He quotes one of Edward Gibbon's less defensible remarks:

> From enthusiasm to imposture the step is perilous and slippery: the daimon of Socrates affords a memorable instance, how a wise man may deceive himself, how a good man may deceive others, how the conscience may slumber in a mixed and middle state between self-illusion and voluntary fraud.[19]

Afterward, in another swoop, Kennan compares Soviet leaders to the family in Thomas Mann's *Buddenbrooks*.

The article is mainly remembered for putting the word "containment" on so many officials' lips, but Kennan's literary airs contributed to the confusion over just what he meant by the term. He introduces the idea with an image of a river in spate that was a commonplace of epic from Homer's time on:

> Its [the USSR's] political action is a fluid stream which moves constantly, wherever it is permitted to move, toward a given goal. Its main concern is to make sure that it has filled every nook and cranny available to it in the basin of world power. But if it finds unassailable

barriers in its path, it accepts these philosophically and accommo-
dates itself to them. The main thing is that there should always be
pressure, unceasing constant pressure, toward the desired goal. . . .
In these circumstances it is clear that the main element of any United
States policy toward the Soviet Union must be that of a long-term,
patient, but firm and vigilant containment of Russian expansive
tendencies.

So America must build dams in front of "every nook and cranny" in
the "basin of world power." What kind of dam? An army barricade, a
stiffened ally, a threat? And what if the stream has already slipped into
some nook—must it be expelled (what would later be called a policy
of "rollback")? Kennan says the United States must use "counterforce."
The "policy of firm containment" will "confront the Russians with
unalterable counterforce at every point where they show signs of encroaching upon the interest of a peaceful and stable world." Kennan
would later claim that he was referring to nonmilitary force—to economic pressure and enticement, to diplomatic maneuver and bargaining. But these are not normally called "force," or "counterforce." He
could claim his innocence of more aggressive intent because his recommendations of sabotage teams to overthrow Communist regimes
were still hidden in classified documents when he wrote his *Memoirs*.

Walter Lippmann was the most trenchant critic of the "X" article.
He wrote twelve newspaper columns attacking it, which were quickly
published in book form.[20] Lippmann thought Kennan's approach too
sweeping, too aggressive, too provocative in anticipating diplomatic
failure and moving toward confrontation. Kennan would admit in his
Memoirs that his piece was "careless and indiscriminate" in its language,
and that he did not make clear that he was not talking about *military*
containment. He used another nature image to describe his own trouble
with the river-in-spate image:

Feeling like one who has inadvertently loosened a large boulder from the top of a cliff and now helplessly witnesses its path of destruction in the valley below, shuddering and wincing at each successive glimpse of disaster, I absorbed the bombardment of press comment that now set in.[21]

Kennan argued later that Lippmann misunderstood his "X" article because the journalist mistakenly thought Kennan was the author of the Truman Doctrine speech. Aside from that, Kennan claimed in his *Memoirs* that he agreed with Lippmann's "excellent and penetrating" book.[22] As with the Long Telegram, Kennan would live for years trying to back off from his most influential writings.

That was not his reaction at the time. Writing again from a sickbed (as when he dictated the Long Telegram), he composed a detailed answer to Lippmann and tried to get it published in *Foreign Service Review*. He was frustrated when that journal's editor, Henry Villard, turned his piece down because of its "personal angle." Kennan wrote a friend, "I don't know what to do with it, and if Chip [Ambassador to Moscow Chester Bohlen] would like to show it to Lippmann, he can." Bohlen did not want to intervene.[23] By the time he had cooled off, in his *Memoirs,* Kennan said he did not send the response to Lippmann because Marshall had taught him that "planners don't talk."

(15) NATIONAL SECURITY ACT (JULY 16, 1947)

The National Security Act was the major reorganization of all the country's military resources. It created the separate air force referred to in an earlier chapter, and it merged this, along with the army and navy, into a single national military establishment (later renamed the Department of Defense), with a new office—that of Secretary of Defense—over the whole establishment. A Secretary of the Army replaced the old Secretary of War. The President created the National Security Council to give him policy advice on security matters outside the State Department. It would become a rival to the State Department, and its classified directives (NSC orders) would authorize much of the secret activity of the Cold War.

Since the main burden of this act was military and centralizing, military intelligence was also centralized, in the new office of Director of Central Intelligence (DCI). Thus the CIA came into being. It was meant to coordinate all the sources of intelligence in one clearinghouse. The information thus gathered was to be made available

(a)   to the President,
(b)   to the heads of departments and agencies of the executive branch,
(c)   to the Chairman of the Joint Chiefs of Staff and senior military commanders, and
(d)   where appropriate, to the Senate and House of Representatives and the committees thereof (National Security Act, Section 103).

The impression would grow up later that the CIA was to report only to the President. That was far from the case. The information could go to the new Department of Defense, which had autonomous authority to act on it (Section 106). Truman would later say he was reluctant to form a spy unit, for fear it could turn into "a Gestapo." He wrote after he left the presidency that he only meant it to be an information-collecting agency, not one licensed to indulge in "strange activities."[24] Yet, despite misgivings expressed by Dean Acheson and others, the act did allow for "covert activities," defined thus: "As used in this title, the term 'covert action' means an activity or activities of the United States Government to influence political, economic, or military conditions abroad, where it is intended that the role of the United States Government will not be apparent or acknowledged publicly" (Section 503 e).

Each covert activity had to be separately based on a written "finding" by the President that "found" the action was "necessary to support identifiable foreign policy objectives of the United States and is important to the national security of the United States" (Section 503 a). "A finding may not authorize any action that would violate the Constitution or any statute of the United States" (Section 503 a5). Furthermore, all covert actions had to be reported to the appropriate members of Congress. Four committees were to be informed on overt acts (the Intelligence and Appropriation committees of each chamber) and two for covert acts (the Intelligence committees), according to Section 504 e2. The DCI "shall keep the congressional intelligence committees *fully and currently* informed of *all* covert actions which are the responsibility of, are engaged in by, or are carried out for or on behalf of, *any* department, agency, or entity of the United States Government *including significant failures*" (Section 503 b1, emphasis added). Furthermore, "Nothing in this Act shall be construed as authority to withhold information from the congressional intelligence committees on the grounds that providing the information to the congressional intelligence committees would constitute the unauthorized disclosure of classified information or information relating to intelligence sources and methods" (501 2e).

These limits would routinely be ignored or defied by future DCIs. Richard Helms made defying them a proud matter of principle, and William Colby would be denounced as a traitor to the Agency when he obeyed them. Daniel Patrick Moynihan resigned in protest from the Senate Intelligence Committee when William Casey defied the Congress. The CIA was not set up to be an illegal body, but it quickly became one.

(16) NSC 4/A, PSYWAR
(DECEMBER 17, 1947)

The NSC set up a separate covert war operation in the CIA, devoted to what was known in the intelligence community as "psywar" (psychological warfare). The Kennan psychological analysis of the USSR was so prevalent, it was felt, that a secret campaign must be undertaken to play on Soviet compulsions, feed their insecurities, and break down their myths—in short, to mess with their minds, on the grounds that they were trying to mess with our minds. As the council put it:

> The USSR is conducting an intensive propaganda campaign directed primarily against the US and is employing coordinated psychological, political and economic measures designed to undermine non-Communist elements in all countries. The ultimate object of this campaign is not merely to undermine the prestige of the US and the effectiveness of its national policy but to weaken and divide world opinion to a point where effective opposition to Soviet designs is no longer attainable by political, economic or military means. In conducting this campaign, the USSR is utilizing all measures available to it through satellite regimes, Communist parties, and organizations susceptible to Communist influence.

The American response, it was argued, should be to mirror our enemies, but to be even more sophisticated in psychological manipulation. I first heard the term "psywar" being used by James Burnham, who had helped recruit William F. Buckley, Jr., right out of Yale, to join the CIA's secret operations in Mexico (under the direction of E. Howard Hunt). Psywar was an Ivy League specialty.

6

COMPLETING THE
APPARATUS (1948–1952)

After the rapid mobilization of national security resources in 1947, several areas remained for extension of the policies already put in place.

(17) NSC 7, COUNTEROFFENSIVE
(MARCH 30, 1948)

This National Security Council document asserts that the USSR's objective is "domination of the world" and warns that "a defensive policy cannot be considered an effectual means of checking the momentum of communist expansion." Already the NSC was moving beyond the goal of "containment." What it secretly called for now was "a world-wide counter-offensive" aimed at "the defeat of the forces of Soviet-directed world communism." This was not simply a matter of foreign pressure, but of countering a domestic threat, since the Soviets were mounting a "worldwide Fifth Column," able to do so only because "communism has been allowed to operate as a legitimate political activity."[1]

(18) NSC 10/2, OFFICE OF POLICY COORDINATION (JUNE 18, 1948)

The covert operations that had been authorized by NSC 4/A were focused on psywar. George Kennan, George Marshall, and James Forrestal decided that more was needed. Armed intervention might be called for. The fears of the time arose from the Italian elections of 1948, when it was suspected that the Communists could win many local elections, or even the national one. In that case, America would be dispensing Marshall Plan moneys to a Communist entity. Kennan said that such an outcome *must* be prevented. He wrote to Marshall on March 15, 1948:

> If Communists were to win election [in Italy] our whole position in Mediterranean, and possibly in western Europe as well, would probably be undermined. I am persuaded Communists could not win without strong factor of intimidation on their side, and it would clearly be better that *elections not take place at all* than that Communists win in these circumstances.
>
> For these reasons I question whether it would not be preferable for Italian government to outlaw Communist party and take strong action against it before elections. Communists would presumably reply with civil war, which would give us grounds for reoccupation of Foggia fields [air base] *or any other facilities we would wish.* This would admittedly result in much violence and *probably a military division of Italy;* but we are getting close to the deadline and I think it might well be preferable to a bloodless election victory, unopposed by ourselves, which would give the Communists the entire peninsula at one coup and send waves of panic to all surrounding areas. (Emphasis added)[2]

James Forrestal tried to take less drastic measures, funneling money and propaganda assistance to the PSDI (Social Democratic Party) in

Italy. He asked the DCI of the time, Admiral Roscoe Hillenkoetter, to use CIA funds for the project. But Hillenkoetter went to the General Counsel of the CIA, Lawrence Houston, for authorization of the funding, and Houston decided that the National Security Act did not give the Agency power to tamper with free elections in other countries—Congress would not have approved that in 1947. Houston said that the act conceived of the CIA as an information-gathering agency. That function was best served by "deep cover" agents who passively acquired knowledge, not endangering their cover by disruptive actions. When Forrestal was turned down, he privately raised funds himself and funneled them to Italy.[3]

But if the CIA could not directly meddle in foreign politics, the NSC decided that it could do so indirectly. Kennan and Marshall got the NSC to authorize a body outside the CIA to direct Marshall Plan funds into covert activities. The new body was given an anodyne title, the Office of Policy Coordination, and the Marshall Plan gave it secret money to spend at will. As Tim Weiner writes, "It was a global money-laundering scheme that stayed secret until well after the Cold War ended."[4] If the original CIA charter was limited, the OPC was given a breathtakingly broad mandate, a secret one not passed through Congress. The growing executive power to carry on secret operations was spelled out brazenly. It said that covert actions were those "that, if uncovered, the U.S. Government can plausibly disclaim responsibility for."

> Specifically, such operations shall include any covert activities related to: propaganda; preventive direct action, including *sabotage,* anti-sabotage, *demolition* and evacuation measures; *subversion* against hostile states, including assistance to *underground resistance movements, guerrillas and refugee liberation groups.* . . . (Emphasis added)[5]

These last named actions always included assassinations—which soon began to take place. The path had been opened toward murderous doings ahead, performed in secret till Frank Church's Senate special committee turned some of them up in 1975.

Kennan, it was noted earlier, said that this kind of operation, kept secret and using unauthorized funds, had to be entrusted to a single director (the Groves model), and he named OSS veteran Frank Wisner as the one man. Wisner, himself unstable (he committed suicide in 1965), attracted a wild crew of operatives, making a general factotum of Carmel Offie, who quickly recruited ex-Nazis to carry out covert operations in what was called Operation Blackstone.[6] As the OPC grew ever more lawless, Kennan came to regret his part in its creation—as he did his more militant writings.[7] Walter Bedell Smith, who became the fourth DCI in 1950, took offense at Wisner's operation outside his control and demanded that the OPC lose its independent status.[8] It was folded into the CIA's own covert activities branch, the Office of Special Operations. But that just meant that some of the wild men were given a new base, from which they were involved in CIA activities like the anti-Castro operations in Cuba.

(19) NSC 20/1, ROLLBACK
(AUGUST 18, 1948)

In the summer of 1948, James Forrestal, now the Secretary of Defense, asked the NSC to clear up the confusion over what "counterforce" meant in the doctrine of "containment." The NSC responded in a document that states what is a theme of this book, the prolonged existence of war in peacetime. It said: "This Government has been forced, for purposes of *the political war now in progress,* to consider more definite and *militant objectives* toward Russia" (emphasis added). Though saying that peacetime does not license all the acts of war, the document asserts that the goal of both peace and war is to "reduce the power and influence of Moscow." And "it must be recognized that the smaller the

gap between peacetime and wartime purposes, the greater the likeli-
hood that a successful military effort will be politically successful as
well." The document goes beyond containment to what would become
known as rollback. "The projection of Russian power beyond its
legitimate limits must be broken up."

In this effort, "it is our objective to bring to the Russian people and
government, *by every means at our disposal,* a more enlightened concept
of international relations" (emphasis added). "With respect to the satellite area, the aim of U.S. policy in time of peace is *to place the greatest
possible strain on the structure of relationship by which the Soviet domination
of this area is maintained,* and gradually, with the aid of the natural and
legitimate forces of Europe, to maneuver the Russians out of their
position of primacy" (emphasis added). Accordingly, "our first aim with
respect to Russia in time of peace is to encourage and promote by
means short of war the gradual *retraction* of undue Russian power and
influence from the present satellite area." And "a major factor in
the achievement of all of these aims without exception would be the
degree to which we might succeed in *penetrating or disrupting the iron
curtain*" (emphasis added).

These pressures might, it is admitted, lead to war. But:

> Granted the relationship of antagonism which is still basic to the entire
> relationships between the Soviet Government and non-communist
> countries at this time, war is an ever-present possibility and no course
> which this Government might adopt would appreciably diminish this
> danger. The converse of the policy set out above, namely to accept
> Soviet domination of the satellite countries and to do nothing to
> oppose it, would not diminish in any way the danger of war. On the
> contrary, it can be argued with considerable logic that the long-term
> danger of war will inevitably be greater if Europe remains split along
> the present lines than it will be if Russian power is peacefully with-
> drawn in good time.

This is a sketchy premonition of what would soon be called "brinkman-ship," the belief that the best chance for peace comes from risking war.[9]

The last section of NSC 20 discusses what the aims should be if war comes. Demanding unconditional surrender, with a takeover of all Soviet territory, is declared an unattainable goal. The aim should be the removal of the Communist Party from power, the freeing of the satellite countries, and the possible partition of the Soviet Union itself. It is hard to see how even these limited goals could be achieved in war without the use of nuclear weapons, though the document is silent on this subject. Even a classified paper like this one could not reveal the nuclear planning that was taking shape around the Strategic Air Command in 1948. It should be remembered that the first Soviet atom bomb was still a year off when NSC 20 was drafted.

(20) NSC 20/4, WAR AIMS
(NOVEMBER 24, 1948)

This codicil to NSC 20 spells out more specifics of the war-in-peace and war-in-war plans of the United States. The codicil admits that the Soviets cannot invade America, or even damage it significantly, but they can take over the Eurasian landmass, and the United States must prevent this, by war if necessary. The document establishes a policy that will shortly be implemented by the formation of the North Atlantic Treaty Organization (NATO).[10]

(21) NORTH ATLANTIC TREATY
(APRIL 4, 1949)

The formation of a defensive alliance to balance the power of the Soviet Union and its satellites was a militarization of the European Recovery

Program. America could take the lead in this alliance, since it brought the indispensable counter to the Soviets' massive ground forces—tactical nuclear weapons. Kennan's Policy Planning Staff went out of its way to say that the military alliance was meant not to replace the economic program but to make it more workable. Assurance about security would allow the affected nations to concentrate on their recovery: "A North Atlantic Security Pact will affect the political war only insofar as it operates to stiffen the self-confidence of the western Europeans in the face of Soviet pressure. Such a stiffening is needed and desirable. But it goes hand in hand with the danger of a general preoccupation with military affairs, to the detriment of economic recovery."[11]

Some European nations were uneasy about this concentration of force, on the grounds it made Europe a Soviet military target, but only Charles de Gaulle advanced from mere resistance to outright refusal of NATO, in order to develop France's independent nuclear strike force (the *force de frappe*). Like other politico-military structures, NATO has perdured after the disappearance of its original rationale (opposition to the Soviet bloc).

(22) NSC 58, FREEING SATELLITE COUNTRIES (SEPTEMBER 14, 1949)

Encouraged by Tito's split from the Soviet Union, this document called for pressuring other satellite countries to follow the same course.[12]

(23) NSC 68, WAR MOBILIZATION (APRIL 14, 1950)

It was mentioned earlier that when Dean Acheson and Paul Nitze urged the President to develop the hydrogen bomb, their description of the Soviet threat laid the groundwork for NSC 68. Earlier National Security Council documents, influenced by George Kennan, had conceded that the Soviet Union could not wage war with the United States and have any hope of winning. NSC 68 said that within a few years, the Soviets could in fact do that. This meant that the defense capabilities of the United States had to be drastically upgraded, perhaps tripling expenditures on them.

Paul Nitze, the principal formulator of NSC 68, was more perturbed than even James Forrestal had been three years before. In the interval the Russians had exploded their own atom bomb, and the Communists had prevailed in China. There was an air of panic in Washington, strengthening all the pressures that had reshaped America in terms of Bomb Power. Now there were two Bomb Powers, and it was urged that American forces had to be dramatically preponderant over Russian forces.

Acheson felt that the same tactic used to promote the Truman Doctrine had to be relied on again. It was time to "scare the hell out of the country." The aim, as Acheson put it in his memoirs, was to increase the (already great) power of the presidency:

> The purpose of NSC 68 was to so bludgeon that mass mind of "top government" that not only could the President make a decision but that the decision could be carried out.[13]

One means to this end was the use of exaggeration as an "educational" tool:

> Qualification must give way to simplicity of statement, nicety and nuance to bluntness, almost brutality, in carrying home a point. . . . If we made our points clearer than truth, we did not differ from most other educators and could hardly do otherwise.[14]

In order to prevent opposition based on cost, NSC 68 just omitted any mention of amounts needed for funding the new program. This was not an oversight.[15] The NSC was a bit awed by its own estimates of how much would eventually be needed. It reasoned that the funds, however great, would come if the groundwork for panic had been thoroughly established. The council hoped to increase the military budget from $13.5 million to $50 million per annum.[16] No wonder it set out to exaggerate the threat.

In the words of the document:

> Any substantial further extension of the area under the domination of the Kremlin would raise the possibility that no coalition adequate to confront the Kremlin with greater strength could be assembled. It is in this context that this Republic and its citizens in the ascendancy of their strength stand in their deepest peril.[17]

A massive stockpiling of atomic weapons of greater strength was called for, but it had to be supplemented with a program of increased defensive forces of all kinds:

> A further increase in the number and power of our atomic weapons is necessary in order to assure the effectiveness of any U.S. retaliatory blow, but would not of itself seem to change the basic logic of the above points. Greatly increased general air, ground and sea strength, and increased air defense and civilian defense programs would also be necessary to provide reasonable assurance that the free world could survive an initial surprise atomic attack of the weight which it is estimated the U.S.S.R. will be capable of delivering by 1954 and still permit the free world to go on to the eventual attainment of its objectives. (416)

The sense of emergency came from a vast overestimation of the Soviet power. This is the time when official documents began to talk of the widening "gap" between Soviet and American military force. "In the face of obviously mounting Soviet military strength ours has declined relatively" (402). "The readiness of the free world to support a war effort is tending to decline relative to that of the Soviet Union" (405). "The Soviet Union is widening the gap between its preparedness for war and the unpreparedness of the free world for war" (409). "It is clear that our present weakness would prevent us from offering effective resistance at any of several vital pressure points" (414). What Acheson presented as a kind of principled exaggeration would serve as just a basis and beginning for fear of manpower gaps, bomber gaps, missile gaps, and throw-weight gaps.[18]

The document calls for a massive war mobilization, the greatest since World War II. Anticipating objection to this as a strain on the economy, the document argues that war measures like those of the 1940s actually strengthened the economy. "Progress in this direction [economic growth] would permit, and might itself be aided by, a buildup of the economic and military strength of the United States and the free world" (407). Of course, as in World War II, governmental regulation and planning would be necessary.

> The capability of the American economy to support a buildup of economic and military strength at home and to assist a buildup abroad is limited not, as in the case of the Soviet Union, so much by the ability to produce as by the decision on the proper allocation of resources to this and other purposes. . . . The programs now planned will not meet the requirement of the free nations. The difficulty does not lie so much in the inadequacy or misdirection of policy as in the inadequacy of planned programs, in terms of timing or impact, to achieve our objectives. (405, 410)

This document lies midway between Acheson's Delta Council speech on government control of the economy and President Truman's seizure of the steel mills as a Korean War measure. It expects Republican objections to higher budgets, bigger government, and interference with the free market, but its authors know that fear of communism can trump these matters.

Since the country was so exposed to peril, the document advocates first use of atomic weapons rather than waiting for a Communist "surprise attack" (414).

It has been suggested that we announce that we will not use atomic weapons except in retaliation against the prior use of such weapons by an aggressor. It has been argued that such a declaration would decrease the danger of an atomic attack against the United States and its allies.

In our present situation of relative unpreparedness in conventional weapons, such a declaration would be interpreted by the U.S.S.R. as an admission of great weakness and by our allies as a clear indication that we intended to abandon them. Furthermore, it is doubtful whether such a declaration would be taken sufficiently seriously by the Kremlin to constitute an important factor in determining whether or not to attack the United States. It is to be anticipated that the Kremlin would weigh the facts of our capability far more heavily than a declaration of what we proposed to do with that capability.

Unless we are prepared to abandon our objects, we cannot make such a declaration in good faith until we are confident that we will be in a position of attaining our objectives without war, or, in the event of war, without recourse to the use of atomic weapons for strategic or tactical purposes. (418)

Such a massive program was bound to be debated in the summer of 1950, but during that summer the North Koreans crossed the thirty-eighth parallel into South Korea, and Truman was braced for war by the time he signed this document as NSC 68/2 on September 30, 1950. The document itself said that no part of the world could be ceded to Communist control. Kennan had objected that the Truman Doctrine did not distinguish central from peripheral concerns. NSC 68 wiped out that distinction entirely. There was no part of the world that did not threaten American security if it adopted communism. This was a zero-sum gain where any Communist gain was an American loss: "The assault on free institutions is worldwide now, and in the context of the present polarization of power a defeat of free institutions anywhere is a defeat everywhere" (389).

That standard would take America into endless conflict in the back alleys of the world. The National Security State was now almost entirely assembled and put at the President's disposal.

(24) PSYCHOLOGICAL STRATEGY BOARD (APRIL 4, 1951)

Though a psywar operation was authorized for the CIA by NSC 4/A in 1947, the President decided to create, by secret directive, a separate organization for this purpose, one geared to the Korean War and under his White House control (it was technically a subcommittee of the NSC). Communist "brainwashing" was a concern at the time, and ways to counter it by imitating it were being explored. These included "gray" and "black" propaganda—propaganda that was not attributed to America but to nonhostile countries (the gray kind), or attributed to "Soviet, Communist, or other hostile sources" (the black kind).[19]

An early investigation by the Psychological Strategy Board found that the Economic Cooperation Administration had 69 persons working on propaganda, while the State Department had 2,724. The PSB was supposed to evaluate the effectiveness of these efforts, improve them, and coordinate them, but bureaucratic turf guarders made them resist outside direction, and Eisenhower as President returned psychological warfare to the CIA and other agencies.

(25) NATIONAL SECURITY AGENCY
INAUGURATED, (NOVEMBER 4, 1952)

As the CIA diversified into more and more actions, its original function of merely collecting information was comparatively neglected.
The NSA was created simply to monitor information (and to protect
it cryptographically); it would soon be doing that by satellite signals,
among other ways. It was not to engage in aggressive actions, overt or
covert. Nor was it to monitor information from United States citizens
domestically—which would violate the Fourth Amendment ban on
warrantless searches of a citizen's domain. In 1975 the Church committee discovered that the Nixon administration had been doing that,
so Congress passed the Foreign Intelligence Surveillance Act (FISA) in
1978, setting up a special court to meet in secret and issue warrants for
surveillance. The Bush administration would violate *that* act. It had an
instrument at hand for doing so in the NSA, and the NSA was ready.
Even before the 9/11 attacks, the head of the NSA, Michael Hayden,
asked the incoming Bush administration for permission to keep a
"powerful, permanent presence" on the commercial networks. He said
he liked to "live on the edge," thus "my spikes will have chalk on them"
(from flirting with the boundaries).[20]

The National Security State was formed in and by the Cold War. It
was modeled on entities from World War II—the OSS, the Manhattan
Project, the wartime FBI, among other things. It was continued
and intensified during the war on terror, with even greater secrecy,
executive unaccountability, and projects like torture and extraordinary
rendition. The whole structure is outside the Constitution. There had
been nothing like it before in American history. Arthur Schlesinger,
Jr., traced some of its more obvious features.

In the 1950s American foreign policy called on the American government to do things no American government had ever tried to do before. The new American approach to world affairs, nurtured in the sense of omnipresent crisis, set new political objectives, developed new military capabilities, devised new diplomatic techniques, invented new instruments of foreign operations and instituted a new hierarchy of values. Every one of these innovations encouraged the displacement of power, both practical and constitutional, from an increasingly acquiescent Congress into an increasingly imperial Presidency.[21]

That passage does not stress enough that the National Security State was riddled with illegalities from the outset, that it was in multiple ways unaccountable to the Congress or the people, was secret and secretly funded, resorting to subversion, sabotage, and assassination. It may be said—it has been said—that all governments do these things. But the United States had not done so in any systematic way before the period after World War II. And other countries do not have the United States Constitution.

Accountability is the essence of democracy. If people do not know what their government is doing, they cannot be truly self-governing. But the National Security State assumes that government's secrets are too important to be shared, that only those in the know can see classified information, that only the President has all the facts, that we must simply trust that our rulers are acting in our interest.

The test of accountability is funding. The activities of the National Security State have relied on many forms of secret funding. According to the National Security Act, Section 504, the CIA must request funds for specific purposes and cannot use them for any other purpose, except in two cases. It can use a Reserve for Contingencies in the CIA for a new purpose if it "has notified the appropriate congressional committees of the intent to make such [money] available to such activity" (504 2c). Or it can use funds on covert action after a presidential finding authorizes it, and Congress must be informed as soon as possible of the use, even if the covert action has been a "significant failure" (503 b1). Such partial and select accounting does not meet the requirements of Article I, Section 9, Clause 7, of the Constitution:

> No money shall be drawn from the Treasury but in consequence of appropriations made by law; and a *regular* statement and account of the receipts and expenditures of *all* public money shall be *published* from time to time. (Emphasis added)

"From time to time" does not mean "occasionally"—that would not meet the test that the account be "regular." In past legal usage, the phrase meant "from [one] time to [the next] time"—that is, without gaps, without leaving unreported times. Why add this phrase when the clause has already said "regular"? The addition accepts the fact that the reporting need not be instantaneous, day by day—it may appear in increments, so long as each new report takes up where the last one left off. We have a perfect parallel to this in the requirement of Article I, Section 5, Clause 3:

> Each House shall keep a journal of its proceedings and *from time to time* publish the same, excepting such parts as may *in their judgment* require secrecy; and the yeas and nays of the members of either house on any question shall, at the desire of one fifth of those present, be entered on the journal. (Emphasis added)

Here, too, the record is to be complete, published from one time to the next publication. Admittedly, this clause allows Congress members to keep some things secret if it is *their judgment* that this is necessary—an exception, be it noted, not contained in the financial reporting clause. Congress is the supreme judge of national security, not the President.

It alone can declare war. It alone can fund war. It alone can call militias into national service. It alone can decide what needs to be kept secret. Not the President.

There is one more use of the term "from time to time" in the Constitution, and it, too, proves that this is a matter of accountability, of establishing a complete record. Article II, Section 3, begins:

> He shall from time to time give to the Congress information of the state of the union, and recommend to their consideration such measures as he shall judge necessary and expedient.

As the Congressional Research Service edition of the Constitution points out, this clause "imposes a duty rather than confers a power."[22] One is required to give reports to a superior, and Congress is the President's superior. The "time to time" phrase, once again, does not mean "randomly"; it means on a continuing basis. So George Washington set the precedent of making the report annually (a time not specified in the Constitution—only its regularity is required, as in the "regular" reporting of expenditures). It is a sign of the inflation of the presidency in modern times that the "State of the Union" address is now treated as a presidential prerogative, not a duty, as his power to set a legislative agenda (far from the "recommending" duty of the clause itself).

On the financial reporting clause, the Congressional Research Service text of the Constitution, edited by Lester Jason and others, declares: "This clause is a limitation upon the power of the Executive Department and does not restrict Congress in appropriating moneys in the Treasury."[23] That is, only Congress can raise money. It cannot give to another branch what the Constitution limits to it. Executive actions that raise money apart from Congress, that hide the money raised from Congress, that fail to report all expended moneys to Congress, are all violations of the Constitution. The Manhattan Project was therefore a violation of the Constitution—a thing perhaps understandable, or forgivable, as a onetime emergency measure in war. But as a standing policy, over decades, extended to many other parts of government, this creates a steady erosion of the constitutional system. The National Security State is in permanent constitutional crisis.

III.

PRESIDENTIAL WARS

7

KOREA

The first opportunity to assert the full prerogative of the Commander in Chief in the Bomb Power era—and to show the force of the fresh-minted NSC 68—came when North Korea crossed the thirty-eighth parallel to invade South Korea in June 1950. Secretary of State Dean Acheson advised President Truman to send American troops without asking Congress to declare war. He did this to protect the authority of the President to respond to the challenges of the nuclear age with maximum flexibility. North Korea did not itself pose a nuclear threat, but exercising the President's supposed autonomy of action protected his possible use of the Bomb in the future. Besides, Korea could escalate to a nuclear threat, since North Korea was seen as doing Stalin's will, and the freedom of the President to act at each stage of any confrontation with the Soviets was at stake. At the very first session planning a response to the invasion, Truman wondered, if the Soviets intervened, whether all the Soviet air bases in the Far East could be wiped out. Air Force Chief of Staff Hoyt Vandenberg said they could "if we used A-Bombs."[1] Later, Truman would admit that use of the Bomb was "under active consideration" in the Korean War.

The real foe, then, was the Soviet Union, not the small power in North Korea, which Acheson called "a Soviet puppet," whose attack was "mounted, supplied, and instigated" by Stalin.[2] Truman would later write: "I expressed the opinion that the Russians were trying to get Korea by default, gambling that we would be afraid of starting a third world war and would offer no resistance."[3] The full power of the United States—which now meant the power of the President—had to be committed to the world struggle outlined in NSC 68. Acheson said that Truman acted as he did because he revered his own "great office," which "he was determined to pass on unimpaired by the slightest loss of power or prestige."[4] Averell Harriman, then Truman's Special Assistant to the President, recalled that Truman told him he could not ask for congressional approval, since that would weaken the hand of future presidents. This, said Harriman, "was characteristic of President Truman. He always kept in mind how his actions would affect future presidential authority."[5] The new status of the Commander in Chief had to be asserted in this first possible vindication of it.

The decision to go to war in Korea was taken within forty-eight hours of the news that North Korea had crossed the thirty-eighth parallel, with no consultation outside the very top executive ranks—even George Kennan was not asked for an opinion. Why the haste? The anti-Communist rationale of NSC 68 gives the underlying motive, but does not explain the precipitous speed. One unspoken but genuine consideration is that the Truman administration was under fierce criticism, from the right-wing "China lobby" and its many congressional devotees, for having "lost China." There had even been some bluster about impeaching Truman for "abandoning" Chiang Kai-shek. The storm of protest anticipated over any further "loss" of Korea exerted a strong pressure on all those around Truman.

The new Commander in Chief power was based on the premise that response to a nuclear threat had to be so rapid that only the President, unchecked by Congress, could act quickly enough to be effective. That same rationale was now applied to the non-nuclear threat in Korea. To wait for Congress to declare war, it was feared, would enfeeble the President. Acheson said that allowing Congress to debate the matter would blunt the full force of American reaction, confuse the public, and demoralize the military. Criticism of a President had now become unpatriotic, a refusal to "support our troops." The President, acting without a congressional declaration of war (which would certainly have been given), could not—said Acheson—ask for even a congressional *resolution* approving his acts, once taken.

Acheson wrote: "Congressional hearings on a resolution of approval at such a time, opening the possibility of endless criticism, would hardly be calculated to support the shaken moral of the troops or the unity that, for the time, prevailed at home."[6] Another administration document said: "The circumstances of the present crisis make *any debate* over prerogatives and power essentially sterile if not dangerous to the success of our foreign policy" (emphasis added).[7] Any debate at all was illegitimate. This would become an official refrain in the era of Bomb Power.

When Senator Robert Taft objected that the President was acting unconstitutionally, Acheson dismissed him: "The ground Senator Taft chose was typical senatorial legalistic ground for differing with the President."[8] "Senatorial legalistic ground" was Acheson's synonym for the Constitution. With typical bravado, Acheson would write: "There has never, I believe, been any serious doubt—in the sense of non-politically inspired doubt [like Taft's]—of the President's constitutional authority to do what he did."[9] To prove this, Acheson had the State Department draw up a list of eighty-three cases where a President sent troops without congressional authorization. But Arthur Schlesinger, Jr.—who, to his later regret, joined Acheson in attacking Taft at the time—took a later and a longer historian's look at this list of eighty-three cases and declared it bogus.

year
1805
JEFFERSON

The precedents invoked by Acheson, the State Department, and [Senator Paul] Douglas were precedents for limited action to suppress pirates or to protect American citizens in conditions of local disorder. They were not precedents for sustained and major war against a sovereign nation.[10]

A favorite "precedent" of defenders of presidential war is Jefferson's and Madison's "Barbary Wars." But Jefferson informed Congress in his first annual message that he had ordered only defensive action when Americans were attacked by Tripolitan pirates, since he was "unauthorized by the Constitution, *without the sanction of Congress,* to go out beyond the line of defense" (emphasis added). "The legislature will doubtless consider whether, by authorizing measures of offence also, they will place our force on an equal footing with that of its adversaries."[11] Jefferson asked for—and got—a mere resolution, not a declaration of war, since the pirates were not a sovereign nation. In fact, as Louis Fisher points out, "Congress enacted ten statutes authorizing action by Presidents Jefferson and Madison in the Barbary Wars."[12] A parallel to the pirates would be the terrorists of modern times, whose acts are not those of a sovereign state.

UN "POLICE ACTION"?

The Truman administration did an end-run around Congress by invoking the UN as its authorizing body, but then it did an end-run around the UN. It used the UN while claiming that the UN was using it. It claimed that it was responding to the call of the Security Council to enforce treaties (the one dividing Korea at the thirty-eighth parallel). But the call was initiated by the United States, which acted before the Security Council resolved that it should—as even Acheson later admitted: "Some American action, said to be in support of the [UN] resolution of June 27, was in fact ordered, and possibly taken, prior to the resolution."[13] He knew very well that the Seventh Fleet had been sent before the resolution was passed.

On the Saturday when Acheson learned of the attack, it was decided at a meeting in the State Department that the UN should be the "aegis" under which to take action. Though it would be hard to assemble the Security Council on a weekend, the Secretary-General, Trygve Lie, was informed that the United States wanted that to happen as soon as possible. Acheson got approval of these first steps from the President in an 11:20 p.m. phone call to Truman's home in Independence, Missouri.[14] Early the next morning, the State Department relayed to Lie, through its representative to the UN, Ernest A. Gross, the statement it wanted from the Security Council, saying: "An attack of the forces of the North Korean regime . . . constitutes a breach of the peace and an act of aggression."[15] When the Security Council met on Sunday afternoon, it issued a statement that dropped the words "act of aggression," waiting for fuller information, but it called upon the North to withdraw from South Korea, and it asked all members to "render every assistance" for accomplishing this.[16]

The United States wanted a specifically military authorization from the UN (since it was already taking military action), and it got it on Tuesday, when a second Security Council meeting called on members to "furnish such assistance to the Republic of Korea as may be necessary to repel the armed attack."[17] It would not have got it, of course, if the Soviet Union had not been boycotting the Security Council because it continued to include the government of Taiwan among its members. If the Russian representative, Yakov Malik, had been in attendance, he would no doubt have used his veto to kill the resolution.

This raised an interesting question at the time. If, as Acheson maintained, North Korea was moving on Stalin's timetable, why did it attack at a time when the Russians were absent from the Security Council?

George Kennan suggested that they probably did not anticipate intervention by the UN in what was more a civil war among Koreans than an international incident: "The Russians were surprised that the United Nations would regard it as within its competence to take cognizance of what was, in the formal sense, a civil war."[18] At any rate, basing American power on the absence of Malik was a shaky proposition, as even right-wing judge Robert Bork wrote in 1971: "The President's constitutional powers can hardly be said to ebb and flow with a veto of the Soviet Union in the Security Council."[19]

This in turn raises another interesting point: What would the United States have done if Malik had been present and vetoed the Security Council resolution? There is no doubt. It would not have made any difference. The troops were already on their way. The NSC had declared that any Communist gain, anywhere, could not be accepted. It was an American war, despite the UN fig leaf. The truth peeped out in a meeting of congressional leaders at the White House on the very day when the second Security Council resolution was passed. Acheson told the members of Congress why military action was necessary to stop the Communist army in Korea. When he finished, a surprised President Truman said, "But Dean, you didn't even mention the UN."[20] Truman felt the need for a UN pretense, which Acheson was not even bothering with. Asked at a press conference, on the day after that congressional meeting, whether the country was at war, Truman answered, "We are not at war." What is it then, the reporter asked—a "police action"? "That is exactly what it amounts to."[21]

But the UN excuse was, in fact, inexcusable. The very UN Charter Truman invoked, he was also violating. To use the UN to circumvent Congress was to violate the UN Charter, which said that Congress had to approve any commitment of U.S. troops to the UN. Congress cannot give away its constitutional monopoly on the right to declare war. If it cannot give it away even to the President, it certainly cannot give it away to some non-U.S. entity—and it never did give it away. Before accepting the UN Charter, Congress made sure that it had a "special agreement," under Article 41 of the charter, that the Congress's UN Participation Act would be honored. Section 6 of that act says that the commitment "shall be subject to the approval of the Congress by appropriate Act or joint resolution."

This understanding of America's participation in the UN had been spelled out in congressional testimony by none other than Dean Acheson when membership in the UN was being debated, and Republican objections to it had to be assuaged. Testifying as Undersecretary of State before the House Committee on Foreign Affairs in 1945, Acheson was asked by John Kee, a House Representative from West Virginia, if a President could ever commit troops to a UN action without the permission of Congress. Acheson answered:

> The answer to that question is "No," that the President may not do that, that such special agreements refer to the special agreement which shall be subject to the approval of the Congress, so that until the special agreement has been negotiated and approved by the Congress, it has no force and effect.[22]

When Republicans moved that approval of UN actions be by the same process as formation of a treaty—by two-thirds of the Senate—this was defeated by a vote of 57–14, on the grounds that *both* houses had to approve a war measure.[23]

The terms of this debate were obvious, since it had all been fought out before, when President Wilson asked Congress to ratify the League of Nations. The request was rejected because it would have given the League power to commit U.S. troops to its requirements. Senator Henry Cabot Lodge of Massachusetts knew his history (he received a Harvard doctorate in the subject from Henry Adams) and he knew the Constitution. He said in the Senate debates that the League as proposed would violate American law.

The United States assumes no obligation to preserve the territorial
integrity or political independence of any other country, or to interfere
in controversies between nations—whether members of the League or
not—under the provisions of Article 10, or to employ other military
or naval forces of the United States under any Article of the treaty for
any purpose, *unless in any particular case the Congress, which, under the
Constitution, has the sole power to declare war or authorize the employment of
the military or naval forces of the United States, shall by Act or joint resolution
so provide.* (Emphasis added)[24]

Wilson's own closest allies—Robert Lansing, Colonel House, Bernard
Baruch, Herbert Hoover, et al.—advised him to accept Lodge's condition for entry into the League, but he refused. According to him, this
would "cut out the heart of this Covenant," allowing Congress to "nullify" a treaty. His stubbornness doomed America's participation in the
League.

Why was he so adamant? Because he was a believer in supreme
executive power when no one else was. In his book *Congressional Government* (1885), he parroted Walter Bagehot's criticisms of the United
States Constitution, which, by dividing up jurisdictions and responsi-
bilities, made the presidency and the judiciary too weak. By the time
he wrote *Constitutional Government in the United States* (1908), Wilson
had seen Theodore Roosevelt invigorate the presidency, a development
he celebrated:

Some of our presidents have deliberately held themselves off from using
the full power they might legitimately have used, because of conscien-
tious scruples, because they are more theorists than statesmen. . . . The
President is at liberty, both in law and conscience, to be as big a man
as he can. . . . The initiative in foreign affairs, which the President pos-
sesses *without any restriction whatever,* is virtually the power to control

them *absolutely.* The President cannot conclude a treaty with a foreign power without the consent of the Senate, but he may guide every step of diplomacy, and to guide diplomacy is to determine what treaties must be made, if the faith and prestige of the government are to be maintained. He need disclose no step of negotiation until it is complete, and when in any critical matter it is complete the government is virtually committed. Whatever its disinclination, the Senate may feel itself committed also. (Emphasis added) [25]

Wilson wrote that as a political scientist and a university president. Eleven years later, he tried to enact what he had formulated "more as a theorist than a statesman," giving the Senate in the Treaty of Versailles what he felt they must be committed to. He wanted the power that Truman would actually wield in 1950. But he did not have the Bomb Power that made Truman able to act in defiance of both the United States Constitution and the United Nations Charter. He had no way to realize that what he envisioned was impossible before the Manhattan Project showed modern Presidents the way.

MacARTHUR'S DISASTER

But Truman's power to start his own war did not guarantee that he had the power to win it. That truth came crashing in on Truman just three months after his war began. On November 1, 1950, as General MacArthur confidently drove up through North Korea and approached the Chinese border at the Yalu River, he was ambushed by 260,000 Chinese troops, who drove him back in what Robert Beisner calls "the worst rout in U.S. military history."[26] There were 11,000 American casualties, which caused a panicky disorientation and dismay in the American public and in the Truman administration. Doomsday

scenarios floated around Washington. Orville Anderson, Comman-
dant of the Air War College, said publicly that the air force was ready
and able to bomb Moscow.[27] Famous "wise man" Bernard Baruch sent
a message to Secretary of State Acheson saying that the American
people wanted Truman to remedy this desperate situation by using
the atom bomb in Korea.[28] Some felt that Truman must take drastic
measures, starting with the firing of Dean Acheson. Senator Joseph
McCarthy of Wisconsin said that Truman and Acheson had led America into "the Korean death trap," and even the influential columnist
Walter Lippmann said that Acheson had to go.[29] George Kennan, fro-
zen out of the decision to enter the Korean War, was called back in
to give advice, and to sound out Yakov Malik at the UN on Soviet
intentions.[30]

Truman, trying to show he could control the disaster, was, like
Baruch, thinking of the Bomb. At a November 30 press conference he
reminded people that no matter how bad things looked, he still had his
"ace in the hole." He would take "whatever steps are necessary to meet
the military situation." One reporter thought he was hinting at the
power given by the ultimate weapon, and directly asked if his statement
included use of the atomic bomb. Truman answered, "That includes
every weapon we have." Was such use under "active consideration"?
Truman replied, "There has always been active consideration of its use."
Another question showed how incredulous the press was at this news.
"Did we understand you clearly that the use of the bomb is under active consideration?" "Always has been. It is one of our weapons."

Another reporter pointed out that the United States was fighting as
part of a UN combined force, under a Security Council mandate.
With that in mind, another reporter asked, "Does that mean we
wouldn't use the atomic bomb except on a United Nations authorization?" Truman replied, "No, it doesn't mean that at all. The action
against Communist China depends on the action of the United

Nations. The military commander in the field will have charge of the use of the weapons, as he always has."[31] The idea that atomic weapons were at the disposal of Douglas MacArthur was supremely upsetting to many people all around the world. In London, Prime Minister Clement Attlee was so disturbed that he said he must fly to the United States immediately to seek a clarification from the President. Acheson tried to quiet the fears of an unleashed MacArthur in a new statement that said, "It should be emphasized that, by law, only the President can authorize the use of the atomic bomb, and no such authorization has been given."

But what Truman said had to be defended as well. The statement also said:

> The President wants to make it certain that there is no misinterpretation of his answers to questions at his press conference today about the use of the atom bomb. Naturally, there has been consideration of this subject since the outbreak of the hostilities in Korea, just as there is consideration of the use of all military weapons whenever our forces are in combat. Consideration of the use of any weapon is always implicit in the very possession of that weapon.[32]

That was not clarification enough for Prime Minister Attlee, who arrived in Washington, on December 1, to express his and his country's misgivings. He was accompanied by his military and Foreign Office advisers, who pleaded with Truman to withdraw from the forlorn effort in Korea and concentrate on the defense of Europe.[33] Attlee would later claim that in a private session with the President, he got a pledge that the United States would not use the Bomb without getting approval from Britain's leaders. That would later be denied by Acheson, among others; but Truman himself told the gathered British and Americans after the private session that the United States "would not consider the use of the Bomb without consulting with the United Kingdom."[34] Attlee tried to get this agreement in writing, but Truman said his word was always good enough.

Acheson was appalled when he heard what Truman said. He took the earliest possible moment to hustle Truman into the Oval Office, with the Prime Minister, where he tactfully warned the President that he was breaking the law (the Atomic Energy Act) if he gave anyone else a veto over the Bomb's use. Besides, it would be politically disastrous to give Britain a veto over a decision even the U.S. Congress was excluded from.[35] Another "clarification" had to be quickly cobbled together, one that Attlee went along with it, but reluctantly. It said:

> The President stated that it was his hope that world conditions would never call for the use of the atomic bomb. The President told the Prime Minister that it was also his desire to keep the Prime Minister at all times informed of developments which might bring about a change in the situation.[36]

After the crushing blow to MacArthur's troops, the logic of NSC 68 began to turn upon its own head—just *because* the Communist menace was everywhere, America's troops should not be massively pinned down in one place. With threats of war elsewhere growing, "Truman's military advisers were increasingly insistent that ways be considered for withdrawing 'with honor' from Korea."[37] As Acheson writes, "The generals saw an increased threat of general war and were clear that it should not be fought in Korea."[38] MacArthur refused to accept a "substitute for victory." He told the Joint Chiefs of Staff that he could prevail if he was allowed "hot pursuit" into China, with air cover, a naval blockade, troops from Nationalist China, and the possible use of tactical atom bombs.[39] On December 29, 1950, the Joint Chiefs sent a message framed by Acheson and Truman telling MacArthur,

"Major war should not be fought in Korea," so the General was to withdraw, inflicting as much damage on his enemies as he could, and begin to consider an "orderly evacuation."[40] MacArthur complained that this was surrendering the ideal of a unified Korea under a non-Communist government. Acheson granted that this was still the ideal, but "United Nations and United States war aims had not included the unification of Korea by armed force *against all comers, and Chinese intervention had now removed this as a practical possibility*" (emphasis added).[41]

The Truman administration now started negotiating for a cease-fire and a return to the two Koreas separated at the thirty-eighth parallel, the status quo ante. The British, still nervous over the atom bomb threat, enthusiastically backed this proposal. But MacArthur was so opposed to it that he issued his own public threat to the Chinese, thus sabotaging the negotiations (as Acheson put it).[42] Truman had heretofore flinched from the obvious need to fire MacArthur. He knew this would be highly unpopular with much of the public and Congress. His standing in the Gallup poll had already sunk to 26 percent, and it would go even lower (to 22 percent) after the firing.[43] This is the lowest for any president since polling records have been kept. Acheson, who knew that MacArthur had long needed firing but could not be fired, gave Truman his feelings over its final occurrence:

> It was summed up, I said, by the story of the family with the beautiful young daughter who lived on the edge of a large army camp. The wife worried continually, and harassed her husband, over the danger to which this exposed their daughter. One afternoon the husband found his wife red-eyed and weeping on the doorstep. The worst had happened, she informed him; their daughter was pregnant! Wiping his brow, he said, "Thank God that's over!"[44]

It was the only relief that could be felt around the White House. Many there now wished they had secured congressional approval of the war, so blame for it could be shared. Instead, even those in Congress who had supported it initially (boisterous cheers were raised in the House when it was announced that troops were being dispatched to Korea) were by now contemptuously calling it "Truman's war." And even after MacArthur was fired on April 11, armistice efforts were protracted on through the rest of Truman's term. Getting rid of Mac-Arthur did not mean getting rid of generals who still thought they could win in Korea. Nor did South Korean President Syngman Rhee want to go along with a return to the status quo ante. Acheson wrote that Rhee had a "mania for reunification" of the whole country under his government.[45]

Peace talks deadlocked over two issues, the truce line and prisoner-of-war exchanges. The United States team wanted to strike a truce at the line of advance UN troops had made into North Korea, and the North wanted a return to the thirty-eighth parallel. Congressional hawks called this latter position a surrender. On the POWs, the North wanted automatic repatriation of all prisoners, but the U.S. wanted only voluntary return, since the return of people to Soviet countries in Europe had been painted as atrocities—Truman said at the time, "We will not buy an armistice by turning over human beings for slaughter or slavery."[46] The war dragged on for two more years. Soldiers in Korea were deserting—a development Truman attributed to "the sabotage press."[47] Faced with continuing casualties, Truman tried to minimize them by citing high death rates from domestic car accidents.[48] Acheson said that the casualties in the two years of stalemate were only 63,200, compared to 78,800 in the first year alone.[49] When Truman announced that he would not run again in 1952, he lost what little leverage remained for him, and he left the war to his successor, as Presidents Johnson and Bush would leave their later wars as unfinished business. Eisenhower, with his great personal standing, could bring America to swallow the bitter pill of a major defeat in war, the first in United States history.

Acheson's "precedents" for waging wars without Congress were bogus. But they left a putative precedent for the future. Korea was not a UN "police action." It was not even a UN war. It was an American war, a President's war—Truman's war. And Truman found out what others would learn after him, that presidential wars may be easy to start but they are almost impossible to end.

8

PERMANENT
EMERGENCY

In the frenzy that followed on MacArthur's disaster near the Yalu River, Acheson advised Truman to declare a state of national emergency. The losing war's impact on the economy was feared, and added powers given to the President would make it easier for him to wield "controls on the economy." Seen in this light, Acheson was just taking the next step after his Delta Council speech of 1947, the one calling for greater economic regulation by the government. Thus the proclamation of a state of emergency, issued December 16, 1950, focused on the economy (among other things). It said:

> I summon our farmers, our workers in industry, and our businessmen to make a mighty production effort to meet the defense requirements of the Nation, and to this end to eliminate all waste and inefficiency and to subordinate all lesser interests to the common good.

In the light of Truman's continuing struggle with labor unions—especially the railroad unions whose strike he had earlier called "communistic" and tried to break by drafting the workers—some claimed this was a move to mobilize the country in dictatorial ways.

There was, in fact, something scary in the rolling out of this proclamation. The *New York Times* ran a screaming banner headline at the top of its front page: PRESIDENT PROCLAIMS A NATIONAL EMERGENCY. Under it was the news of a freeze on auto prices. The proclamation itself began:

> Recent events in Korea and elsewhere constitute a grave threat to the peace of the world and imperil the efforts of this county. . . . World conquest by communist imperialism is the goal of the forces of aggression that have been loosed upon the world.

So it was not just South Korea that was under attack, but the whole world. Any restrictions on American freedom were to be seen as protecting larger freedoms:

> If the goal of communist imperialism were to be achieved, the people of this country would no longer enjoy the full and rich life they have with God's help built for themselves and their children; they would no longer enjoy the blessings of the freedom of worshipping as they severally choose, the freedom of reading and listening to what they choose, the right of free speech including the right to criticize their Government, the right to choose those who conduct their government, the right to engage freely in collective bargaining, the right to engage freely in their own business enterprises, and the many other freedoms and rights which are a part of our life.

All these rights would be taken away by the Communists when they defeated us, so the only way to save them was to sacrifice some of them now to defeat the Communists.

Foes of Truman saw something sinister in this call for new power. At the December 13, 1950, White House session where Truman revealed his intentions to congressional leaders, Senator Kenneth Wherry of Nebraska jotted advice to his fellow Republicans—not to grant the new powers, since Truman was planning to use them to prevent his impeachment.[1] That is how far Truman had fallen, dragged down by his unwinnable war.

States of national emergency had traditionally been declared in times of war (as martial law) or internal rebellion (as insurrectionary law) or natural disaster (as emergency relief). The collapse of U.S. troops in Korea seemed to have elements of all three. But Truman was disposed to see emergency as a continuing thing that had been with him from the moment he became President. Being poised for hair-trigger response to nuclear threat was now the normal state of the presidency. After VJ Day ended the world war, he had wanted to put America on a permanent military alert by giving the citizens Universal Military Training (UMT).

UMT

This was an attractive idea to Truman, since it gave more formal expression to the growing sense that the President was the Commander in Chief of all the people, not just of the military. Truman doggedly promoted UMT from the time he first discussed it at a press conference in June of 1945. Later that year (October 23) he presented UMT to a joint session of Congress. It called for a year of military training for every male on completion of high school, followed by six years in the General Reserve. He returned to the idea in a message on January 21, 1946. Only during the Korean War did he cease pressing for this favorite idea, since the military men needed to conduct the training in this large program were now occupied overseas.[2]

DRAFTING RAILROAD WORKERS

The first opportunity Truman had been given to exercise emergency powers was during the railroad workers strike of 1945. President Roosevelt had extracted no-strike pledges from some unions during the war, and there was a stalling of wage raises that the unions meant to remedy after VJ Day. Business, too, was quick to throw off wartime price controls. On December 3, 1945, Truman asked Congress to set up an arbitration board to consider grievances, calling for a thirty-day no-strike period while the board made its findings. When Congress did not give him this at once, Truman set up the board himself. This body tried—and failed—to settle a dispute between General Motors and its workers. The Office of Price Administration tried—and failed—to hold down steel prices. When John L. Lewis took coal workers out on strike on April 1, 1946, Truman ordered Julius Krug, his Secretary of the Interior, to seize the mines and order the strikers back to work. Krug could not enforce the order, so the companies surrendered to Lewis's terms.[3]

By this time, Truman was in a towering rage at the unions. How dare they disobey the Commander in Chief? When the railroad unions went on strike in May of 1946, Truman handwrote a seven-page frothing-at-the-mouth speech denouncing them. It is a speech that even Truman's adoring biographer, David McCullough, calls "appalling."[4] Truman wrote:

> First came the threatened automobile strike. Your President asked for legislation to cool off and consider the situation. A weak-kneed Congress didn't have the intestinal fortitude to pass the bill.
>
> Mr. [Phil] Murray [of the CIO] and his Communist friends had a conniption fit and Congress had labor jitters. Nothing happened. . . .
> Every single one of the strikers and their demagogue leaders have been living in luxury, working when they pleased. . . .

I am tired of the government's being flouted, vilified and misrepresented. Now I want you men who are my comrades in arms, you men who fought the battles to save the nation just as I did twenty-five years ago, to come along with me and eliminate the [John L.] Lewises, the [A. F.] Whitneys [of the trainmen's union], the [Alvanley] Johnstons [of the railway union], the Communist [Harry] Bridges [of the longshoremen's union] and the Russian Senators and Representatives and really make this a government of, by and for the people. I think no more of the Wall Street crowd than I do of Lewis and Whitney.

Let us give the country back to the people. Let's put transportation and production back to work, hang a few traitors, make our own country safe for democracy, tell the Russians where to get off and make the United Nations work. Come on boys, let's do the job.

Truman meant to match these extreme words with equally extreme action. If the strikers would not return to work, he would draft them into the army. That, you may remember, was what General Groves wanted to do with the scientists he was putting to work. When Truman's Attorney General, Tom Clark, said he did not think that action legal, the President said, "We'll draft them and think about the law later."[5]

Truman meant to deliver his pyrotechnic speech on the radio the next night at ten o'clock. But his press secretary, Charlie Ross, persuaded him to let Clark Clifford tone the speech down.[6] Clifford removed the personal insults, and put more stress on national security as the basis for Truman's action—that was usually the trump card in the National Security State. The revised speech said:

I come before the American people tonight at a time of great crisis, the greatest crisis in this country since Pearl Harbor. The crisis of Pearl Harbor was the result of action by a foreign enemy. The crisis tonight is caused by a group of men within our own country who place their private interest above the welfare of the nation. . . . It is inconceivable that in our democracy any two men [Johnston and Whitney] should be placed in a position where they can completely stifle our economy and ultimately *destroy our country.* (Emphasis added)

Truman said nothing on the radio about drafting the strikers—he was saving that for his address to Congress the next day. But he said he would call out troops to break the strike if the unions did not return to work by four o'clock the next day.

The next afternoon, the President went before Congress to ask for emergency legislation to draft the strikers into the army. In the midst of his speech he was handed a note that said the unions had given in to his demands. He stopped, smiled, and read the note out loud; he received warmer applause than he had ever received before, or would receive after, from the Congress. But he nonetheless read the speech prepared by Clifford to the very end.[7] Congress refused to vote him the power to draft the workers, but by then it was a moot matter.

SEIZING STEEL MILLS

Truman won the next round in the union wars, but by going to the courts, not to Congress. John L. Lewis threatened another miners strike, and Truman asked a federal court to issue a restraining order. When Lewis ignored the order, the judge found him and the union guilty of criminal and civil contempt, and fined the union $3.5 million and Lewis $1,000. The Supreme Court upheld the conviction (by a 5–4 decision) but reduced the fines. Lewis won in the end, though, after a disaster in the Centralia mine that killed eleven men. Public sympathy for the victims let Lewis negotiate a new contract, and the fines were dropped.[8] But Truman won another fight in the courts when the trainmen's union went out in February 1949. The President again threatened to call out troops against union officials acting "like a bunch of Russians." But the court settled the matter with another conviction of contempt and fines.

Things were very different during the steel strike of 1952. In Korea, the nation was teetering on the edge of disaster, and Truman used his Commander in Chief powers to seize eighty-six steel mills, saying their product was vital to the war. In a radio address explaining his action to the nation, he resorted to his Bomb Power for authorization: If steel production stops, he said, we will have to "cut down and delay the atomic energy program."[9] The speech was written by Clark Clifford, who again compared the present crisis to the challenge of Pearl Harbor. That was becoming an all-occasion excuse.

Truman was assured by his friend and appointee Chief Justice of the Supreme Court Fred Vinson that seizing the mills was the President's prerogative. But even Truman's admiring biographer had to disapprove of this action by a Chief Justice:

> Such counsel clearly violated the division between branches of govern-
> ment and was particularly improper in this instance, since a seizure
> of the steel industry was bound to be challenged in the courts and
> thus Vinson himself, very likely, would wind up having to weigh
> the case.[10]

That is exactly what happened. Truman had used the Interior Department when he tried to commandeer the railroads. For the steel companies he used his Secretary of Commerce, Charles W. Sawyer. That is why, when the Youngstown Iron Sheet and Tube Company joined other companies bringing suit against the government's action, the case reached the Supreme Court as *Youngstown Sheet and Tube Co. et al. v. Sawyer*. And, sure enough, Justice Vinson presided over the case, though he should have recused himself after consulting with the President before the mills were taken over.

Vinson joined with two other lightweights, Justices Stanley Reed and Sherman Minton, in defending the President's actions.[11] Vinson wrote the dissenting opinion for the three. Six heavier hitters made the majority ruling against the seizure. Hugo Black wrote the majority's opinion, and concurrences were written by Felix Frankfurter, William O. Douglas, Robert Jackson, Harold Burton, and Thomas Clark.[12] Truman was especially stunned that his old friend and his own appointee as Justice, former Attorney General Clark, voted against him. He wrote off the six in the majority as second-raters (though his four nominations for the Court were generally inferior to the five placed there by Roosevelt): "I could not help but wonder what the decision might have been had there been on the Court a Holmes, a Hughes, a Brandeis, a Stone. . . . I think Chief Justice Vinson's dissenting opinion hit the nail right on the head, and I am sure that someday his view will come to be recognized as the correct one."[13]

That has clearly not happened. Black's majority opinion relied on the most important point. Article I of the Constitution states: "*All legislative powers* herein granted shall be vested in a Congress of the United States" (emphasis added). Truman was trying to make law on his own. Some people defend wide-ranging executive orders as fulfilling the presidential duty, spelled out in Article II, Section 3, to "take care that the laws be faithfully executed." But Black points out, "The President's power to see that the laws are faithfully executed refutes the idea that he is to be a lawmaker. The Constitution limits his functions in the lawmaking process to the recommending of laws he thinks wise and the vetoing of laws he thinks bad." The laws he is to execute come from the source of "all legislative powers herein granted." Speaking to Truman's executive order in this case, Black says, "The President's order does not direct that a congressional policy be executed in a manner prescribed by Congress—it directs that a presidential policy be executed in a manner prescribed by the President." In this case, Congress had actually made clear that it did *not* want to authorize confiscation in strike situations:

Moreover, the use of the seizure technique to solve labor disputes in order to prevent work stoppages was not only not authorized by any congressional enactment; prior to this controversy, Congress had refused to adopt that method of settling labor disputes. When the Taft–Hartley Act was under consideration in 1947, Congress rejected an amendment which would have authorized such governmental seizures in cases of emergency. Apparently, it was thought that the technique of seizure, like that of compulsory arbitration, would interfere with the process of collective bargaining. Consequently, the plan Congress adopted in that Act did not provide for seizure under any circumstances. Instead, the plan sought to bring about settlements by use of the customary devices of mediation, conciliation, investigation by boards of inquiry, and public reports. In some instances temporary injunctions were authorized to provide cooling-off periods. All this failing, unions were left free to strike after a secret vote by employees as to whether they wished to accept their employers' final settlement offer.

If the Congress wants to change its legislation, that is its prerogative, not the President's.[14] "This is a job for the Nation's lawmakers, not for its military authorities."

EXECUTIVE ORDERS

The ruling in the steel case applies to many modern executive orders, though it is not often invoked. Executive orders have been issued in blizzards since World War II, going far beyond their original rationale. It is licit for a President to decide the best way of implementing laws, and to instruct whichever departments he chooses for implementing them. These are little more than housekeeping rules, and they fall within the constitutional grant of power at Article II, Section 2, Clause

1: "he may require the opinion, in writing, of the principal officer in each of the executive departments, upon any subject relating to the duties of their respective offices." This clause has puzzled some as otiose, but it is the residue of a debate over the presidency in the Philadelphia convention. Many delegates feared giving all executive power to a single man, since that smacked of the king they had rebelled against. Some wanted a presidential council to advise the President, others a plural presidency made up of three representatives of different regions. What won the day for a single-man executive was James Wilson's argument that a single center of power could be held more accountable—how do you impeach one or more members of a plural body?

> In order to control the legislative authority, you must divide it. In order to control the executive, you must unite it. One man will be more responsible than three. Three will contend among themselves, till one becomes the master of his colleagues. In the triumvirates of Rome, first Caesar, then Augustus, are witnesses of this truth. The kings of Sparta and the consuls of Rome prove also the factious consequences of dividing the executive magistracy.[15]

It is no wonder, then, that the Constitution ended up saying that all executive departments must report to the President, who was to be held responsible for all their actions.

The majority of early executive orders, therefore, were simply housekeeping rules between the departments, or the choice of means to achieve the goal set by Congress in its laws. In the nineteenth century, many of these were personnel decisions to conform with civil service standards, or dispositions of the federal territory turned over to the executive by Congress. Other rules continue to be celebratory or symbolic, a kind of executive department cheerleading—which medals to give out, when to fly the flag at half-mast, and so on.

The trouble begins with executive orders that set policy and can stand in for laws. The tendency of modern executive orders to make law has been tracked in much of the literature, legal as well as political scientific. A change came in with the hyperactive presidency of Theodore Roosevelt: "Theodore Roosevelt issued 1,091 orders during his two terms, nearly as many as had been issued by all previous Presidents over the prior 111 years (1,259)."[16] Executive orders became more important from then on.[17] The rate increased throughout the twentieth century. Exceptional early policy directives tended to occur at times of emergency—with Washington's orders in the Whiskey Rebellion, for instance, or Lincoln's during the great insurrection. But a change has occurred since World War II, when we have been in a condition of permanent emergency, of war in peace—or so Presidents claim as they issue orders in increasing number and with increasing scope.

As one might expect, the Civil War was an emergency that Lincoln responded to with a number of executive orders, the Emancipation Proclamation among them, and several orders suspending habeas corpus and imposing martial law outside the immediate theater of battle. After the war, the Supreme Court found the suspension of habeas corpus by anyone but Congress illegitimate, except in places (like conquered Louisiana) where civil courts were not in operation.[18] But Chief Justice Roger B. Taney had made a one-judge ruling while on circuit duty in 1861, saying that only Congress can suspend habeas corpus rights.[19] Lincoln defied this ruling with an executive order of September 24, 1862, saying in part:

> Be it ordered:
>
> First, that during the existing insurrection as a necessary measure for suppressing the same, all rebels and insurgents, their aiders and abettors within the United States, and all persons discouraging voluntary enlistments, resisting militia drafts, or guilty of any disloyal practice affording aid and comfort to rebels against the authority of the United

States, shall be subject to martial law and liable to trial and punishment by court martial or military commission.

Second, that the writ of habeas corpus is suspended in respect to all persons arrested, or who are now, or hereafter during the rebellion shall be, imprisoned in any fort, camp, arsenal, military prison, or other place of confinement by any military authority or by the sentence of any court martial or military commission.[20]

On March 3, 1863, Congress would meet Taney's objections by passing its own Habeas Corpus Act suspending the right for military prisoners.

It should be noted that Lincoln operated under insurrectionary law throughout the rebellion. No declaration of war was called for, he maintained, since there was no war. His position throughout was that the Confederacy was not a separate and sovereign nation but a group of lawbreaking citizens.[21] When he issued the Emancipation Proclamation, it was as a method of quelling a riot. He stressed the limited *military* purpose of the emancipation as affecting *only* states in rebellion, and *only* if they did not give up their rebellion by a certain date. Had they put down arms, they could have retained their slaves. The Proclamation presented itself as a "necessary war measure."[22] The aim was to damage the rebellious army and recruit blacks into the anti–rebellion enforcers. He wrote that "the emancipation policy, and the use of colored troops, constitute the heaviest blow yet dealt to the rebellion."[23] He also said: "The original proclamation has no constitutional or legal justification, except as a military measure."[24]

His edict applied only to the theater of war.[25] The federal prosecutor Richard H. Dana said, before the war's end: "[The Proclamation] is a military act and not a decree of a legislator. It has no legal effect by its own force on the status of the slave. . . . If you [in the South] sustain the war, you must expect to see the war work out emancipation."[26] A *general* emancipation, Lincoln said, was not within his executive power. That would have to come by the amending action of the Congress and the states—as it did, with the Thirteenth Amendment.

Recent Presidents have defended their own runaway practice of issuing executive orders by using Lincoln as a precedent. His situation was unique—our only great national insurrection—and he was careful in limiting his actions to partial martial law. But it has now become common to let Presidents give orders for anything they want. Congress is simply left out of consideration, or openly defied. To take a simple instance: President George W. Bush wanted a program to have government fund religious charities—what he called the Faith-Based Initiative. He could easily have got this from Congress, which already had a similar bill (called Charitable Choice) under consideration. But Bush had his proposal presented to Congress by what his first director of the Faith-Based Initiative called the extreme positions of "the most far-right Republicans," and when he did not get what he wanted from Congress, he just launched the program on his own by executive order.[27]

It is common now for a President to preclude action by Congress for the sake of an option he personally prefers. As political scientist William G. Howell wrote: "Pre-empting Congress, Nixon used an executive order to design the Environmental Protection Agency, not as an independent agency, as Congress would have liked, but as an agency beholden directly to the President."[28] President Clinton, when Congress would not give him funds to help the Mexican economy, took money by executive order from the Exchange Stabilization Fund set up in 1934 to keep the dollar viable.[29] Sometimes people come to like the outcome of executive orders. Jefferson purchased Louisiana by executive order, though he admitted privately that this was an unconstitutional step.[30]

John F. Kennedy set up the Peace Corps and funded it from his discretionary funds because he did not want to take a chance on Congress setting it up and funding it the constitutional way.[31] Jimmy Carter, with an executive order, used emergency economic funds to pay off

Iran for returning hostages.[32] Sometimes the action becomes a matter of regret and reparations, as when Franklin Roosevelt imprisoned American Japanese by executive order during World War II. But the important thing is that increasing numbers of executive orders, of increasing importance, are now accepted as the ordinary course of legislation, so that they are rarely challenged by Congress or the courts, and the challenges are rarely successful.[33]

The most momentous executive actions have to do with war, defense, and national security—such as when George W. Bush set up an alternative justice system, secret and unaccountable, to "fight terror." But the advantage of permanent emergency, for the executive, is that even trivial things can routinely be accomplished by the crisis presidency. If everything is an emergency, all power is emergency power. And if a President can start a war on his own say-so, what can he not do?

Why have Congress and the courts let modern Presidents make so many unilateral laws on their own? The main reason is the Bomb. Anything that makes a President look weak lessens his authority for the Main Thing, makes him less imposing to potential enemies. By a paradox, the very thing that makes a President strong requires that he anticipate and be defended against any sign of weakness. But the President has always had many advantages in conflict with the other parts of government. The fact that other Presidents did not use these powers before World War II (Lincoln excepted) supports the idea that Presidents in the Bomb Power era have more confidence in their general ability to control events, and the other actors are more hesitant or intimidated.

Kenneth Mayer counts off ways that Congress and the courts start at a disadvantage in contests with the President. He can make a first move, achieving a fait accompli that others find difficult to undo, or to do so quickly. He is a single actor, and the Congress must work through a complicated layering of subcommittees, committees, majority factions, and minority factions. The courts must wait for a grievance to be brought to them, with subsequent appeals and procedural delays. It is often too late for the toothpaste to be put back into the tube. Once the President has put executive departments or officers to work on his project, those agents have an investment in their own prerogative and power that they will defend. In all these ways, the Presidents have reversed the logic of James Wilson's argument at the constitutional convention. He said the presidency must be single, not plural, to make it more accountable. The new way is to use the singleness of power to make it *less* accountable.

Besides, a President in the Bomb Power era can delay or abort action against the executive by denying access to evidence through the classification process. It has become common to deny courts what are labeled "state secrets," even when the secrets have no military importance. The key NSC 68, for instance, was not declassified for publication for a quarter of a century after it was written. There were leaks, of course, but legal action cannot be taken on the basis of leaks. Legal action requires hard evidence, original documents, or a cumbersome declassification of things classified in a wholesale way. In fact, all the NSC directives considered in earlier chapters were originally classified, meaning they could not be challenged for lack of knowledge about their scope or intent. They were classified, indeed, *by executive order*. Catch-22.

IV.

INFORMATION POWER

9

SECRECY AS EMBARRASSMENT COVER

Bomb Power translates directly to information power. Secrecy emanated from the Manhattan Project like a giant radiation emission. Anything connected with the Bomb—its development, scientific advisers, protection, deployment, possible use—was, as Senator Daniel Patrick Moynihan said, "born secret." It was self-classifying. General Groves himself said that "security" was born of the Bomb: "The Army as a whole didn't deal with matters of security until after the atomic bomb burst on the world, because it was the first time that the Army really knew there was such a thing [as security]."[1]

And the power of secrecy that enveloped the Bomb became a model for the planning or execution of Anything Important, as guarded by Important People. Because the government was the keeper of the great secret, it began to specialize in secret keeping:

What is especially striking about debates over classification and secrecy is that presidents have asserted almost complete command over the institutions and processes that both produce and protect secret information. . . . In practice, classification remains an outpost of almost absolute executive prerogative.[2]

The National Security State has a de facto monopoly on secrets— which, as Max Weber said, is a very desirable thing:

> Every bureaucracy seeks to increase the superiority of the profession- ally informed by keeping their knowledge and intentions secret. . . . The concept of the "official secret" is the specific invention of bureaucracy, and nothing is so fanatically defended by the bureaucracy as this attitude.[3]

Storing secrets is a source and sign of power. Allowing access to secrets is a favor that obliges those so favored. It is also a sign of prestige. "Clearance" to see classified documents is a badge of prestige in Wash- ington. We have seen in an earlier chapter how Robert Oppenheimer was stripped of influence by denying him clearance to read classified material.

The storehouse of secrets grows for many reasons, most not really having to do with national security. Senator Moynihan noted that there should have been less need to classify information after the Cold War ended and we were no longer locked in a struggle with the Soviet Union. But in fact the rate of classification was not only maintained but increased. In 1996, for instance, there were 62 percent more materials classified (almost six million documents) than in the preced- ing year.[4] And the dam on such secreting really broke with the 9/11 terrorist attacks in 2001: "In the year following the September 11 attacks, the government classified 11.3 million documents, which jumped to 14.2 million the following year, and 15.6 the year thereafter."[5] Many of these classified items are trivial.[6]

And the hope of decreasing the mountains of secrecy is vanishing or gone. Shrinking the stockpile of secrets is difficult, since the declassifying process is cumbersome and costly. As Lynne Duke reported in the *Washington Post,* in 2006, four hundred million pages of classified material were declared ready for review—*but:* "Fifty archivists can process 40 million pages in a year, but now they are facing 400 million. The backlog, inside the National Archives II facility in College Park [Maryland], measures 160,000 cubic feet."[7] All this would be true even if the government were seriously cooperating in the declassification. But the Bush II administration put the brakes on releasing presidential papers and dealing with Freedom of Information Act (FOIA) requests. As law professor Peter Shane writes:

> According to a study of twenty-two agencies by the Coalition of Jour-
> nalists for Open Government, the use of FOIA exemptions to deny
> requests jumped by 21 percent between 2000 and 2004, even though
> the total number of FOIA requests processed by these agencies, the
> largest volume handlers of FOIA requests, dropped by 13 percent.[8]

One of the principal aims of creating secrecy around govern-ment documents is to cover up criminal or bungling acts of the government. In 1957, Attorney General Herbert Brownell told Presi-dent Eisenhower that classification procedures were "so broadly drawn and loosely administered as to make it possible for government offi-cials to cover up their own mistakes and even their wrongdoing under the guise of protecting national security."[9] And in 1989, Erwin Gris-wold, who as Solicitor General had argued against publication of the Pentagon Papers, confessed that there were no state secrets in those papers, and published an op-ed column in the *Washington Post* saying, "It quickly became apparent to any person who has considerable experience with classified material that there is massive overclassifica-tion, and that the *principal concern of the classifiers* is not with national security but rather *with governmental embarrassment* of one sort or another" (emphasis added).[10]

The invocation of state secrets to prevent prosecution of things like the Reagan administration's trading of arms for hostages in Iran is a growing trend. From 1952 to 1976, the state-secrets privilege was used to deny evidence in five court cases. From 1977 to 2000, it was used sixty-two times. In the first four years of George W. Bush's administration, it was invoked thirty-nine times.[11] If anyone doubts whether the government was hiding something, he or she should reflect on the fact that the Supreme Court case on which withholding of evidence is based was itself a cover-up of a crime.

UNITED STATES V. REYNOLDS ET AL. (1953)

On October 6, 1948, an air force plane exploded and fell out of the sky in Georgia. It was doing experimental work on a guided missile system called Banshee. Five of the eight crew members aboard, and four of the five civilians, died. The other four parachuted to safety. It came out in an interview with the one surviving civilian that he and his non–air force fellows had not been instructed in the use of escape hatches; and there had been trouble with fires on other B-29s, so there seemed a prima facie case of criminal neglect in the civilians' deaths. Three of them were electrical engineers working on Banshee under contract with the Radio Corporation of America (RCA). Their young widows decided to sue the air force in a Pennsylvania district court. Their lawyer, Charles Biddle, asked for information in the air force's keeping—the official accident report and depositions from the three surviving crewmen. The air force refused to surrender the documents, saying the report was classified and the depositions were "hearsay." If the plaintiffs wanted such "hearsay," they could take their own depositions from the survivors.

The right to classify the report was said to derive from the house-keeping privilege, which dates back to a 1789 statute known as the

Housekeeping Statute, which directs agency heads to keep custody of their records (but does not say their information cannot be shared for good reason).[12] Biddle, a very sharp lawyer, probably wondered why this statute was cited, rather than some more exigent form of executive privilege. He did not know what later came out—that, sure enough, the accident report was routinely classified, as were all crash reports, but it was at the lowest grade of secrecy at the time—restricted—not secret or top secret. "Restricted" is defined as "for official use only, or when disclosure should be limited for reasons of administrative privacy."[13]

As the report had been routinely classified in 1948, it and all the other accident reports would be routinely declassified in 1996. All Biddle knew at this point was that the air force showed a ferocious determination not to give up the documents he was requesting. Could they really have state secrets in them? Was the accident caused by secret Banshee experiments? Did the air force depositions of survivors have things the survivors would not say now to the plaintiffs' lawyers? There was no way of knowing any of this, since the government blocked all access to information.

The Pennsylvania district judge, William Kirkpatrick, was not impressed by the air force argument. He ordered the government to turn over the documents or pay the damages the plaintiffs were demanding, saying he would review the material in camera to see if its release would be dangerous (the solution John Marshall reached when he called for Thomas Jefferson to turn over letters in the Aaron Burr case).[14] The air force argued that testimony by the three surviving crewmen should be enough for the plaintiffs' purposes, without their first depositions. (Why these first depositions of people in the plane were called "hearsay" when they spoke just after the crash, but not a year later, was not explained.)

The air force was now so wed to the idea of new depositions that it would fly the crewmen to the trial at its own expense. Biddle claimed that he could not knowledgeably question them without the accident report. Judge Kirkpatrick agreed. He wryly noted that the crewmen "are employees of the defendant, in military service and subject to military authority. . . . [T]hey will not be encouraged to disclose, voluntarily, any information which might fix responsibility upon the Air Force."[15] Still the air force refused to release the documents, and Judge Kirkpatrick awarded the women their damages.

The air force appealed this decision to the Third Circuit Court, with a famous jurist, Albert Maris, presiding over its three-judge panel. Here the air force went beyond the housekeeping privilege and alleged there were state secrets that had to be protected, for the sake of national security. Judge Maris said he would therefore review the information in camera before releasing it, but the air force refused to produce it even for this purpose, so the panel unanimously affirmed the women's award. The air force lawyers took their appeal to the final arbiter, the Supreme Court.

The Court that accepted the case was headed by Chief Justice Fred Vinson, whom we have already met defending his friend Harry Truman's seizure of the steel mills in 1952. That case, remember, linked Vinson with two others in a minority that was overruled by a majority of six that contained two of the "Greats" (Hugo Black and Felix Frankfurter) and two "Near Greats" (Robert Jackson and William O. Douglas).[16] Biddle must have taken heart from the fact that the Court went against the government in the steel case, decided just one year before his case against the air force. But an odd inversion occurred. This time the lightweights were in the majority supporting the air force, and the heavy hitters were in the minority. Black, Frankfurter, and Jackson stood with the lower courts, and Douglas at first voted with them—though at the last minute he said Vinson could add his name to that of the majority, made up of Vinson, Sherman Minton, Stanley Reed, Tom Clark, and Harold Burton. Vinson wrote the majority decision, saying that the plaintiffs forfeited their claim to more information when they declined to take what was offered them (new depositions from the crewmen). Vinson refused to call for an in camera look at the air force documents, and decided that the Korean War made it important to respect state secrets. In his decision, he assumed that the classified documents, which he had not seen, dealt with the Banshee experiment:

> In the instant case we cannot escape judicial notice that this is a time of vigorous preparation for national defense. Experience in the past war has made it common knowledge that air power is one of the most potent weapons in our scheme of defense, and that newly developing electronic devices have greatly enhanced the effective use of air power. It is equally apparent that these electronic devices must be kept secret if their full military advantage is to be exploited in the national interests. On the record before the trial court it appears that this accident occurred to a military plane which had gone aloft to test secret electronic equipment. Certainly there was a reasonable danger that the accident investigation report could contain references to the secret electronic equipment which was the primary concern of the mission.[17]

In reversing the appeal, the majority sent the case back to the original court for any further proceedings "consistent with the views expressed in this opinion."[18] Biddle saw little point in going back. But the air force was very anxious to get rid of this case, and it agreed to settle for an award close to the one first granted, if the women would agree to a "final release" of all claims against the government. The story seemed to be over, and it was—for roughly half a century (forty-seven years).

In 2000, the accident report that was withheld from the Court saw the light of day. The daughter of one of the RCA engineers who died in the crash, Judy Palya Loether, was only seven weeks old at the time of the accident, but she grew up with a great curiosity about the father she never knew. She was also a constant surfer of all things online. In 2000, while looking around on her computer for information about what her father did and how he died, she came across an entry, "Accident-Report.com," which promised to supply people with records of government airplane crashes. She did not know that there had been a Supreme Court case that hinged on the production of such a report, but she wanted to know if she could find anything about her father's crash.

Accident-Report.com belonged to Michael Stowe, a studious collector of aviation information. He had learned in 1996 that the Clinton administration, fighting the overclassification of documents, had declassified the air force accident reports with low (restricted) rank and an expired date. Stowe determined, at great cost, to acquire the microfilms of these reports—one thousand reels of them, at thirty dollars each. To help support his research hobby, he began supplying information on crashes, for a small sum, over the Internet. From this fortuitous connection between Ms. Loether and Mr. Stowe, the whole story of the air force's concern with the cause of a particular crash was finally revealed.

Ms. Loether purchased the report of her father's last flight, and sought out other relatives of the RCA engineers, to show them the report—all 220 pages of it (with fifteen photos of the wreckage). They read the report carefully, looking for details of any secret project the plane was involved in. There were none. Instead, the report told a horror story of incompetence, neglect, bungling, and tragic error. The plane had a troubled history, and it took off without heat shields that would keep the engines from overheating. When the outer left engine lost power during the plane's climb, the pilot tried to turn it off but inadvertently turned off the outer right engine. The copilot cut power to the left engine, but it was soon in flames. The inner left engine then went out, and the one working engine on the right side kicked the plane into a hard swerve to the left. The pilot, with only one of his four engines working, could not feed that engine more power without accelerating a spin. An expert who studied the report later said that the only way he could maintain speed and avoid a stall was to dive down to an altitude where it was safe to bail out.[19] Meanwhile, the first engine that caused trouble was about to explode.

The front tire bay, one of the escape routes, was blocked, and the opening of the bomb bay, the main escape route, created a drag that increased the plane's spin and threatened to stall it. The copilot kicked his way through the front wheel bay, but the pilot's chute caught on the plane and was disabled as he got out. Only two of the five civilians were close enough to the front bay to follow the copilot through it— and one of them, Judy Loether's father, died because his parachute would not fully open. This story was disgraceful to the air force, and that, not national security, explains the hard determination of the government not to let the story come out. The only protection of the wronged women was a Supreme Court that would follow the path of the excellent lower judgments and demand a look at the evidence in camera. The Vinson Court failed that test.

Ms. Loether, who did not know there had been a Supreme Court case when she first got the accident report, soon learned about the trials from the relatives of the other dead civilians. She asked several lawyers to look at this new evidence, at first without success. But when she went to the firm that had originally pled the case before the Court, she found a man who would take up again the cause of Charles Biddle (now dead)—Wilson Brown. It took Brown a while to find a strategy for reopening the case. The firm could not bring a new action against the air force, since the plaintiffs had signed a pledge not to do that. Instead, it could ask the Supreme Court to restore the first judgment on damages awarded the women, on the grounds that they had been deprived of them by a fraud practiced on the Court itself. The vehicle for this was the little-used writ of error *coram nobis,* which

shows that a judgment was based on fraudulent information—a writ
that had been used successfully in 1983, when the District Court of
San Francisco threw out the conviction of Fred Korematsu for disobeying
an order for the internment of Japanese-Americans on the grounds
that the Solicitor General of the United States had suppressed exoner-
ating evidence in his plea before the Supreme Court in 1944.[20]

Thirty-nine years passed between the conviction and the reversal
in that case. Why should a fifty-year interval (1952–2003) be ruled
out in Ms. Loether's case? The difference between the award for the
women first granted by the Court and what the air force settled for
was not great (fifty-five thousand dollars), but with compound interest over the years it had reached over a million dollars in 2003 cur-
rency.[21] But the important thing was to show that all invocations of a
state secret on the basis of *United States v. Reynolds* were based on a
governmental lie.

In the sixty-two cases between 1977 and 2001 where the government withheld evidence by citing *United States v. Reynolds,* some courts
not only reaffirmed the decision but broadened its application by a
"mosaic theory": they said that information not directly concerned
with national security may be pieced together with other parts of the
"mosaic" to give a different picture. Only government experts, not lay
observers or even judges, are qualified to see such technical connec-
tions.[22] By this test, almost any information can be presumed to have
a subtle connection with national security. The government now had a
greater stake than ever in retaining the validity of *United States v.
Reynolds.*

Chief Justice William Rehnquist's Court was very deferential to the
government in 2003—and no wonder. Before Nixon appointed him
to the Supreme Court, Rehnquist had been his Assistant Attorney
General, in which office he wrote a legal rationale for Nixon's secret
bombings of a neutral country (Cambodia), arguing that Presidents
have "a grant of substantive authority" to send military forces "into

conflict with foreign powers on their own initiative," without congressional authorization—against the National Security Act's provisions, not to say Article I of the Constitution. When faced with the new evidence of fraud in the state-secrets case, Rehnquist asked the Solicitor General at the time, Theodore Olson, whether he should take the *Reynolds* plea *coram nobis*.[23] Before becoming Solicitor General, Olson had successfully pled George Bush's case in *Bush v. Gore,* which gave Bush the Florida election and the presidency. Not surprisingly, Olson said the Court should not take the case, and he used the mosaic theory as his reason. The accident report did not have national security information, but it "might lead to disclosure" of connected things that would pertain to national security.[24] On June 23, 2003, in one sentence, the Court denied the right to file the writ *coram nobis*. Brown then took the case back to the district court, where he lost, as he did at the appeals level. The case now was, finally, over.

But its legacy lives on, in all the cases where evidence is denied a court on the basis of *United States v. Reynolds*. How many of those, too, are based on fraud and the covering up of official crime? The *Reynolds* case exists to make it impossible for us to find out.

10

SECRECY AS CONGRESS DECEIVER

IRAN-CONTRA

Since American hostages held by Iran helped bring down the presidency of Jimmy Carter, the administration of his successor, Ronald Reagan, was anxious to free other hostages held in Lebanon. An attempt was therefore made, in 1986, to bring the hostages out by giving ostensibly moderate Iranians American missiles, funneled through Israel. For such a secret operation, you may recall, the National Security Act required authorization by a presidential finding that it was necessary. But in this case, three findings were created, none of which adhered to the act's definition of that instrument. The act demanded that the Director of Central Intelligence "shall keep the congressional intelligence committees *fully and currently* informed of *all covert actions* which are the responsibility of, are engaged in by, or are carried out for or on behalf of, *any* department, agency, or entity of the United States Government, *including significant failures*" (emphasis added).[1] An amendment to the act in 1958 re-emphasized that all covert actions of the government, not simply those of the CIA, must be reported to the congressional intelligence committees.

Yet President Reagan authorized a finding on January 17, 1986, that told the CIA: "Because of the extreme sensitivity of this project, it is recommended that you exercise your statutory [non-existent] prerogative to withhold notification of the Finding to the Congressional oversight committees."[2] This project was so secret that the President not only failed to inform Congress of it, but did not inform his Secretary of State (George Shultz) or his Secretary of Defense (Caspar Weinberger), because he knew that both of them would declare the project illegal and politically foolish. Reagan's sympathetic biographer Lou Cannon finds it especially significant that Reagan did not even let his wife, Nancy, in on the plan, since she had great antennae for things that could embarrass or imperil her husband.

The finding just quoted was a third attempt to authorize, retroactively, activities that were already taking place. The second finding, which Reagan signed on January 6, 1986, was so secret that Admiral John Poindexter, the National Security Adviser who had presented it to Reagan, refused to send it to the CIA, which is the point of such a finding. Instead, he locked it in his office safe and, when it was later demanded, he furtively took it from the safe and destroyed it. That finding had been written by a lower staff member on his National Security Council, Lieutenant Colonel Oliver North.

North had also written the first finding, of December 5, 1985, with the help of Stanley Sporkin, the Legal Counsel of the CIA. That one said:

I direct the Director of Central Intelligence not to brief the Congress of the United States, as provided for in Section 501 of the National Security Act of 1947, as amended, until such time as I may direct otherwise. . . . Certain materials and munitions may be provided to the

Government of Iran which is taking steps to facilitate the release of the American hostages. . . . All prior actions taken by U.S. Government officials in furtherance of this effort are hereby ratified.[3]

The President, in signing this finding, did not notice that it promised munitions to *the government* of Iran—though he had been buying the story that the missiles went to "moderates" trying to change the Khomeini government.

That is only part of what was wrong with the first finding. Findings are supposed to precede the actions they authorize. This one had to be hurriedly cobbled together because Oliver North had already illegally promised missiles to Israel if Israel would clandestinely supply missiles to Iran. When the Israelis could not deliver the missiles to an arranged staging area in Portugal (Lisbon denied them landing rights), North went for help to a CIA ally in another of his secret projects—illegally funding Nicaraguan rebels ("Contras") against the Sandinista regime. North's CIA ally was Duane "Dewey" Clarridge. Those two tried to divert a plane already scheduled to fly to Nicaragua, and use it instead for the Iranian project. When the plane was not turned over to them, they used another CIA "proprietary" to fly the missiles from Israel to Iran. The Iranians said that the *anti-tank* missiles delivered this way were of no use to them. They thought they were getting *anti-aircraft* missiles.[4]

After John McMahon, the CIA's Deputy Director, learned that a CIA plane had been used to take missiles to Iran, he realized that this exposed the CIA to legal jeopardy. He told Sporkin that they had to get a finding and it had to say that it authorized the flight retroactively.[5] This is when Sporkin called on North to get the necessary authorization from the White House. That first finding left National Security Adviser Poindexter troubled, and he had North draw up another one, which did not say the "aid" was going to the Iranian *government*. Poindexter took the new one to Reagan, and said that he should show it to

Shultz and Weinberger before signing it. Reagan signed it, but he disregarded the advice about informing his Secretaries of State and Defense about it. He knew they were opposed to it, and he did not mention it when these men met the next day. This is the finding Poindexter put in his safe and later destroyed.

After Shultz and Weinberger heard that the operation was going forward despite their opposition, Poindexter and North recruited Attorney General Edwin Meese to assure Reagan that he was within his legal rights in ordering the exchange, and they created the third finding on the basis of that legal counsel. There was nothing legal about anything in these activities—not the trade with Iran; not the support for the Contras (outlawed by the Boland Amendment, which forbade giving money to the Contras); not the shipment of missiles not released by requisition procedures; not the channeling of funds through untraceable Swiss bank accounts; not the use of CIA airplanes; not the withholding of information from Congress; not the money skimmed off for personal use; not the many and entangled lies to rationalize, deny, or misrepresent each element in the operation.[6] In fact, six of those involved in the Iran-Contra affair would be convicted of withholding information from Congress, among other crimes—Oliver North, Dewey Clarridge, Elliott Abrams, Robert "Bud" McFarlane, Alan Fiers, and Clair George—and Caspar Weinberger was indicted but not tried because of a pre-emptive presidential pardon.

None of the participants was punished severely. The worst suffering that resulted from the plot was self-inflicted, when former National Security Adviser McFarlane tried to commit suicide after White House Chief of Staff Don Regan blamed the whole affair on him. The hapless McFarlane, Poindexter's predecessor as National Security Adviser, had been trying to serve Ronald Reagan's obsession with freeing the hostages. Reagan was repeatedly told that what he was doing was illegal, but Weinberger, in notes taken on the spot, quoted him as saying he "could answer charges of illegality, but he couldn't answer the charge that 'big, strong President Reagan passed up a chance to free hostages.' "[7]

Though many secrets came out in this case, executive information power won in the end. The most serious charges against Oliver North—conspiracy and diversion of funds—had to be withdrawn by the prosecution for lack of evidence, since the White House denied it classified information.[8]

Those convicted continued to prosper after President George H. W. Bush pardoned them all. North, whom Reagan called "a national hero," became a right-wing celebrity and ran for the Senate. Elliott Abrams returned to government service. Vice President George H. W. Bush, who had gone along with the arms-for-hostages deal when he learned of it, gave different and mutually contradicting versions of his involvement and, coached by the television guru Roger Ailes, launched a personal diatribe against Dan Rather when the television anchor tried to discuss the hostage operation.[9]

"SECRET BOMBING"

One of my favorite *Doonesbury* comic strips shows the Vietnamese character Phred visiting a devastated Cambodia. Phred asks a Cambodian couple if the destruction of their home occurred "during the secret bombings." The man answers: "SECRET Bombings? . . . There wasn't any secret. I said, 'Look, Martha, here come the bombs.'" His wife chimes in: "It's true. He did." The comic strip illustrates a recurring and favorite use of government secrecy. It is meant not to fool the enemy, which knows what is going on. It is for fooling Congress and the American people.

The double use of secrecy—kept from one's own but revealed to the foe—is perfectly illustrated by President Nixon's bombing of Cambodia, a state not formally at war with the U.S. Nixon had claimed, in his 1968 comeback run for the presidency, that he had a way to end the Vietnam War, a war whose frustrating prolongation forced Lyndon Johnson to give up any hope of re-election. Nixon's new approach was to convince the enemy of his willingness to escalate the war endlessly, frenziedly, while hiding that intent from an electorate that had no appetite for such endless expansion of battle. He had explained this approach to his close aide H. R. "Bob" Haldeman during the campaign:

> I call it the Madman theory, Bob. I want the North Vietnamese to believe I've reached the point where I might do anything to stop the war. We'll just say the word to them that "For God's sake, you know Nixon is obsessed about Communism. We can't restrain him when he's angry—and he has his hand on the nuclear button" [always Bomb Power]—and Ho Chi Minh himself will be in Paris in two days begging for peace.

But how would he demonstrate his unrestrained fury to the Communists while hiding it from his fellow citizens? Less than two months after he took office, he was given what seemed to him an ideal way to accomplish this. From Vietnam, General Creighton Abrams claimed that he had finally located the long-sought center of operational control for the North Vietnamese troops (COSVN, the Central Office for South Vietnam). It was over the border in neutral Cambodia. Abrams said that an air strike could take this headquarters out. Nixon authorized the strike so long as it could be kept absolutely secret—secret not only from Congress but from the State Department and from the Secretary and Chief of Staff of the air force.[10] To maintain this secrecy, the after-bombing reports were falsified, identifying targets within Vietnam. The crews that flew these raids were given a first (fake) briefing with stated Vietnamese goals, then quietly told to disregard the alleged instructions and follow radar guidance into Cambodia.[11]

The first raids did not find COSVN—Secretary of Defense Melvin Laird would soon admit that the entity never existed.[12] But the raids gave Nixon the laboratory for testing his "madman theory." After twenty thousand tons of explosives were dropped on the first two sites said to be sheltering COSVN, the bombings went northward to four other places in Cambodia.[13] In all, the secret raids totaled 3,630 bombing runs over a fourteen-month period.[14] At first, a few sympathetic congressmen were quietly told of what was going on, without formal notification to the oversight committees. Only after two months of bombing had occurred were the intelligence committees told of it. Congress at large did not find out about this unauthorized invasion of a neutral country for another four years. When it did, congressional opposition, which was what Nixon had been trying to avoid, finally erupted. The House impeachment committee would name the secret bombings of Cambodia as one count for Nixon's impeachment in 1973, though the full House did not pursue that matter.

The uproar that would have followed the secret attacks was made clear when Nixon openly invaded Cambodia on April 30, 1970. Four of Henry Kissinger's top advisers—Roger Morris, Anthony Lake, William Watts, and Larry Lynn—angrily resigned from his National Security Council staff.[15] Over two hundred Foreign Service and State Department officers signed a petition of protest at the invasion. Nixon called an Undersecretary of State in the middle of the night and said, "Fire them all!"[16] Student protests broke out instantly on 1,350 college campuses, forcing 536 of them to suspend classes, 51 of them for the rest of the year.[17] *Esquire* magazine predicted it would not be possible to open the next school year, and a "Princeton Plan" was organized to coax them back to campus in the fall by giving them time off for protest without academic penalty. Fifteen students were shot in an anti-war demonstration at Kent State University, and four died. Fourteen students were shot and two were killed at Jackson State College. Congress reacted with the Cooper-Church Amendment, refusing funds for further military action in Cambodia. At first, in June of 1973, only the Senate passed the amendment, but both houses of Congress sent it to Nixon in December. Nixon, who had threatened a veto on the bill to which the amendment was attached, finally signed it, when it allowed bombing to interdict supply routes. The President told his staff, "I want this purpose interpreted very broadly," and went on to ignore the congressional directive.[18]

CUBA

Just how dangerous it is to exclude Congress from secret operations can be illustrated by Operation Mongoose, the Kennedy brothers' large-scale effort to oust Fidel Castro after the failure of the Bay of Pigs invasion of Cuba. This was a later act in the drama that had begun with the success of Castro's revolution. In 1959, toward the end of President Eisenhower's second term as President, CIA Director Allen Dulles was given a broad mandate to overthrow or kill putatively hostile rulers, and he went quickly to work planning the elimination of Castro. One fruit of this effort was the disastrous 1961 invasion of the Bay of Pigs, planned under President Eisenhower but conducted by President Kennedy. Another result was the hatching of various plots to murder Castro. Since the Mafia had run the drug, gambling, and prostitution rings in Cuba before Castro kicked the mob out, Dulles figured that mobsters like Sam Giancana, Johnny Roselli, and Santo Trafficante had the contacts, skills, and revenge motive to help end Castro's life.[19] The CIA gave Roselli powerful poison pills and trusted him to get them into Castro's food.[20]

The CIA agent running anti-Castro schemes was the hard-drinking and talkative William Harvey. (J. Edgar Hoover had eased him out of the FBI because of his drunkenness.)[21] Since Harvey liked to boast of his activities in Miami circles, there was no reason for Castro to be surprised by the Bay of Pigs assault. Once again, the enemy knew it was coming but Americans were kept in the dark. Even Secretary of State Dean Rusk and Adlai Stevenson, our ambassador to the UN, were not informed about America's role in the invasion.[22] The opening air strike against Cuba prompted an emergency meeting of the UN General Assembly's Political Committee, where Stevenson showed a faked photograph of a plane, one supplied him by the CIA, and said that no Americans were involved with the invasion.

In this whole cycle of hidden acts and public lies, there is a poignant personal note in the lie to Adlai Stevenson. Alistair Cooke, the British broadcaster stationed in New York, was a close friend of Stevenson's, and he recorded that this was "the supreme humiliation of Stevenson's public career." With false data, Stevenson grandly rejected charges that America had launched the attack on Cuba, reminding his audience that President Kennedy had publicly stated "there will not be, under any conditions, an intervention in Cuba by the United States armed forces." Immediately after his speech, Stevenson was praised and applauded in the UN dining room—but he was intercepted on his way out of lunch by a White House emissary who said, "The President thinks you ought to know *it was our show*."[23]

The failure of the Bay of Pigs invasion, so early in Kennedy's presidency, made Castro a Kennedy obsession. Robert McNamara later told the Church committee, "We were hysterical about Castro."[24] The CIA was determined to make up for its bungling of the operation. The President was displeased. Robert Kennedy took it as his personal mission to destroy Castro. He supervised Operation Mongoose, the anti–Castro task force in the National Security Council. Though he was the Attorney General, an official of the Justice Department, he appointed himself to the NSC's Special Group, making it the Special Group (Augmented). He demanded action, fast and furious. He wanted daily meetings to deal with Cuba. He said, "My idea is to stir things up on [the] island with espionage, sabotage, general disorder."[25]

Even Robert Kennedy's fan and friend, Arthur Schlesinger, admits that he lost all perspective in his frenzy over Castro:

> The Attorney General was always dissatisfied with Mongoose. He wanted it to do more, the terrors of the earth, but what they were he knew not. . . . Castro was high on his list of emotion, much lower on his list of informed concerns. When he was able to come to meetings of the Special Group (Augmented), as he did his best to do, he made up in pressure for what he lacked in knowledge. . . . He conveyed acute impatience and urgency.[26]

Of course, Congress was not informed of any of this activity. The required finding was never written. Rather, Kennedy extracted from his Justice Department a legal opinion that the President can use "any means necessary to combat the measures taken by the Communist bloc . . . *without express statutory authorization*" (emphasis added). That is the kind of unconstitutional activity that can backfire disastrously—as it was about to do.

Kennedy put Edward Lansdale, whose counterinsurgency activities in the Philippines and Vietnam he admired, in charge of planning the attacks on Cuba. But Lansdale still had on his team the blow-hard William Harvey running around Miami looking for Cuban collaborators against Castro. That, along with the scale of the Mongoose project, alerted Castro to various efforts at sabotaging Cuban harbors, mines, sugar crops, and businesses. Like the Cambodians later "secretly" bombed, Castro knew what the American public was not allowed to know. The elaboration of Mongoose was meant to make up for the skimpy arrangements at the Bay of Pigs:

> Task Force W, the CIA unit for Mongoose, soon had four hundred American employees in Washington and Miami, over fifty proprietary fronts, its own navy of fast boasts, a rudimentary air force and two

thousand Cuban agents. The Miami headquarters became for a season the largest CIA station in the world. All this cost over $50 million a year [in 1962 dollars].[27]

The scurry of this activity convinced Castro that America was preparing to invade his island—which was, indeed, the wish of many around Mongoose. The Joint Chiefs of Staff hoped that Castro would be provoked into an act that would give the rationale for outright invasion and conquest of Cuba.[28]

RUSSIAN MISSILES

The direct consequence of Mongoose was Castro's acceptance of the Russian offer of nuclear missiles on his island. His small nation could not win in an all-out clash with its giant northern neighbor—not unless it had tactical nuclear weapons to greet American invaders on Cuban beaches.[29] But Castro could use those only if a nuclear response from America was precluded by retaliatory intermediate-range missiles reaching Washington and other American cities.

Soviet Premier Nikita Khrushchev's aim was both to protect the Communist beachhead in the Americas that Castro had created and to deter America from a long-range nuclear attack on the Soviet Union. The Russians did not yet have intercontinental missiles to reach the United States. But the missiles in Cuba would deter just as much as if Khrushchev had equaled the United States in air capacity. Khrushchev reasoned that the missiles were no more a provocation to war than were the American missiles based just over the Soviet border in Turkey.[30] Unless Castro believed that he needed the missiles to prevent or defeat an American invasion, it made no sense to make his island a target for nuclear incineration by America. He wanted no exchange that would totally obliterate Cuba. He wanted the missiles only as a deterrent against invasion of his land.

But Kennedy could not admit that there was a defensive rationale for Cuba's missiles, since that would involve admitting to the Mongoose threat. The trouble with protecting secrets is that new forms of secrecy have to be invented to guard the original ones. That had happened in the 1950s, when the government could not use evidence against American Communists at their trials because that would mean revealing that the government's VENONA program had broken the Soviets' code during World War II. (Actually, the Soviets knew this because their spy Kim Philby had informed them of the development—another case of a secret being kept from the American people though the enemy knew about it.)[31]

The way this played out in the Cuban missile crisis is that Khrushchev and Castro, who knew about Mongoose, truthfully called the missiles defensive. Kennedy, who could not let Americans in on the Mongoose secret, lied in his dramatic speech to the nation on October 22, 1962. He said the only reason for the presence of the missiles was not defensive but aggressive, "none other than to provide a nuclear strike capability against the Western Hemisphere." He said that the Soviets had lied when they promised that only defensive weapons would go to Cuba—the missiles were "clearly offensive weapons."

> Only last Thursday, as evidence of this rapid offensive buildup was already in my hand, Soviet Foreign Minister Gromyko told me in my office that he was instructed to make it clear once again, as he said his government had already done, that Soviet assistance to Cuba, and I quote, "pursued solely the purpose of contributing to the defense capabilities of Cuba," that, and I quote him, "training by Soviet specialists of Cuban nationals in handling defensive armaments was by no means offensive, and if it were otherwise," Mr. Gromyko went on, "the

Soviet Government would never become involved in rendering such assistance." That statement also was false.

By framing the issue this way, Kennedy irresponsibly raised the temperature of the crisis. If the missiles were there only to attack America, they had to be removed by any means, at any cost, even that of nuclear war. There could be no negotiating. Kennedy delivered an ultimatum, backed up by a blockade of Cuba (an act of war in international law). When Adlai Stevenson suggested a trade—removal of our missiles from Turkey if Khrushchev removed the Cuban missiles—Kennedy dismissed the idea contemptuously. He told his journalist friend Clayton Fritchey, "Adlai wanted a Munich."[32]

In fact, Kennedy ended up making the Turkish trade-off, but insisted to the Russians that they keep this secret, so he could tell more lies to the American people, saying he would not bargain with the foe. He risked nuclear war to keep his secrets. Kennedy has been praised extravagantly, ever after, for being wise and restrained. The man who was restrained and responsible was Khrushchev, who accepted the trade along with a humiliating submission to the secrecy pledge. The Cuban affair ended as it had begun, in a cloud of secrecy protected by lies. Each lie entailed further ones, as Kennedy moved from the Bay of Pigs to Mongoose to his television speech to his deal with Khrushchev. And throughout, the only ones deceived—deprived of knowledge, kept out of participation in what was being done in their name—were the American people. This was the supreme example of the use of secrecy as a Congress deceiver.

11

SECRECY AS
POLICY DISABLER

In 1990, when the Senate was debating whether to give President George H. W. Bush authority for war in Kuwait, the former Chairman of the Joint Chiefs of Staff, Admiral William Crowe, told the Armed Services Committee that he believed the effectiveness of sanctions had not been tested enough. Secretary of State James Baker then appeared before the committee and dismissed Admiral Crowe's views, on the grounds that he no longer had top security clearance to read classified documents.[1] Whatever the merits of the argument in this case, the answer surely limits sharply the kinds of expertise one can draw on. The clearance patricians need not pay any attention to "outside" opinion, since it is by definition ill-informed. The insiders listen only to themselves. A broader spectrum of knowledge is excluded. Many examples of this occur in our recent history.

BAY OF PIGS

Very early in his presidency, John F. Kennedy—an admirer of John Buchan novels, of James Bond, of counterinsurgency "experts," and of what would soon be called Green Berets—believed Richard Bissell, the CIA Director of Plans, when Bissell told him that an assault on Cuba would be successful. Arthur Schlesinger, the John Kennedy hagiographer, admits that his hero succumbed to the fake omniscience of insiders:

> Intelligence agencies, sealed off by walls of secrecy from the rest of the community, tend to form societies of their own. Prolonged immersion in the self-contained, self-justifying, ultimately hallucinatory world of clandestinity and deception erodes the reality principle. So intelligence operatives, in the CIA as well as the FBI, had begun to see themselves as the appointed guardians of the Republic, infinitely more devoted and knowledgeable than transient elected officials, morally authorized to do on their own whatever they believed the nation's security demanded. Let others interfere at their peril. J. D. Esterline, the CIA's supervisor of planning for the Bay of Pigs, bitterly told the board of inquiry, "As long as decisions by professionals can be set aside by people who know not whereof they speak, you won't succeed."[2]

In fact, those "in the know" were extremely ignorant about Cuba in 1961. Senator Moynihan makes the same point that Professor Schlesinger did. Moynihan points out that respectable academic polling showed a high degree of support for Castro in the aftermath of his revolution, and little support among Cubans for any attempt to overthrow him. This knowledge was readily available and entirely trustworthy. It was confirmed not only in academic studies but in State Department and British statements.[3] It had only one disadvantage, Moynihan wryly notes—it was not classified, so it was not taken seriously. "In a culture of secrecy, that which is not secret is easily disregarded or dismissed."[4] The CIA was listening to its own contacts and hired spies, who were disposed to oppose Castro—the same thing would happen when George W. Bush's cabinet was disposed to heed exiles like Ahmed Chalabi and others saying it would be easy to win in Iraq.

Kennedy was so secretive about the Cuban invasion that even his "alter ego," Theodore Sorensen, was kept in the dark: "I knew nothing of the operation until after it was over."[5] Nor, astonishingly, did Kennedy's new Secretary of State, Dean Rusk.[6] Secrecy so excluded expertise in the case of the Bay of Pigs that Richard Bissell kept his plan secret from the CIA's own experts: "Bissell had cut out the analytical side of the CIA, and thereby deprived himself of experts who might have cautioned him against being too optimistic."[7] Bissell had become his own expert, buoyed by successes like his creation of the U-2 program. His assistant Bob King said of Bissell: "He wanted [White House] backing, but he did not want a lot of advice. He had a lot of confidence."[8] He reveled in the secret wars the CIA had waged under Eisenhower. The Agency had been successful (in the short run) in replacing the governments of Iran and Guatemala. Cuba would just be another notch in the CIA's gun. CIA Director Allen Dulles told Kennedy about the Bay of Pigs: "I was certain our Guatemalan operation would succeed, and, Mr. President, the prospects for this plan are even better than they were for that one."[9]

Bissell assembled the same team that had toppled Jacobo Arbenz Guzmán in Guatemala—the Cuban Brigade was already being trained in post-Arbenz Guatemala. Immediately after Kennedy's election and before his inauguration, Bissell explained to Kennedy his plan for the attack on Cuba. Kennedy wanted to keep America's connection with the anti-Castro Cubans secret. He changed the invasion site to an out-of-the-way place (the Bay of Pigs) as if that would hide it from the world. He cut the American air cover in half; and he said the brigade must land at night—as if the world would not notice so long as the invasion was what Kennedy called "less noisy." In this process, he distanced the invasion from the mountains the attackers were supposed to "fade into" if they were failing. Without that mountain refuge, the brigade was left with "no fallback plan."[10] The only thing that could save it in this case would be an open American intervention.

It is hard to know how Eisenhower would have conducted the invasion (if he had finally approved it), but it is certain he would not have moved with insufficient force. He knew when military actions were futile—as he proved when refusing to give the French ground support in Vietnam or to prolong the war in Korea.[11] In the one open military action of his presidency, the landing of troops in Lebanon, Eisenhower had flooded the beach with men, precluding any hostile response to such numbers.[12] For the invasion of the Bay of Pigs, Eisenhower had set up certain preconditions, including a functioning government in exile by the Cuban insurgents—a condition not met by Kennedy.[13] In his memoirs Eisenhower wrote: "Inefficient functioning of government organization, bringing about indecision and untimely counter-orders, was apparently part of the cause for the 1961 Bay of Pigs fiasco."[14]

In one of the shrewdest assessments of the Eisenhower presidency, Murray Kempton said that one of Ike's guiding rules was: "Do nothing unless you know exactly what you will do if it turns out to have been the wrong thing."[15] Contrast that maxim with what Theodore Sorensen wrote after the Bay of Pigs: "No realistic appraisal was made of the chances for success or the consequences of failure. . . . The possibilities of failure were never properly considered."[16]

When Kennedy's invasion fell apart and he did not know what to do (except lie to the UN), Eisenhower wrote in his diary that, from reports on the operation, it was "a very dreary account of mismanagement, indecision, and timidity at the wrong time," in fact "a Profile in Timidity."[17] When Kennedy asked Eisenhower to join him at Camp David after the invasion's failure, Eisenhower went away from the meeting convinced that "he had no idea of the complexity of the job [of President]." Kennedy had made much of the way he got rid of the cumbersome staff system of Eisenhower—his people would scramble, like a basketball team making up plays on the run, not huddle like a football team calling a preformed play. But at Camp David, Eisenhower asked: "Mr. President, before you approved this plan did you have everybody in front of you debating the thing, so you got pros and cons yourself and then made your decision, or did you talk to these people one at a time?"[18] Kennedy admitted he had never submitted the plan to his National Security Council at all.

Why did the CIA go ahead with a plan that Kennedy had perilously shrunk? The agents thought they were still working for Eisenhower, who in a crunch supplied what was needed—as he had when the Guatemala coup was foundering and he flew in last-minute support. At his Camp David encounter with Kennedy, the ex-President said: "I believe there is only one thing to do when you go into this kind of thing. It must be a success."[19] Eisenhower had told Allen Dulles, "If you commit the American flag, you commit it to win."[20] Though Kennedy felt that the CIA had misled him, the CIA people felt that he had let them down—when they asked for air support and supplies for the trapped invaders, Kennedy refused. He could have kept the cover story—that the Cuban Brigade was made up of "freedom fighters" acting on their own—but said that America could not stand by and watch these brave rebels being slaughtered. Bissell later complained, "I thought Kennedy was tough, that he wouldn't cancel air strikes and lose his first major effort."[21] Tracy Barnes, another CIA leader involved in the invasion, said later that he felt betrayed by Kennedy.[22] Theodore Sorensen mused with wonder: "Their [the CIA's] planning, it turned out, proceeded almost as if open U.S. intervention were assumed."[23] In fact, CIA operatives had told the invaders themselves that America would come to their aid if it was needed.[24]

It was noted in the last chapter that the Bay of Pigs preparations turned out to be another case, like the "secret bombing" of Cambodia, where secrecy affected only the American people. Castro was aware of the preparations being made in Miami and Guatemala. They were two hives of gossip about the coming invasion: "By now all pretense of discretion was gone. Talk was unrestrained in the motels and bars."[25] A Miami reporter turned in an article on the subject to the *New York Times*. Managing editor Turner Catledge asked his Washington bureau chief, James Reston, whether the paper should run it. Reston said no—keeping the secrets is instilled as a duty in the Bomb Power era. But Arthur Schlesinger concluded that a national disaster might have been averted if the paper had acted "irresponsibly," breaking the secret.[26]

Cubans inside and outside the actual brigade gladly spread word to their countrymen that rescue was coming, Castro was doomed, and the United States would ride to the rescue. Bissell belatedly lamented that "Cubans don't know how to keep a secret."[27] But the CIA was no better at hiding its intention.

> The CIA even dictated battle communiqués to a Madison Avenue public relations firm representing the exiles' political front. After all the military limitations accepted in order to keep this nation's role covert, that role was not only obvious but exaggerated.[28]

Aides to Kennedy, frightened by these reports, urged him to say that the United States was not planning action in Cuba. Compliantly, he claimed in a press conference what Adlai Stevenson would later quote: "There will not be, under any conditions, an intervention in Cuba by the United States Armed Forces."[29] By the law of inverted reality under national security lying, Castro did not believe that. Nor did the rebels. Nor did CIA leaders. Only the Americans, as always, were left out. They believed their President.

PENTAGON PAPERS

Another example of secrecy as a precluder of good advice comes from the Pentagon Papers affair. The classified Papers, which Daniel Ellsberg leaked to both the *New York Times* and the *Washington Post,* provide a test of the supposed benefits of classifying information. Did the Papers show the benefits of keeping national security secrets away from the public, or did they reveal the poor information and bad planning that lay at the heart of a major activity of the government, and thus prevented the government from getting better information and advice? The Papers prove that the latter hypothesis is the true one. When the Nixon administration made this a showdown before the Supreme Court, even its own Solicitor General ended up saying that there were no national security secrets in the documents he had asked the Supreme Court to keep sacred.

What were the famous Papers, which few have read, including the people who claimed they were too important to be read? They were seven thousand pages of material printed in forty-seven volumes. The Papers were compiled by the Department of Defense at the request of the Secretary of Defense, Robert McNamara. Secretary McNamara was a prime example of what seemed glamorous on John Kennedy's "New Frontier." He was a driving entrepreneur (for Ford Motors) with intellectual aspirations (he read Teilhard de Chardin). The most famous Defense Secretary before him was Charles "Engine Charlie" Wilson of General Motors, who said, "What is good for General Motors is good for America." McNamara was supposed to be the anti-Charlie, philosophical but able to bring rational cost-effectiveness to the military. As part of that program, he asked for what was, in effect, a market analysis of the Vietnam War—what were its benefits, what was its cost, what improvements could be made? He wanted a long period covered, from

1945 to 1967, the year he issued the order for the study. He brought
in dozens of Ivy League and think-tank-intellectual types to do the
research.

Lyndon Johnson said that the public would realize how wise had
been his conduct of the war if only it could read the classified material
he did. When Daniel Ellsberg gave people the opportunity to do just
that, President Nixon tried to prevent them from doing so. The
Department of Justice sent the *New York Times* a notice that if it
continued publishing the Papers it would cause "irreparable injury to
the defense interests of the United States."[30] The Papers were, after all,
stamped top secret, the highest classification at the time, one reserved
"only to that information or material the defense aspect of which is
paramount, and the unauthorized disclosure of which could result in
exceptionally grave damage to the nation such as leading to a definite
break in diplomatic relations affecting the defense of the United States,
an armed attack against the United States or its allies, a war, or the
compromise of military or defense plans or intelligence operations, or
scientific or technological developments vital to the national defense."[31]
Since all seven thousand pages of the Papers were top secret, every
page, it was claimed, contained material as damaging as the classification proclaimed. No wonder many people thought Daniel Ellsberg an
enemy to his country, a traitor who had exposed us to enemy response
of the most catastrophic sort.

Both friends and foes thought Ellsberg was acting from deeply leftist and ideological motives. I knew better. I first met him months before
he gave the Papers to the *New York Times*. He came to a meeting of
the fellows and board members of the Institute for Policy Studies. He
had been working with the founders of the institute, Richard Barnet
and Marcus Raskin, on a book critical of the Vietnam War. Ellsberg
did not come from a leftist upbringing. Though he would later be
radicalized (in part by the Nixon administration's frenzy to destroy
him), he was for a long time deeply embedded in the Establishment,

and especially in institutions of the National Security State—the Pentagon, the military mission in Vietnam, the RAND Corporation. A Harvard graduate with a Ph.D. in economics, he became one of McNamara's "whiz kids" in the Pentagon. Then he went to Vietnam as a believer in the war, and worked for two years on the staff of the counterinsurgency guru Edward Lansdale—when Kissinger and Nixon visited Lansdale in Vietnam, Ellsberg was present while they were being briefed.[32] He came back to a position at the RAND Corporation, the government's favorite defense think tank, from which he was called to contribute to the formation of the Pentagon Papers (which is why he knew about them in the first place).

When I heard him speak at the Institute for Policy Studies, he said that his disillusionment with the government came from an economist's disgust with inefficiency. At RAND, he drafted a study of nuclear command conditions.[33] With his top security clearance, he was allowed once to inspect the most secret kinds of material in the Pentagon, the plans for response to nuclear attack. For access to these one had to enter a cage, with no pencil or paper for taking notes, and, under constant surveillance, study the Single Integrated Operational Plan (SIOP) for nuclear war. To his horror Ellsberg found the plan confused and inconsistent, with incompatible elements. He concluded, over time, that the government had no business conducting nuclear war on such a basis.

He felt the same way as he would later, when he read the Pentagon Papers through. He had been an enthusiastic supporter of the war. It dismayed him to discover the confusion, doubt, lack of knowledge, lack of clear plans, and lack of firm confidence revealed in the Papers. While administration figures had been projecting confidence and optimism, the Papers were full of discouraging reports and borderline despair. The sheer ineptitude of the government was what struck Ellsberg. Far from seeing LBJ's wisdom after reading what he was cleared to read, the public might turn against the war even more than it was disposed to do when kept in the dark.

The great secret of the Pentagon Papers was that they had no great secrets. Ellsberg and a more radical colleague at RAND, Anthony Russo, took one of the few complete sets of the Papers out of a RAND safe and painstakingly photocopied them, working late at night for weeks on end.[34] Ellsberg first tried to get Senate and House war critics to publish the papers in the *Congressional Record*. Senator William J. Fulbright of the Senate's Foreign Relations Committee asked Secretary of Defense Melvin Laird to declassify the documents and release them to his committee. When the Pentagon refused, Fulbright gave up the project. Ellsberg then gave the Papers to reporter Neil Sheehan at the *New York Times* and to editor Ben Bagdikian at the *Washington Post*. The *Times* held the Papers for two months, preparing them for publication while the paper's lawyers were consulted. When the *Times* began to publish on Sunday morning, June 13, 1971, the front page had a picture of Nixon and daughter Julie at her wedding the day before. But a first installment of the Papers was also begun on the front page and ran on six inner pages.

This came as a total surprise to the administration. The instant reaction of Nixon and Kissinger was to think the publication posed no threat to them. The Papers ended their record in 1967, a year before Nixon's election, and any criticism arising from them would apply to Presidents Kennedy and Johnson, not Nixon. Nixon's immediate response to his aide H. R. Haldeman was that his staff should "keep out of it." Kissinger, too, called Nixon to say that the Papers "could help us a bit," since they describe "massive mismanagement," but they "pin it all on Kennedy and Johnson." Only Kissinger's assistant Al Haig seemed upset at the outset, alleging the Democrats had stolen the Papers to hurt Nixon's re-election chances.[35]

But suspicion about the source of this massive leak very quickly centered on three men—Daniel Ellsberg at RAND, Leslie Gelb at the Brookings Institution, and Morton Halperin at the Council on Foreign Relations. They were all known as "Kissinger's boys"—they had been his teaching assistants at Harvard. Ellsberg and Halperin were both brought by Kissinger into Nixon's transition team, compiling advice on the war between Nixon's 1968 election and 1969 inauguration; Gelb had directed the production of the Pentagon Papers, and had consulted Kissinger while they were being assembled.[36] Nixon referred pointedly to Ellsberg as "Kissinger's friend."[37] In a panicky desire to dissociate himself from embarrassing company, Kissinger became the fiercest administration critic of the release of the Papers. White House aide for domestic policy John Ehrlichman wrote: "Without Henry's stimulus . . . the President and the rest of us might have concluded that the Papers were Lyndon Johnson's problem, not ours," but Kissinger "fanned Richard Nixon's flame white hot."[38] Naturally, in his memoirs, Kissinger deplored the excesses he had prodded the President into committing.[39]

Members of the Nixon administration—including Daniel Patrick Moynihan, Leonard Garment, and William Safire—attribute Nixon's downfall to his obsession with secrecy growing out of the Pentagon Papers affair. Safire wrote: "Nixon let his anger undermine his political judgment. The Pentagon Papers case led him into an overreaction that led to his most fundamental mistakes . . . to defend his privacy at the expense of everyone else's right to privacy and to create the climate that led to Watergate."[40] Nixon lashed out in several directions. First he banned all *New York Times* personnel from the White House and from Air Force One. He ordered his staff to have no dealings with "any of those Jews." Then he told Attorney General John Mitchell to prosecute the publication of the Papers under the ancient Espionage Act, to "put those bastards . . . at the *New York Times* in jail."[41]

When it was confirmed that Ellsberg had leaked the Papers, Mitchell convened a grand jury to indict him and give immunity to his RAND colleagues if they would testify against him. Nixon sent burglars to rifle the records of Ellsberg's psychiatrist, looking for dirt in his private life. E. Howard Hunt and G. Gordon Liddy brought Cubans

up from Miami to heckle and assault Ellsberg at an anti-war demonstration.[42] Nixon also wanted to *expand* hints in the Papers that President
Kennedy had backed the assassination of South Vietnam's president,
Ngo Dinh Diem. Convinced that proof of this was at the Brookings
Institution, he ordered it, too, to be burgled, and Charles Colson
invented a scheme to set a fire and have the burglars enter disguised as
firemen.[43] In his frenzy over secrecy, Nixon committed more crimes
that had to be kept secret, and used bribes to hush up these secrets. He
also corrupted the CIA and FBI to create more walls of silence around
his crazed efforts to destroy his foes.

But the tragedy of Richard Nixon is not as devastating as the harm
done to the nation for all those years when the President was making
sound judgment impossible by relying only on classified information
that was woefully deficient. The closed circle of "cleared" experts did
not want or heed sounder judgments. They relied on the magic of
secret "knowledge" that was in fact ignorance. Robert McNamara later
admitted that the responsible officials in the U.S. government had little
knowledge of Vietnamese culture.

Despite all the denunciations of Ellsberg for revealing state secrets,
there were none in the Papers. One of the favorite themes, both in
public and in the court actions, was that foreign governments could
not trust or confide in us if we published their messages. But Ellsberg
never released the four volumes of diplomatic correspondence from
foreign countries. Another theme was that troop movements were sig-
naled to the enemy by the publication. But the latest record in the
Papers was from 1967, four years before the Papers were printed. Any
information contained in the Papers was obsolete by that time—the
troops had already done, or failed to do, what was envisaged in
the earlier reports. At first it was feared that cryptographic secrets were
in the Papers, but the Pentagon said that was impossible.[44] When
the government argued that the Papers contained secret information
about a supposed Vietnamese attack on an American destroyer in the

Gulf of Tonkin, used by President Johnson to get congressional approval of his actions, the defense quickly proved that this material had already been published in the *Washington Post*—and it later turned out that the report in the Papers had not come from secret information anyway.[45]

The government's account of what was in the Papers proved weak, largely because the government's lawyers had been given insufficient time to read them. The government's rush to court precluded adequate study of the Papers' content. The government instantly won a temporary restraint on publication. But when a hearing on the restraint failed to result in an injunction, the government went immediately to an appeals court. The same process was repeated when the *Washington Post* began publishing its copy of the Papers. John Mitchell ordered his Solicitor General, Erwin Griswold, to conduct the appeal, though Solicitors General normally appear only before the Supreme Court. Nixon even toyed with the thought of pleading the case himself before the Supreme Court.

When Griswold lost the appeal, he took the case to the Supreme Court, where the *Times* and *Post* cases were combined. The action had moved so fast that Griswold had still not read the Papers. Since he could not introduce classified material in open court, he filed a secret brief that only the justices could read. To draw it up, he asked for one expert from the Pentagon, one from the State Department, and one from the National Security Council to inform him on what each considered the most salient threats to the nation revealed in the Papers. He interviewed them separately for a half hour each, drew up what he thought were the forty most serious matters, boiled them down to eleven items he felt he could argue most persuasively, and based his secret brief on them.[46]

The Supreme Court, by a majority of 6–3, rejected the government's appeal and allowed publication to proceed.[47] Those who later tried to claim that national security secrets were revealed in the Papers rely almost exclusively on the eleven matters in the secret brief, now that it has been declassified; but John Prados and Margaret Pratt Porter studied each of the eleven in detail and concluded that none of them revealed anything dangerous to the nation.[48] But we do not have to take their word on the subject. Erwin Griswold, the man who chose the eleven items and wrote the secret brief, later said that his own case had no merit. Earlier, I gave a brief quote from his article, but more should be put down here:

> I have never seen any trace of a threat to the national security from the publication. Indeed, I have never seen it even suggested that there was such an actual threat. . . . I doubt if there is more than a handful of persons who have ever undertaken to examine the Pentagon Papers in any detail—either with respect to national security or with respect to the policies of the country relating to Vietnam. . . . It quickly became apparent to any person who has considerable experience with classified material that there is massive overclassification, and the principal concern of the classifier is not with national security but rather with governmental embarrassment of one sort or another. There may be some basis for short-term classification while plans are being made, or negotiations are going on, but apart from details of weapons systems, there is very rarely any real risk to current national security from the publication of facts relating to transactions in the past, even the fairly recent past. This is the lesson of the Pentagon Papers experience.[49]

The nation was not hurt by the release of the Pentagon Papers. It had been hurt by keeping them secret—as policy is often disabled by the withholding of information from knowledgeable critics.

12

SECRECY AS CRIME CONCEALER

In 2004, photographs from the Abu Ghraib prison in Iraq were published, and they horrified Americans. It was suddenly possible to ask "unthinkable" questions about our country. Had we really become a sponsor of torture around the world? Denunciations of the Bush administration were commonplace. But this was not an isolated thing, an aberration. It fit in with a pattern we had glimpses of thirty years earlier in congressional investigations of the CIA. In 1975, we learned about an American campaign of assassinations planned, abetted, encouraged, and sometimes accomplished. The CIA had at least *tried* to murder leaders around the world—General René Schneider of Chile, Rafael Trujillo of the Dominican Republic, Patrice Lumumba of the Congo, Zhou Enlai of China, the Diem brothers of Vietnam, Fidel Castro of Cuba.[1] This does not count the killing of lesser functionaries as part of the subversion of leftist regimes, or of support for right-wing dictators—especially by death squads trained in the United States Army School of the Americas.[2] These activities were even worse than the crimes committed at Abu Ghraib, since murder is worse than torture. One maims life, the other entirely removes it. Lyndon Johnson once said that the CIA was "running a Murder, Inc."

What made so many American officials feel they had the right to roam the world secretly killing "undesirables"? The right grew out of one of the requisites of Bomb Power. The American empire was not built primarily to acquire territory (like the empire of Alexander the Great), or financial tribute (like that of Athens), or resources and trade goods (like that of the British). It was more like the Venetian empire, which was meant to secure safe harbors and emporia for its trading fleet. America, after the acquisition of the Bomb, needed secure places for planes and ships carrying nuclear weapons, and secure regimes providing storage facilities and launching pads for our missiles. This soon extended into a network of espionage and counter-subversion activities meant to gather intelligence to direct our nuclear (and other) activities. Any "unfriendly" regime threatened to increase the Soviets' influence and intelligence operations. It was a duty, in our role as protector of world freedom against all the tentacles of Soviet expansion, to eliminate any regimes that denied us access to what we needed to ensure our activities.

We toppled regimes in a high-handed way, which gave us license to kill those who might uphold dangerous regimes, even democratically elected ones. After all, killing one or two troublemakers was preferable to destroying whole governments, though sometimes the one led to the other. Thus we overthrew or undermined the Mossadegh government in Iran, the Arbenz one in Guatemala, the Sukarno one in Indonesia, the Lumumba one in the Congo, the Diem one in Vietnam, Goulart's in Brazil, Allende's in Chile, the Bosch forces in the Dominican Republic, the Bishop reign in Grenada, the Noriega one in Panama. The lesson for other countries seemed to be: "Don't bother with leaders America doesn't like—they'll just get knocked off." By the careful count of Stephen Kinzer, a longtime *New York Times* reporter, the United States overthrew foreign governments 114 times over the last century or so—not counting many cases where we tried but failed to bring a regime down. He also does not count the cases where our role was simply supporting an indigenous coup.[3]

The U.S. government tried repeatedly, by sabotage and economic pressure, by secret aggression and outright invasion, to do in the Castro regime in Cuba. It used money from the sale of missiles to the Ayatollah Khomeini in an effort to unseat the Ortega government in Nicaragua. The Church and Pike committees—respectively, the Senate and House bodies investigating CIA wrongdoing in 1975—turned up a sickeningly long list of leaders and followers who had been "snuffed," or targeted for snuffing, as part of the CIA's official duties. And of course all these acts had to be kept secret. The secrecy was not the least part of the duties. Americans must not know what was being done for their own good—since, once again, the supposed enemies knew or suspected what was being plotted inside their borders. The secret subversions were guarded so carefully that their nickname in the Agency was "the family jewels." When, under subpoena, William Colby revealed secrets, Agency loyalists and their right-wing supporters treated this as an act of treason. He had betrayed the protectors of the nation. When Richard Helms defied Congress, and when William Casey lied to Congress, they were considered the true patriots.

IKE'S SECRET ARMIES

One of the more surprising revelations among the family jewels was the patronage of international insurgency by President Dwight Eisenhower. With his sunny smile and scrambled grammar, "Ike" had long been considered the very epitome of things benign and avuncular. But the political scientist Fred Greenstein's book, *The Hidden-Hand Presidency,* probed behind the mask and found an efficiency in the man bordering on the ruthless. That was borne out (though Greenstein did not emphasize this side of him) in the way Eisenhower secretly toppled governments. His hit teams accomplished or contributed to the fall of rulers like Mohammad Mossadegh in Iran, Jacobo Arbenz Guzmán in Guatemala, and Patrice Lumumba in Congo. They also tried to over-throw the governments of Indonesia and Syria. Ike had many notches on his gun.

The CIA's paramilitary operations had ballooned during the Korean War. In 1951, the year before Eisenhower's election, the budget for the CIA's covert operations was three times that of intelligence gathering and analysis (the CIA's original mission).[4] Eisenhower meant to make full use of CIA black operatives, relying on the team of Dulles broth-ers, John Foster at State and Allen at CIA. "This is the first and only time in American history," Kinzer writes, "that siblings ran the overt and covert arms of foreign policy."[5]

Ike's first target was Iran. Ancient and unfair grants had allowed the British oil industry, largely owned by the British government, to take a huge share of oil profits from the country, supporting the oil-driven navy that dominated the British Empire. The Anglo-Iranian Oil Com-pany claimed to be remitting 16 percent of the oil profits to the Iranian people, but the claim was doubtful—the Iranians said it was only 8 percent. In 1950 alone, Britain made more from oil than it had paid to Iran in the preceding half century.[6] When the nationalist Prime Minister Mohammad Mossadegh proposed a new profit-sharing arrangement, splitting the proceeds fifty-fifty, the British refused. With the approval of his parliament, Mossadegh began the nationalization of the oil wells in his country, arguing that the British themselves had just nationalized their own coal and steel companies.

The British reacted with a worldwide embargo on the shipping of Iranian oil, which they tried to get other countries to support. When this was not sufficient to break the Mossadegh government, the British began to plan its overthrow. President Truman would not back this attempt to bring down Iran's government.[7] When Mossadegh discovered the British coup attempt, he closed the British embassy in Iran and expelled British intelligence agents. Now England needed new resources, and (of course) money. The British Foreign Secretary, Anthony Eden, approached the new President, Dwight Eisenhower, in 1953 and proposed a joint operation by the British Secret Service and the CIA to oust Mossadegh.[8] Eisenhower was hesitant at first, saying it would be cheaper to give Mossadegh ten million dollars than to invest in risky subversion. But British agents played on the anti-communism of the Dulles brothers, alleging Soviet control over Mossadegh, and "the Dulles brothers had developed an excellent sense of how to bring their boss around to their way of thinking."[9]

Kermit "Kim" Roosevelt, the CIA man put in charge of the coup, called his plan Operation Ajax. He schemed to recall the exiled Shah of Iran, who shied from the challenge. Though Roosevelt spoke no Middle Eastern language, he had the help of three brothers, royalists of the Rashidian family, to organize teams of street brawlers, some purportedly Communist, some anti-Communist, to create such chaos that a chosen strongman (General Fazlollah Zahedi) had to be called on to restore order and take the reins from Mossadegh. As soon as Zahedi had accomplished this, Roosevelt ousted him and reinstated the exiled Shah. Operation Ajax became the CIA's shining example of how America could create just the kind of regime it wanted in any foreign country. President Eisenhower felt he had a secret weapon he could use at will.

But a fuse was lit that would smolder for years and lead to the anti-American revolution of the Ayatollah Khomeini, the capture of American hostages, the downfall of Jimmy Carter's presidency, the bargaining of Oliver North for later hostages, the disgracing of President Reagan, and the conviction of six high American officials for breaking the law in a trade-off of arms for hostages with Iran. As James Bill notes, the price of Eisenhower's "success" in Iran was high and took a long time paying out:

This direct covert operation left a running wound that bled for twenty-five years and contaminated America's relations with the Islamic Republic of Iran following the revolution of 1978–79. From Iran's perspective, the manner in which the United States intervened in Iran's internal affairs was at least as reprehensible as the decision to intervene itself. . . . After the fall of Mossadegh the acronym CIA became the most pejorative political term in the vocabulary of Iranian nationalism.[10]

Despite this long-term cost, Kim Roosevelt continued to boast of his Ajax success for many years, writing a book to celebrate (and, critics say, to exaggerate) his role in it.[11] The Pulitzer Prize–winning investigative reporter Thomas Powers wrote: "Restoring the Shah to power is probably the happiest memory of Roosevelt's life."[12]

What America did for the Anglo-Iranian Oil Company in Iran it should do, some wealthy Republicans thought, for America's own company, the United Fruit Company in Guatemala. That corporation was deeply interwoven, at one and the same time, in Guatemala's economy and in the United States government's Republican elite class. The company was not only Guatemala's largest landowner and employer—it also owned half of the shares of the shipper of its fruit, the International Railways of Central America, and much of the Electric Bond and Share power company. The lawyer for all three companies had been none other than the United States Secretary of State, John Foster Dulles. Some of his peers in government—and in his law firm (Sullivan & Cromwell)—were also heavily involved in the company:

> Allen Dulles, Director of the CIA, had done legal work for United Fruit and held shares in it.
> Thomas Dudley Cabot, Director of International Security Affairs in the State Department, had been president of the company.
> Robert Cutler, of the National Security Council, had been its chairman of the board.

John J. McCloy, President of the International Bank for
  Reconstruction and Development, was a former board
  member.
Walter Bedell Smith, Undersecretary of State, would join the
  board when he left government.
Robert Hill, the Ambassador to Costa Rica, was also a future
  board member.[13]

No wonder the United States was alarmed when Arbenz in Guatemala,
like Mossadegh in Iran, tried to regain some control over his country's
natural resources. Any form of redistribution was considered a lurch
toward communism—even though the Iranian Communist Party
(Tudeh) had been inconsequential, and the Communists in Guatemala
held only four of the sixty-one votes in Arbenz's coalition.[14]

Allen Dulles turned over the Guatemalan coup—called Operation
Success—to Frank Wisner, who recruited the help of Tracy Barnes,
Richard Bissell, and E. Howard Hunt.[15] They found a figurehead for
the "insurgents," Carlos Castillo Armas, trained in Honduras and Florida, and launched the coup in 1954 with the help of radio and pamphlet
"psywar" and small CIA air attacks. When the coup seemed to stall,
Allen Dulles asked President Eisenhower for two more airplanes for
raids to terrorize the populace. Unlike Kennedy at the Bay of Pigs,
Eisenhower authorized the air cover.[16] The coup succeeded, like that
in Iran, with minimal forces and cost. The CIA seemed on a winning
streak.

The plot that overthrew Rafael Trujillo in the Dominican Republic was also begun under Eisenhower, though Trujillo was assassinated
four months after Kennedy's inauguration. An earlier killing was done
late in Eisenhower's second term. Richard Bissell said that Eisenhower
ordered the assassination of Congo's Patrice Lumumba, and the CIA
initially delivered poisons for that purpose.[17] The later coup that actually killed Lumumba was partly prompted and supplied by the CIA.[18]

Ike's CIA was not always successful in its subversive campaigns. Indeed, the apparent ease with which Iran and Guatemala were toppled made Kim Roosevelt too cocky about overthrowing the Syrian and Indonesian governments. The Indonesia effort foundered in 1957 when an American bomber was shot down and its pilot revealed the plot.[19] In Syria, the plan to assassinate Abdul Hamid Serraj was badly bungled and the American ambassador was expelled from the country.[20] These failures, Thomas Powers claims, showed that "the Dulles brothers had grown fond of the quick and dirty approach without regard to the real strength of local allies."[21] Still, four out of six is not a bad record for Eisenhower, the destroyer of governments.

LATER PRESIDENTS

John F. Kennedy, who followed Eisenhower in office, was not as successful at overthrowing governments. His administration did abet the killing of the Diem brothers, but he failed over and over to topple Cuba and kill Castro. Lyndon Johnson's CIA lent support to the coups that brought down João Goulart in Brazil (1964) and Sukarno in Indonesia (1967). Richard Nixon's primary subversion, if we do not count Vietnam and Cambodia, occurred in Chile. The CIA poured two million dollars into an attempt to block the election of a leftist, Salvador Allende, as President of Chile.[22] When Allende was elected, Richard Nixon and Henry Kissinger refused to accept the results of a free election in a nation not theirs. Kissinger put it clearly: "I don't see why we have to let a country go Marxist just because its people are irresponsible."[23]

Kissinger and the CIA, without informing the Secretaries of State and Defense, set up parallel operations (Track I and Track II) to oust Allende.[24] Track I was a propaganda and bribery operation to prevent Allende's election from being confirmed by the Chilean congress.

Track II fomented a military coup against Allende. Track II ran into a problem when the Chilean army's Commander in Chief, René Schneider, refused to go along with the coup plot. The CIA then supplied weapons to kill Schneider. The weapons were not used, since a rival Chilean military leader stepped in and did the job on his own.[25] Over the next three years, the CIA supported the insurgency of Augusto Pinochet, whose forces were besieging the President's palace when Allende committed suicide rather than be taken. Pinochet, with American support, ruled as a cruel dictator for sixteen years (1974–1990).

Jimmy Carter, a believer in human rights, did not destroy any foreign regimes, a fact that made the right wing consider him a wimp. As his successor, Ronald Reagan, said after invading Grenada, "Our days of weakness are over."[26] Ronald Reagan failed to bring down the junta in Nicaragua with covert support of the Contras, but in general the age of covert subversion and coups was giving way to overt invasion as a way of overthrowing governments—Ronald Reagan in Grenada, George H. W. Bush in Kuwait and Panama, Bill Clinton in Haiti, George W. Bush in Afghanistan and Iraq. Secrecy was not necessary to these operations. (With Bush II, of course, there were concealed crimes in the detention centers.)

Stephen Kinzer argues that in the 114 cases where we denied a country the right to choose its own government, long-term results were usually damaging to the United States.[27] These overthrows normally involved violations of international law, as well as intrusion into sovereign bodies, and they created ill will from other nations and distrust or cynicism in our own. Crime, that is, did not pay. And secrecy did not let us escape its cost.

V.

EXECUTIVE USURPATIONS

13

"WAR POWERS"

In republican government the legislative authority, necessarily, predominates.

—JAMES MADISON, *The Federalist* 51

The conventional account of the later decades of the twentieth century claims that the "imperial presidency" reached a climax in the Vietnam War and Watergate and suffered a rebuke from Congress and the public. Then, at the beginning of the twenty-first century, prompted by worldwide terrorist threats, the executive branch clawed its way back into supremacy. There is some truth in this construction. But the earlier blows to the presidency were glancing ones, and the arc of executive power continued to rise throughout the supposed time of decline, when presidential wars kept occurring despite the War Powers Resolution that was supposed to check them. The reining in of the presidency was meant to happen after the War Powers Resolution (1973), the Ethics in Government Act (1978), the Independent Counsel Act (1978), the Foreign Intelligence Surveillance Act (1978), and the Presidential Records Act (1978). Of these, the one most resented by Dick Cheney was the War Powers Resolution (WPR).

The WPR was caused by Congress's long-delayed regret over its being stampeded into authorizing Vietnam actions by the Tonkin Gulf Resolution of 1964. On August 2 of that year, an American destroyer fired on three gunboats off the shore of North Vietnam. Expecting retaliation on August 4, the destroyer fired at phantom attackers in bad weather, and President Johnson instantly authorized air strikes at the harbor from which the attack boats were supposed to have been launched. After explaining his action on television that night, Johnson asked for authorization to defend South Vietnam under the Southeast Asia Collective Defense Treaty of 1954—as Truman had claimed authority for the Korean War under the UN Charter. The House voted unanimously to give Johnson the power he requested (and had already exercised), and only two Senators voted against it in the other house. Thus, without a declaration of war, Congress retroactively approved Johnson's air strikes as necessary "to assist any member or protocol state of the Southeast Asia Collective Defense Treaty request- ing assistance in defense of its freedom." After declassified NSA documents showed that there had been no August 4 attack, the Congress repealed its Tonkin Gulf Resolution in 1971 and began deliberating on a war-restricting act that was finally passed two years later.

As liberals like Senator Thomas Eagleton and Congresswoman Bella Abzug pointed out at the time, this "encroachment" on presiden- tial power was actually a surrender of Congress's constitutional monopoly on the right to go to war. The WPR institutionalized a *joint* authority that is denied in the Constitution. James Madison could not have been clearer about the document he had so great a role in drafting and defin- ing and defending:

> A declaration that there shall be war is not an execution of laws: it does
> not suppose pre-existing laws to be executed; it is not in any respect
> an act merely executive. It is, on the contrary, one of the most delib-
> erative acts that can be performed. . . . In the general distribution of
> powers, we find that of declaring war expressly vested in the Congress,
> where every other legislative power is declared to be vested, and with-
> out any other qualification than what is common to every other

legislative act. The constitutional idea of this power would seem then clearly to be that it is of a legislative and not an executive nature. . . . Those who are to *conduct* a war cannot in the nature of things be proper or safe judges whether a war ought to be *commenced, continued,* or *concluded.* They are barred from the latter functions by a great principle in free government analogous to that which separates the sword from the purse, or the power of executing from the power of enacting laws. (Madison's own emphasis)[1]

"War power" is not a term that occurs in the Constitution, much less "war powers," as something to be divided between the President and Congress. Admittedly, it is said that "the executive *power* shall be vested in a president." But what he is *executing,* in a war, is the severely circumscribed role of Commander in Chief. Recall the terms: "The President shall be Commander in Chief of the Army and Navy of the United States; and of the Militia of the several states, when called into the actual service of the United States." This does not say he has the power to initiate, authorize, or determine war. He does not even have the power to call the militias to national service, or to organize the army and navy and militias. Those are all reserved to Congress. They are among the many grants of power given Congress. The fullness of those powers bears out what Madison said about the legislature as the predominant body in a republic. Consider the list of powers, and how many of them have to do with war and armed services.

The congress shall have *power*

> To lay and collect taxes, duties, imposts, and excises, to pay the debts and *provide for the common defense* and general welfare of the United States; but all duties, imposts, and excises shall be uniform throughout the United States.
>
> To borrow money on the credit of the United States.

To regulate commerce with foreign nations, and among the several states, and with the Indian tribes.

To establish an uniform rule of naturalization, and uniform laws on the subject of bankruptcies, throughout the United States.

To coin money, regulate the value thereof, and of foreign coin and fix the standard of weights and measures.

To provide for the punishment of counterfeiting the securities and current coin of the United States.

To establish post-offices and post-roads.

To promote the progress of science and useful arts, by securing for limited times to authors and inventors the exclusive right to their respective writings and discoveries.

To constitute tribunals inferior to the supreme court.

To define and punish piracies and felonies committed on the high seas, and offences against the law of nations.

To declare war, grant letters of marque and reprisal, and make rules concerning captures on land and water.

To raise and support armies, but no appropriation of money to that use shall be for a longer term than two years.

To provide and maintain a navy.

To make rules for the government and regulation of the land and naval forces.

To provide for calling forth the militia to execute the laws of the union, suppress insurrections, and repel invasions.

To provide for organizing, arming, and disciplining the militia, and for governing such part of them as may be employed in the service of the United States, reserving to the states respectively the appointment of the officers and the authority of training the militia according to the discipline prescribed by Congress.

To exercise exclusive legislation in all cases whatsoever over such district (not exceeding ten miles square) as may, by cession of particular states and the acceptance of Congress, become the seat of the government of the United States, and to exercise like authority over all places purchased by the consent of the legislature of the state in which the same shall be, for the *erection of forts, magazines, arsenals,* dockyards, and other needful buildings. And

To make all laws which shall be necessary and proper for carrying into execution the foregoing powers, and all other powers vested by this constitution in the government of the United States, or in any department or officer thereof. (Emphasis added)

It will be noticed that the grants are, with only one exception (and that exception is expressly made), *exclusive* grants. That is, no other entity may coin money, determine naturalization, and so on. The exception is that once the militia is provided for and regulated and funded by Congress, the states may appoint officers and carry out the training. There is thus no reason to think Congress does not have *exclusive* power to declare war, regulate captures, make laws for the land and water services, call forth the militia, and so on.

Yet the War Powers Resolution did not maintain this congressional monopoly prescribed by the Constitution. The Resolution was passed, as it says, "to insure that the *collective* judgment of *both* the Congress and the President will apply to the introduction of United States Armed Forces into hostilities." It is a sign of the modern cult of the presidency that this abdication of power was widely treated as a congressional usurpation of power—certainly that is how Dick Cheney treated it from the moment when it was first proposed.

The resolution goes on: "The President *in every possible instance* shall *consult with* Congress before introducing United States Armed Forces into hostilities . . . and after every such introduction shall *consult* regularly with the Congress." It was easy to predict what events soon proved, that Presidents would not think prior consultation "possible," and that the "consulting" would be perfunctory if undertaken at all.

The resolution provides ridiculously inadequate means for guaranteeing consultation. It says that once a President decides to commit troops, he has forty-eight hours to explain why he is doing it, and he must withdraw in sixty days unless Congress gives him an extra thirty days to complete the mission. No President has observed these conditions, and most have denied their validity. John Yoo, the lawyer at the Justice Department's Office of Legal Counsel who would write the "torture memos" for dealing with Iraq War captives, wrote in 2005: "Presidents have never acknowledged the WPR's constitutionality, and their recent actions have ignored its terms."[2] The legal scholar Peter Irons has written: "[The WPR] was badly drafted, replete with loopholes, and has been simply ignored by every president—seven in number from Richard Nixon to George W. Bush—since its enactment."[3]

In 1975, when President Ford sent forces to rescue sailors from the American merchant ship *Mayagüez,* which had been seized by Cambodians, he informed Congress, but said he was acting by his authority as Commander in Chief and needed no permission from Congress.[4] In 1980, when President Carter sent a rescue team to get U.S. hostages out of Iran, he not only failed to consult Congress—he did not even tell his Secretary of State, Cyrus Vance, what he was doing.[5] Vance resigned his office in protest.

When terrorists blew up a disco in West Berlin in 1986, killing an American serviceman, President Reagan decided that Muammar Qaddafi was responsible and readied an attack on his Libyan headquarters. Before he could launch it, some in Congress said that he needed to consult them, in accord with the WPR. Then-Congressman Dick Cheney said, however, that the President had classified intelligence the Congress lacked, and he should be trusted to take the proper actions based on that intelligence, with no second-guessing from Cheney's fellow congressmen. Cheney said at the time:

If the president of the United States reviews it and feels it's adequate . . .
I am satisfied that I know all I need to know at this point, and I
would disagree with what we often hear from the Hill, the cry for
consultation in advance, let us in on the decision, we want to share
responsibility. . . . It seems to me that this is a clear-cut case where the
president as Commander in Chief . . . is justified in taking whatever
action he deems appropriate and discussing the details with us after
the fact.[6]

Reagan sent the bombers on their raid, without consulting Congress
or getting its authorization. Like Truman in Korea he said he was
acting from "my authority as Commander in Chief."[7]

When President George H. W. Bush was contemplating whether
to send a letter asking Congress for authorization to launch the Gulf
War, Cheney (now the Secretary of Defense) urgently advised him not
to. The *Washington Post* reporter Bob Woodward wrote of this moment: "Cheney cautioned about sending the letter. The simple act of
requesting the resolution would carry immense implications. No matter how the President's letter was phrased, it would be interpreted to
mean that the President thought he needed a vote."[8] When the President sent the letter anyway, and Cheney testified before the Senate
Armed Services Committee, he stressed that the letter was merely a
matter of courtesy, not anything the President needed to do. He told
Senator Edward Kennedy at the hearing: "I do not believe the President requires any additional authorization from the Congress before
committing U.S. forces to achieve our objectives in the Gulf."

Cheney brought up again Dean Acheson's ancient claim that "there
have been some 200 times, more than 200 times, in our history when
presidents have committed U.S. forces."[9] Secretary of State James Baker
made the same point before the Senate Foreign Relations Committee:
"We should not have a constitutional argument, it does not seem to

me, about whether or not the President, as Commander in Chief, has the constitutional authority to commit forces. It has been done going all the way back, I think, to World War II."[10] President Bush agreed with his advisers: "I didn't have to get permission from some old goat in the United States Congress to kick Saddam Hussein out of Kuwait."[11]

Reagan sent troops to Grenada, George H. W. Bush sent them to Panama, Clinton sent them to Haiti, without consulting Congress. Presidents have routinely ignored the WPR. This makes one wonder why the right wing resents it so much. Why not just accept its dismissal as a victory? But when President Reagan won election in 1980, Dick Cheney told Reagan's first Chief of Staff, James Baker, that his first priority should be the expunging of the WPR. Baker's notes of the conversation begin: "Pres. seriously weakened in recent yrs. Restor power & auth. to Exec. Branch—Need strong ldr'ship. Get rid of War Powers Act—restore independent rights [of the President]."[12] When Cheney became Vice President in 2001, he and his legal adviser, David Addington, asked the Justice Department's Office of Legal Counsel to rule that the President, and he alone, has all authority over war— exactly the opposite of the constitutional grant of all such authority to Congress. That is what Cheney had been saying for years, but now he wanted formal confirmation of his view.

John Yoo, the lawyer Cheney was relying on in the Office of Legal Counsel to uphold his constitutional oddities, had to deal with Congress's constitutional rights to declare war. He did this with a flimsy philological fantasy. He said that in the eighteenth century, "declare" did not mean "initiate" or "authorize." Relying on only one source, Samuel Johnson's eighteenth-century dictionary, Yoo said that the verb "declare" has only five meanings, none of which is "make." They are all variants on the sense of "publish," so that is all that Congress can do with regard to war—publish the fact that it is occurring *once the President has initiated it*. In Yoo's words, "declaring war recognized a state of affairs."[13] In fact, we all know many more uses of "declare," including such enacting phrases as "I now declare you man and wife," or "The Court declares you innocent." And the standard historical survey of usage, the *Oxford Dictionary of the English Language,* has a separate entry for "declare war," which as early as the sixteenth century glosses the legal term with *bellum judicare* (decree war).[14] It takes a fierce determination to ignore the obvious source and sense of the phrase "declare war" to play these word games with it.

Besides, Yoo utterly neglects the legislative history. The article as it was proposed in the Federal Convention gave Congress the power to "make war." But Rufus King successfully noted at the convention that "*make* war might be understood to *conduct* it, which was an executive function."[15] This is the same distinction we have seen Madison make in his "Helvidius" letter. Since to conduct a war is a weaker sense than to start a war, the drafters brought in "declare" as the stronger sense and assigned it to Congress. Yoo cannot logically argue that "declare" simply means "publish" in Article III, Section 3: "The Congress shall have power to declare the punishment of treason." Congress there is not simply announcing the punishment, it is defining it.

To buttress his weak case, Yoo adds further absurdities. He says, for instance, that if the framers wanted to make "declare war" mean initiate it, they should have used the phrase "levy war," as the Constitution does in the treason clause (Article III). But "levy" there means prepare or support, not merely initiate. It is a looser term, not a stricter one— its first meanings are to "assess, collect, recruit." It extends beyond actual war, as we can see in the parallel clauses, "adhering to their [the United States'] enemies, giving them aid and comfort." Then Yoo says that the ban on states' "engaging" in war on their own (Article I, Section 10, Clause 3) would have been a clearer definition of the war-making power. But the danger envisaged in the states' ban was the possibility of being drawn into the wars of neighboring powers (Indian tribes, Canada, Mexico) where the war would not be one the states initiated but took some part in. Again, the terminology is looser, not tighter, as Yoo claims. Yoo's supposed philology is all a web of misconstruals woven together to veil the obvious meaning of "declare war."

The extremism of the reaction to the WPR cannot be overstated. In a fury that the Congress had dared to say the President had *joint* power over war (which he does not, under the Constitution), the administration of George W. Bush asserted that the President had *sole* power over its initiation and conduct. The monopoly on nuclear war that was given at the dawn of Bomb Power was now extended to all aspects of war.

14

CHALLENGING
SECRECY

The brain trust of President George W. Bush—principally Dick Cheney and Donald Rumsfeld—took office with him in 2001 to lead what they considered a counter-revolution. They denounced a congressional "coup" that had hampered executive power in the 1970s. Cheney was serving in the seventies as President Ford's Chief of Staff. Rumsfeld was the Secretary of Defense. They had long nurtured an angry feeling that Congress overreacted to the Watergate scandal and to the military loss in Vietnam. A whole series of laws and reforms assailed them—not only acts mentioned earlier (the War Powers Resolution, Ethics in Government Act, Independent Counsel Act, Foreign Intelligence Surveillance Act, and Presidential Records Act [1978]), but especially the recommendations of the Church (Senate) and Pike (House) committees for reforming the CIA.

Against the long period of presidential prerogative that began with the President's sole custody of the Bomb, Congress began finally and timidly, in the 1970s, to challenge the secrecy and unaccountability of the National Security State. The focus of congressional action was the CIA, which had meddled in the Watergate cover-up and failed to inform Congress of many covert activities, thus violating the National Security Act of 1947. The Ford administration tried to abort the congressional investigations. When that failed, Secretary Kissinger became furious at what he called "a runaway Congress." After CIA Director William Colby submitted to congressional oversight, he became in Kissinger's eyes "a runaway CIA director."[1]

It is appropriate that the first major challenge to the National Security State should center on the CIA, since—as Thomas Powers wrote—"the history of the CIA is the secret history of the Cold War."[2] All the themes of executive power are sounded in the Agency: secrecy, secret money, unaccountability to Congress, outside operatives under contract, executive escape from constitutional checks and balances. These were all subjects of conflict in what came to be called "the year of intelligence"—1975.

The immediate cause of the investigations was a series of articles in the *New York Times* written by Seymour Hersh. The reporter who broke the My Lai massacre story in 1969 (which brought him a Pulitzer Prize and a job at the *New York Times*), Hersh had begun ferreting out CIA secrets in 1973. In January of 1974, he was ready to write about the CIA's project for retrieving a sunken Soviet submarine with a special ship (*Glomar Explorer*) built by one of Howard Hughes's companies. CIA Director William Colby knew of the story before it was submitted, and he went to plead with Hersh's editor, Bill Kovach, and *Times* publisher Arthur O. Sulzberger not to publish it, since the project was ongoing, and alerting the Soviets might abort it. The *Times,* as usual, complied.[3]

In July 1974 the *Glomar* mission failed, breaking up the sub while trying to draw it to the surface. Meanwhile, the *Los Angeles Times* had picked up on the story. Colby pleaded with its editors not to publish, and the paper held off for a while—as did the *New York Times,* once again—but other journalists were getting the story, so the Los Angeles paper ran its account on February 7, 1975.[4] That freed the *New York*

Times to run Hersh's article on March 19, 1975. By this time, the White House had many reasons for anger at Hersh, and Dick Cheney decided to give Hersh the same treatment Richard Nixon had given Daniel Ellsberg. In a series of secret memos Cheney recommended that Hersh and the *Times* be indicted, and Hersh's apartment searched, "to discourage the NYT and other publications from similar action."[5] But the Attorney General at the time, Edward Levi, blocked any legal action against Hersh.[6] Years later, when he became Vice President, Cheney would find a far different Attorney General in Alberto Gonzales.

Sandwiched between the *Glomar* skirmishes was the real bombshell in Hersh's coverage of the CIA. On December 22, 1974, he broke the story of the CIA's spying on U.S. citizens, a thing forbidden by the CIA's charter. The knowledge of that activity had been sequestered in what was known as the supersecret report on improper activities, a document called "the family jewels." If Hersh had found out about that, what else in the family jewels was now available to him? There was deep panic at the CIA and in the White House. The CIA's recently retired Director, Richard Helms, warned Kissinger about the scale of the danger. The two men were both in peril because of the way they had worked together to overthrow Salvador Allende. But many people were at risk, including Democrats—Helms assured Kissinger that proof was in the documents that Robert Kennedy ordered the attempt to kill Fidel Castro.[7] Kissinger told President Ford about this, and urged him to head off further revelations and investigations. Ford tried to do just that, but in a clumsy way.

The President invited the editors of the *Times* to the White House for an off-the-record lunch. He pleaded with them, for the good of the nation, not to publish any more Hersh articles on the CIA. The secret material Hersh was turning up could destroy the reputation of every President going back to Harry Truman. *Times* managing editor A. M. Rosenthal asked what kind of secret Ford was talking about. The

President answered: "Like assassinations."[8] Thomas Powers remained stunned, years later, "that a President told the CIA's darkest secret to a *newspaper*" (emphasis in the original).[9]

The *Times* editors were barred from reporting this shocker by off-the-record rules, but Ford should have known they would talk about this conversation, challenging other news channels to find other sources for it. The first to do this was CBS reporter Daniel Schorr, who broadcast Ford's comment on his February 28, 1975, broadcast. CIA assassinations were now in the news. The anger of the administration can be gauged from Richard Helms's denunciation of Schorr. As Helms was leaving Vice President Nelson Rockefeller's office, he ran into Schorr, and shouted with reporters present: "You son of a bitch! You killer! You cocksucker! Killer Schorr—that's what they ought to call you."[10]

ROCKEFELLER COMMISSION

The White House had gone into full damage control immediately after Hersh's December 22, 1974, article on domestic spying by the CIA. Hoping to head off or blunt congressional curiosity, the White House hastily set up its own board on January 4, 1975, a commission to "investigate" itself, under the chairmanship of Vice President Rockefeller. Dick Cheney argued that this investigation would give Ford an excuse for dodging questions about the CIA—he could say he was waiting for the results of the investigation (an excuse Cheney would recycle when he refused to discuss leaks about Joseph Wilson's CIA wife in the "Plamegate" affair). Kissinger said that Rockefeller should be instructed to limit the investigation to domestic spying, the subject Hersh began with. The White House assembled a plausible but conservative group of distinguished Americans (including the ex-governor of California, Ronald Reagan) to serve on the Rockefeller Commission.

William Colby, the principal witness before the commission, says it was incurious—only one member (Erwin Griswold) asked probing questions, and Rockefeller took Colby aside to say he did not want too much candor:

> Bill, do you really have to present all this material to us? We realize that there are secrets that you fellows need to keep and so nobody here is going to take it amiss if you feel that there are some questions you can't answer quite as fully as you feel you have to.[11]

The investigative staff was led by David Belin, who had worked for the Warren Commission when Ford was a member of it. Since Belin fancied himself an expert on assassination, he had to advert to the assassination stories that began two months after the commission was set up. Belin compared such talk with his work on the Warren Commission, subtly reducing the charges to "conspiracy theories." The assassination charges were kept out of that Rockefeller report, which had only this to say of them:

> [On those charges] the Commission's staff began the required inquiry, but time did not permit a full investigation before this report was due. The President therefore requested that the materials in the possession of the Commission which bear on these allegations be turned over to him. This has been done.

The pressure to keep the scope of the commission's work narrow was not all that the White House applied. It limited the documents that could be turned over to the investigation. It kept most of the family jewels tucked away. The commission did mention the program called MK–ULTRA, in which the CIA had experimented with LSD and other drugs to effect "mind control." But it was limited by the fact that Richard Helms had destroyed all the papers of MK–ULTRA, along with all the recordings made in his office, just before he left the directorship.[12]

CHURCH COMMITTEE

White House hopes to preclude other investigations by setting up the Rockefeller Commission were soon disappointed. On January 27, scarcely more than three weeks after the Rockefeller Commission was authorized, the Senate set up a select committee to investigate the CIA. Less than four weeks after that (February 19), the House created its own special committee to pursue the matter. The Senate panel was named for its chairman, Frank Church of Idaho. Colby, in consultation with Senator Church, agreed to hand over all requested materials. That horrified the White House. Church would get all the family jewels. Kissinger asked Ford to fire Colby and replace him with the conservative Laurence Silberman, then serving as Deputy Attorney General.[13] Silberman declined, but apparently he ran an errand for Kissinger. Colby relates that Silberman called him in to the Justice Department and said that by reporting the crimes in the family jewels he could be indicted for crime himself—which seems a blatant attempt to get Colby to suppress the evidence, in order to protect himself.[14]

The source of this panic was the compilation of all CIA activities that could be considered unlawful. The Watergate investigation had proved that some CIA members cooperated with ex–CIA officer E. Howard Hunt in the raid on the office of Ellsberg's psychiatrist.[15] When Colby's predecessor as DCI, James Schlesinger, had learned of this in 1973, he asked what else had been done under Helms without reporting it. He ordered that all "dubious" actions in the past be assembled for his inspection. A summary of these actions ran to twenty pages, but the reports themselves added up to almost seven hundred pages. A memorandum on the whole collection, numbering seventy pages, was what became known as the family jewels.[16] Colby, as Director, told the White House about this explosive collection after Hersh learned about it:

> I bundled them [the reports on dubious actions] together and briefed my two [congressional oversight] chairmen on it, and I let the skeleton sit quietly in the closet, hoping they would stay there. Obviously someone has gotten a smell of a certain number of those. I think a certain number of ex-employees—Hersh put these two tracks [surveillance of peace activists and mail openings] into one track.

Kissinger clearly thought the jewels should have been destroyed—as Helms had destroyed the mind-control papers. But it was too late for that now. Enough was out that destroying them would be clear evidence of crime. Colby, indeed, believed destroying them would destroy the CIA, which he meant to save.

But if the evidence could not be destroyed, it did have to be withheld. Kissinger asked Ford to invoke executive privilege against its release—the resort George W. Bush would get away with later on. But Ford thought using executive privilege would look too much like a cover-up, and it might destroy *him* (Nixon's impeachment was dangerously recent, as was Ford's pardon of him). Still, Ford did refuse to issue an order to all agencies to cooperate with the Church committee.[17] Though Kissinger said the committee's request should be refused, lest documents harm the reputation of America abroad, he knew that his own reputation would take an earlier and more certain blow. His efforts to unseat Salvador Allende by an unauthorized Track II was one of the obvious things that would come out.

Kissinger found Colby's actions so despicable that he professes not to know what possible motive Colby could have possessed. He could come up with only two intentions—that Colby had weighed the balance of power in Washington and taken the side of Congress against the President, or that he had taken the side of radical war protesters against the nation.

> [CIA Deputy Director Vernon] Walters argues that Colby came to believe that a fundamental shift in the Washington power balance had made Congress so dominant that the only way to preserve the CIA was to open its secrets to congressional committees, however unreasonable their requests or however reckless the attendant publicity. . . . Colby in effect threw the CIA on the mercy of Congress. . . . [Or]: It may well be that Colby was seeking to purify his country by cooperating with the strategies of the protest movement.[18]

In private, Kissinger derided Colby's "Catholic conscience," and said that he confused testifying before Congress with going into the confessional.[19]

Actually, Colby was drawing on traditions older than the Catholic one. Before he went to testify before the Church committee, he went to a lecture by an old wartime friend of his, the classical scholar Bernard Knox, Director of Washington's Center for Hellenic Studies. Knox was lecturing on Sophocles at George Washington University that term, and Colby deliberately went to his lecture on *Antigone,* the play whose heroine defies a ruler in order to serve a deeper loyalty.[20] Colby felt that the only way to save the CIA he loved was to divorce it from the bad parts of its history—both internally and before the public—to salvage its good parts. He did not volunteer the family jewels—but he did not refuse to turn them over when Congress officially asked him to.[21] He knew that many in the administration, and in the Agency itself, would despise him for this. According to his sympathetic biographer, Thomas Powers, "Institutional survival required personal tragedy for Colby."[22] The intense hatred felt for Colby was such that several CIA veterans told Powers that Colby must have been "an enemy agent" to do such harm.[23]

THE PIKE COMMITTEE

The House investigation of the CIA was for five months the Nedzi Committee, named for its first chairman, Lucien "Lou" Nedzi from Michigan. The House select committee was more lopsided (seven Democrats to three Republicans) than the Church one (six Democrats to five Republicans) and more aggressive. In forming the select committee, Speaker of the House Carl Albert and Majority Leader Thomas "Tip" O'Neill made a mistake in appointing so many more liberal Democrats than conservative Republicans. The committee was divided against itself from the outset. Some members thought Nedzi was too cozy with William Colby. Nedzi was the only House member whom Colby had briefed on the family jewels in 1973 (even before the Daniel Schorr broadcast), in Nedzi's capacity as chairman of the Armed Services Subcommittee on Intelligence. (Nedzi was investigating the Watergate break-in at the time.) Some on the committee felt they should have been let in on the secrets back then.

When internal resentments on the committee led Nedzi to resign, the full House voted to retain him, but he refused to stay on. The committee had to be reconstituted with more members (thirteen instead of ten) and a different chairman, Otis Pike of New York. But the ideological split continued, and the White House was able to play on that. Colby, who had worked out arrangements to safeguard classified material with the Rockefeller and Church panels, was never able to get reassurances from Pike, who said the House had its own security rules. Since the reconstituted committee got off to a late start (July), it had only five months to work before its mandate ran out. This made it perfunctory and rushed in its work. It would end up writing divergent reports, so little reconcilable that no final report was issued. Colby, who thought that the Rockefeller and Church inquiries acted responsibly, condemned the Pike investigation as "a pretty awful mess."[24] Even the liberal media came to agree with that judgment.

Colby had hired an outside lawyer to represent him, the civil rights attorney Mitchell Rogovin, who had been the lawyer for Neil Sheehan of the *New York Times* when Sheehan published the Pentagon Papers. Henry Kissinger thought Colby was going further off the reservation when he hired so liberal a man as his protector, but Kissinger should have been happy to see Rogovin fight off unreasonable demands from the Pike committee. Pike accomplished what Church never did: In September, he made the White House so angry by releasing classified material that President Ford ordered all such material returned to the White House.[25] When Pike refused to do that, the President ordered all executive personnel to stop cooperating with Pike. Within a month Pike had to back away from his uncompromising stance.

The deepest hatred of Colby came from the notion that he had ratted out Richard Helms. In answer to the command to report all CIA misdeeds, one of Colby's subordinates pointed out that Helms, in his confirmation hearings to become ambassador to Iran, had denied any complicity in the Track II scheme against Allende in Chile. That was not true. Colby turned an investigation of Helms's actions over to a three-man CIA review panel, where only one member was firm in saying that Helms had committed perjury. Colby reluctantly referred the matter to the Justice Department, and this time two men strongly recommended prosecution.[26] President Carter's new Attorney General, Griffin Bell, was also reluctant to proceed, but he felt he could not simply dismiss the allegation. He proposed a deal to Helms's attorney, Edward Bennett Williams, in 1977—a nolo contendere plea to two misdeeds, with no jail and no fine. Helms, convinced of the righteousness of his cause, wanted to reject the deal, and he worried that the nolo plea would make him forfeit his government pension. To secure the pension, he agreed to accept one count of lying to Congress, with a two-thousand-dollar fine and two years of prison suspended. He called this guilty plea a badge of honor.[27]

Kissinger felt that Helms was the true martyr of the CIA probes.

> The most conspicuous casualty of this process was Richard Helms, one of the most distinguished public servants I have known. He was charged with having committed perjury while testifying in 1973 before the Senate Foreign Relations Committee during confirmation hearings for his appointment as ambassador to Iran. Technically, he had testified incompletely; substantively, it was a grave injustice. . . . What made the indictment which ruined Helms's public career and blighted his life particularly egregious was that the alleged perjury had been brought to the attention of the Attorney General by Helms's successor, William Colby, who had in turn been pressed to do so by a subordinate CIA official.[28]

Helms was given a slap on the wrist, retained his pension, and was a greater hero than ever to the right wing. In 1983, President Reagan gave him the National Security Medal. A truer picture of his treatment is that of Helms's biographer:

> If the history of Watergate illustrated any general principle of politics and jurisprudence, it is the principle that political indictments should be narrowly framed. Thus Nixon was charged with obstruction of justice—a pettifogging choice, considering the range of his abuses of his office—and Richard Helms was charged with lying. No one seriously proposed that he be charged with conspiracy to kill Castro, or conspiracy to violate the mails, or conspiracy to commit a burglary, or conspiracy to obstruct justice for having withheld evidence in the Watergate matter, or any of the other doubtful enterprises to which so many people outside the CIA were equally involved—not only those

in the White House who gave or transmitted the orders, but those in Congress who actively collaborated or passively acquiesced. Crimes in the legal sense might have been extracted from the facts of such endeavors, but they would have violated the Watergate principle. As a result Helms was not charged with what he did, but more narrowly for having lied about it.[29]

This is a better example of what was noted earlier, that executive misdeeds are rarely punished, or are punished lightly and pardoned.

Kissinger shed copious tears over the belief that, as he put it, Congress had hamstrung the intelligence community. He even blamed the Church and Pike committees for Oliver North. With the CIA incapacitated, he wrote, "operational control has sometimes fallen into the hands of romantics, not strategists, as in the case of Iran-contra."[30] What Kissinger fails to mention is that North was working for the Contras in coordination with CIA Director William Casey. Casey was so little hamstrung that Daniel Patrick Moynihan had to resign from the Senate oversight committee to protest the CIA's failure to report its covert mining of Nicaraguan harbors. But what Kissinger considered hamstringing came out in his remark to the National Security Council: "It is an act of insanity and national humiliation to have a law prohibiting the president from ordering assassination."[31]

Dick Cheney and Donald Rumsfeld also felt the presidency had been incapacitated by the War Powers Resolution and the CIA investigations. This was the mind-forming experience of their political lives, and they would spend the next four decades trying to reverse this trend. At first they seemed beaten; but they meant to take back a power wrongly wrenched from them. As the French say, they gathered their forces to make a better lunge (*reculer pour mieux sauter*). It would not take them long.

15

THE UNITARY
EXECUTIVE

The weakened presidency, attributed by conservatives to congressional overreach during President Ford's term, lasted only four
years—the years of Jimmy Carter's failed single term. Though Carter
achieved important things—notably the Panama Canal Treaties (1977),
the Camp David Accords between Anwar Sadat and Menachem Begin
(1978), and a foreign policy based on human rights—he managed the
economy miserably. The Iranian hostage crisis, caused by his admission
of the Shah to the United States, put the seal on a series of defeats,
including the failure of a rescue raid to free the hostages in Iran
(Operation Eagle Claw) and the boycott of the 1980 Moscow Olympics
(to punish the Soviet Union for invading Afghanistan). Unfortunate
symbolism dogged him—a collapse while jogging, a supposed attack
on his boat by a swimming rabbit, a supposed indictment of American
"malaise." Most people attributed his poor showing to personal failings;
but the Reagan Republicans were ready with an "I told you so," saying
weak Presidents come from strong Congresses doing things like passing
a War Powers Resolution or investigating the CIA. Edwin Meese,
Reagan's Attorney General, made the case:

Another major threat to constitutional government which the Reagan administration faced was the legislative opportunism that arose out of the Watergate controversy during the early 1970s. Congress had used this episode to expand its power in various ways vis-à-vis the executive branch.[1]

Ronald Reagan came to Washington determined to make the presidency powerful again. He would interpret the Constitution independently of the courts, deny congressional oversight of federal agencies, and remove many of the regulatory standards enacted under Carter, especially those having to do with energy use. Thomas Friedman has paid belated tribute to the way Carter responded to OPEC pressures with a comprehensive conservation program. In response to the first "oil shock" of 1973, the Ford administration had passed the Energy Policy and Conservation Act. Carter expanded and enforced its provisions, adding the establishment of the Department of Energy (1977) and the National Energy Act (1978). The NEA continued mandatory mileage requirements for cars, tax subsidies to solar and wind energy, new energy standards for federal operations, and anti-pollution measures for industry. According to Friedman:

> Not surprisingly, it all worked. Between 1975 and 1985, American passenger vehicle mileage went from around 13.5 miles per gallon to 27.5, while light truck mileage increased from 11.6 miles per gallon to 19.5—all of which helped to create a global oil glut from the mid-1980s to the mid-1990s, which not only weakened OPEC but also helped to unravel the Soviet Union, then the world's second-largest producer.[2]

This network of regulations was a perfect example of what Reagan meant when he said, in his first inaugural address, that "government is not a solution to our problem; government is the problem." He began systematically dismantling his predecessor's energy program. He removed the subsidies to wind and solar production, so that technology pioneered by American tax money was sold to foreign firms. He relaxed pollution and mileage standards. Reagan stocked the agencies with people who did not like what they did. They were there to gut what they were supposed to be promoting. That was true of James Watt at the Department of the Interior. It was true of Anne Gorsuch Burford at the Environmental Protection Agency. It was true of Rita Lavelle in the disposal of hazardous waste products. The results are described by Reagan's generally sympathetic biographer Lou Cannon:

> Overall, Reagan left a ruinous regulatory legacy. Deregulation of oil prices led to the waste of irreplaceable energy resources. The early laxity of regulatory enforcement at EPA increased the hazardous waste problem. And relaxation of regulatory restraints on thrift institutions contributed to the savings-and-loan scandal. The combined effect of these policies was to destroy public confidence in deregulation. "If you thought about deregulation in 1979, it seemed a brave new world," said Urban Institute analyst Michael Fix. "Now the very idea seems disreputable. People at the outset thought we were drowning in government red tape. Now they think we're not being protected."[3]

When it was objected that Reagan was perverting the purpose of agencies set up by Congress to maintain certain standards, Ed Meese turned to conservative young lawyers in the Department of Justice to craft a new theory of the Constitution, one they called the unitary executive. They based it on the fact that the executive branch is the only one in our government filled by one man. Since the founders feared monarchy, there was at first a movement to diffuse executive authority throughout an executive council—George Mason of Virginia recommended a plural presidency, with two men chosen from each of three different sections of the country.[4] This was rejected for two reasons—one, championed by Alexander Hamilton (who did not fear monarchy as the others did), was that a President needed "secrecy and dispatch" to discharge his duties toward other nations, and the second reason, voiced by James Wilson, held that a single authority would be more accountable.[5] After all, whom would you impeach if there were a number of loci in the executive?

The conservatives in Meese's office turned Wilson's logic upside down. They made the single executive an argument for less accountability to the other two branches, not more. Since only the President can run the agencies, they must answer to him, as parts of the unitary executive, and not to outside forces—like congressional oversight committees. As one of those who invented the theory for Mr. Meese, Steven Calabresi, a founder of the Federalist Society, argued, executive agencies should not be responsible to anyone other than the chief executive. One of his favorite examples was the Independent Counsel Act, which let judges appoint the special prosecutor, and thus violated the constitutional separation of powers.[6]

By the logic of this theory, once Congress has established an agency, it must have nothing more to do with it. All further supervision is purely executive and outside its legislative purview. This neglects the fact that Congress has the right to impeach any federal official, legislative or judicial, not just the President—and that involves, of necessity, investigating the performance and overseeing the standards it mandated. The lesser powers are presumed in the greater one (the power to remove from office).

The unitary theory was originally created for a narrow purpose—to let the President get rid of those pesky regulations. To the horror of the first inventors, they found in time that they had been Frankensteins birthing a monster. Calabresi protests that his first theory was extended and distorted when President Bush II and Vice President Cheney made it an authorization for the President, on his sole authority, to set up military tribunals, wage undeclared wars, deprive prisoners of habeas corpus, order extraordinary renditions, hold trials with undisclosed evidence, and unilaterally abrogate the Geneva Conventions subscribed to by Congress:

> We generally reject broad claims of presidential power to deprive peo-
> ple of life, liberty, or property in the absence of statutory authority.
> The classic vision of the unitary executive grew up as an argument that
> the president had a constitutional right to direct and fire officials wield-
> ing executive authority. It had absolutely nothing to do with claims of
> implied, inherent presidential domestic and foreign policy power
> of the kind asserted by the current [Bush] administration. . . . The
> cost of the bad legal advice that he received is that Bush has discredited
> the theory of the unitary executive by associating it not with presiden-
> tial authority to remove and direct subordinate executive officials but
> with implied, inherent foreign policy powers, some of which, at least,
> the president simply does not possess.[7]

Despite their protestations, the first champions of the unitary theory had no reason to think it would be confined to a narrow purpose. It is easy to see how it pushes toward extremes by the rigidity of its first formulation of a totally separate executive power. Henry Kissinger, for instance, was adopting something like the narrow view of the unitary theory when he argued that William Colby, as head of the CIA, should be responsible only to the executive of which he was a part, not to Messrs. Church and Pike in Congress:

> Not even an independent department, the CIA was created under
> the National Security Act of 1947 as an advisory body to the National
> Security Council, which is headed by the President. The traditional
> approach would have been for Colby to leave the constitutional issue
> for the President.[8]

But what starts as a matter of departmental housekeeping—the executive must mind its own affairs—soon becomes a cover for things like assassination attempts by an agency whose charter demands a reporting to Congress of *all* clandestine activities. Colby had said he was obeying the Constitution in his response to a congressional subpoena. Kissinger said he had no right to act that way, apart from the President, who would handle "the constitutional issue."

The constitutional issue was one that Mr. Meese's department soon found itself engaged in while unilaterally wiping away regulations ordered by Congress. In a speech at Tulane Law School, Meese said that the President has the right and duty to interpret the Constitution on his own, declaring some laws unconstitutional even as he signs them into law. He alleged that Abraham Lincoln's resistance to the *Dred Scott* decision was his warrant for saying this. He granted that Lincoln allowed the court authority over Dred Scott, his owner, and his family, but Lincoln said in his debate with Stephen Douglas in Quincy, Illinois, "We nevertheless do oppose [*Dred Scott*] . . . as a political rule which shall be binding on the voter."[9] Before turning to the actual use Meese made of Lincoln, it is best to give a fuller citation from Lincoln's Quincy debate than Meese's truncated bit. Lincoln said:

> We oppose the Dred Scott decision *in a certain way,* upon which I ought perhaps to address to you a few words. We do not propose that when Dred Scott has been decided to be a slave by the court, we, *as a mob,* will decide him to be free. We do not propose that, when any other one, or one thousand, shall be decided by that court to be slaves, we will in any violent way *disturb the rights of property thus settled;* but we nevertheless do oppose that decision as a political rule which shall be binding on the voter to vote for nobody which *thinks* it wrong, which shall be binding on the members of Congress or the president to favor no measure that does not actually concur *with the principles* of that decision. We do not propose to be bound by it as a political rule *in that way,*

because we think it lays the foundation, not merely of enlarging and spreading out what we *consider* an evil, but it lays the foundation for spreading that evil into the states themselves. We propose *so* resisting it as to have it reversed, *if we can,* and a new *judicial rule* established upon this subject. (Emphasis added)[10]

Lincoln was not President at the time he said this, and he did not mention any special role for a President. He was not declaring the *Dred Scott* decision unconstitutional. He admitted the decision was binding in the law. He argued with its political theory, and wanted a debate that could bring about a revision of the principle behind it (a revision through the normal political process, not by presidential fiat). He was describing the intellectual freedom of any citizen (he uses "we" throughout) to think the decision wrong while not advocating disobedience to it. But Meese used the main point of his Tulane speech—that there is a difference between the Constitution and any decision of the Supreme Court—to justify President Reagan's power to declare a law unconstitutional *even as he was signing it into law,* and to say that *he would not enforce it* insofar as it was wrong. Clearly this has nothing to do with what Lincoln said of *Dred Scott.*

Prompted by Meese and his right-wing lawyers, Reagan made an unparalleled (up to that time) use of signing statements—presidential pronouncements at the time of signing a law sent to him by Congress. The Constitution provides that laws will not go into effect until signed by the President, but that merely means that he has received and recognized the law given him for execution. The Constitution does not make his signature a part of the legislating of the act, and it makes no mention of a signing *statement* as part of the process.

Earlier in our history, signing statements were added to the ceremony of signing the law, but they had been *mere* ceremony, fulfilling the function the Supreme Court had granted them in 1899: "It has properly been the practice of the President to inform Congress by message of his approval of bills, so that the fact may be recorded."[11] Sometimes a President would use the occasion to congratulate those who helped pass the law, or to refer to those who would benefit by it, or to praise its object—ceremonial remarks. Only rarely had a President quarreled with anything substantive in the law, and John Quincy Adams led a congressional rebuke to President Tyler for doing so.[12] Under the first thirty-five presidents, who made thousands of signing statements, there were only thirty mentions of anything substantive about the law itself. Under the next five presidents (Lyndon Johnson through Ronald Reagan), there were objections to 367 bills and to thousands of items within them—and after Reagan there would be a veritable explosion of such statements.[13]

Meese moved to have presidential signing statements made part of the official legislative record of a bill, by including them in the *U.S. Code Congressional and Administrative News,* with the President's views on law to be considered along with the congressional intent. Meese said:

> To make sure that the President's own understanding of what's in a bill . . . is given consideration at the time of statutory construction later on by a court, we have now arranged with West Publishing Company that the presidential statement on the signing of a bill will accompany the legislative history from Congress so that all can be available to the court for future *construction of what the statute really means.* (Emphasis added)[14]

Meese wanted the President to be co-drafter of legislation, with his view ranked along with that of Congress.

The Meese Justice Department was busy exploring all the possible uses of signing statements. Meese asked the acting head of the Office of Legal Counsel, Ralph Tarr, for a memo on the subject. After listing several possible uses of such statements, Tarr added: "It might also give

[us] an additional tool—the threat of a *potential* signing statement—with which to negotiate concessions from Congress" (while the law is being drafted).[15] Meese gave the same assignment to the department's Litigation Strategy Working Group, where the future Supreme Court Justice Samuel Alito was at that time a lawyer. Alito wrote that the department had to be careful, since "Congress is likely to resent the fact that the president will get in the last word on questions of interpretation." He said the innovation had to be insinuated gradually:

> As an introductory step, our interpretive statements should be of moderate size and scope. Only relatively important questions should be addressed. We should concentrate on points of true ambiguity rather than issuing interpretations that may seem to conflict with those of Congress. The first step will be to convince the courts that presidential signing statements are valuable interpretive tools.[16]

That caution was initially needed can be seen from a rare early judicial rebuke to a signing statement. President Reagan signed the 1984 Competition in Contracting Act (CICA) but said that the law gave the Comptroller General too much independence, and he ordered the agencies not to observe this aspect of the law. When a corporation (AMERON) lost a contract that the Comptroller General would have given it, the corporation sued the agency involved for rejecting its bid. The Third District court upheld AMERON, and the Tenth Circuit ruled for it on appeal. Even so the Reagan administration defied the law, until Congress threatened to withhold funds for the Justice Department until it complied with the law—and the White House backed down.[17]

This in no way discouraged future Presidents from recourse to signing statements. The lesson the government drew from the experience was to avoid the kind of specificity that would give a plaintiff standing to take the matter to court. AMERON (and other companies) could show that it was rejected precisely because of the presidential defiance of the law. From now on, signing statements would avoid, so far as possible, specific instructions that allowed evasions of the law—or would bring in matters (like terrorism) where the objects of the statement could have no standing in any case. Political scientist Phillip Cooper points out:

> One of the problems is that the language in the statements has often been so broad that it is very difficult for anyone not trained in constitutional and administrative law to understand what is actually intended. . . . In such circumstances, it is extremely difficult for a party to demonstrate at the other end of the policy implementation process that a particular problem can be traced directly to a signing statement.[18]

Ronald Reagan, using the Meese department arguments, objected to 95 sections of the bills he signed—more than any President before him. But this was just a beginning. President George H. W. Bush challenged 232 sections, and his son would object to over 1,400 sections in the first six years of his presidency—twice as many as had been objected to by *all forty-two* earlier Presidents taken together.[19] He called unconstitutional thirty-two items in a single bill (the Consolidated Appropriations Act of 2004).[20] As Christopher Kelley, one of the first scholars to study modern signing statements, told Charlie Savage: "What we haven't seen until this administration is the sheer number of objections that are being raised on every bill passed through the White House. That is what is staggering. The numbers are well out of the norm from any previous administration."[21] There has also been an increase in the gravity of the objections to each law. President Reagan objected on constitutional grounds in 34 percent of his signing statements, President Bush I did so in 47 percent, President Clinton in 18 percent, but President Bush II in 78 percent.[22]

Once Meese had built the structure of the unitary executive theory and the signing statement strategy for augmenting presidential power, George H. W. Bush became blatant in using the structure. The President himself said at Princeton in 1991: "On many occasions during my presidency I have stated that statutory provisions violating the Constitution have no binding legal force." The White House had become more artful, as well as more frequent, in its use of the signing statement. Bush did not use his Attorney General (Richard Thornburgh) to draft his signing statements, but turned to his in-house counsel, C. Boyden Gray, who worked with Republicans in Congress to plant ambiguities and debates in the legislative process to make it easier for the President to give his own twist to a law. For instance, to counter affirmative action requirements in the Civil Rights Act of 1991, Robert Dole brought up objections on the floor of the Senate which, though not voted into the bill itself, allowed the President to claim there was disagreement in the congressional process that he could rely on to say he was not bound by the law. Law professor Charles Tiefer describes the strategy.

> Members sympathetic to the administration position, albeit lacking the votes to win, would preplant legislative history. Although those members would lose in Congress, their legislative history would be deemed authoritative in post-enactment presidential signing statements. This strategy would revise the law beyond what the executive could obtain within the lawmaking process by traditional methods—vetoes, veto threats, bargaining, and public debate.[23]

The grounds for calling a law unconstitutional were as important as was the particular item being condemned. In his first term alone, George W. Bush cited the unitary executive theory eighty-two times to explain why he was rejecting some aspect of a bill.[24] He rejected other legislation as infringements of his sole authority over foreign policy (seventy-seven times), his power to withhold information from

Congress (forty-eight times), and his role as Commander in Chief (thirty-seven times). As we saw earlier, Attorney General Meese, when he got the U.S. Code to include the President's signing statements in the legislative history of any bill, hoped that courts would begin citing them as binding guides to interpretation. Planting these claims to extreme presidential power in the statements increases the odds of getting some such sanction into a court decision.

The strategy began to work in 2006, when Justice Antonin Scalia dissented from the majority decision (5–3) in *Hamdan v. Rumsfeld*, which ruled the military commissions set up by George W. Bush to be unconstitutional. Scalia scolded the Court: "In its discussion of legislative history the Court wholly ignores the President's signing statement" (Dissent, I C).

Signing statements have become the recent norm, despite the fact that they do one or more of four things, all of them illegal.

1. Impoundment. If the signing statement denies the expenditure of funds ordered by Congress on some aspect of the bill, it is an impoundment. The federal courts have upheld the law that forbids this, the Impoundment Control Act of 1974.
2. Line-item veto. If the statement says that some part of the law is not to be observed, the President is using an illicit part veto. Although Congress passed a law allowing this in 1996 (the Line Item Veto Act), a federal court struck this down in 1998, and the Supreme Court ruled the same (*Clinton v. City of New York*).
3. Veto without override. If the statement rejects part of the law, this is a form of veto that denies Congress's right to override it.
4. Nullification. States have been denied the ability to nullify laws they do not approve of. The executive branch, too, lacks that authority.

Looked at from any angle, the signing statements clearly go against the Constitution's structure, in which the legislature makes law and the President executes it. In 2006, the American Bar Association set up a balanced panel of legal experts to study the admissibility of signing statements. It concluded that the use of them to block Congress's intent is illegitimate, and it recommended that Congress introduce legislation to block such uses. One proposal was that Congress give itself standing to take the matter to court—or that the President be required to take his own objections to constitutionality to court. A model for this is the way President Clinton responded to a bill in which Congressman Robert Dornan had inserted an instruction that all military personnel with AIDS be dismissed from service. President Clinton said this was unconstitutional and he would not require its enforcement, but his Justice Department said that this was only in anticipation of a court ruling. White House Counsel Jack Quinn said in a press briefing that "in circumstances where you don't have the benefit of such a prior judicial holding, it's appropriate and necessary to enforce it." And Assistant Attorney General Walter Dellinger explained:

> When the President's obligation to execute laws enacted by Congress is in tension with his responsibility to act in accordance to the Constitution, questions arise that really go to the very heart of the system, and the President can decline to comply with the law, in our view, only where there is a judgment that the Supreme Court has resolved the issue.[25]

President Clinton did not always act in this manner. But all Presidents should.

16

AMERICAN MONARCH

All the forces traced in this book have moved toward a concentration of power in the presidency, far from the design of the framers of the Constitution, who were determined not to have a monarch like the king they had just rebelled against. From World War II, the secrecy and unchecked power of Leslie Groves set a pattern repeated in the CIA, the NSA, and the President's private monopoly over nuclear weaponry. The undeclared wars against Korea and Vietnam endorsed presidential control of military power and created a cult of the President as Commander in Chief. The attempt to push back with the War Powers Resolution, CIA oversight, and the FISA court did little or nothing to check Presidents defying the WPR in Lebanon, Grenada, Panama, Libya, Haiti, Kosovo, Bosnia, and elsewhere. But these foreign adventures cannot compare with the full-court press of warmaking powers asserted by the administration of George W. Bush.

The trend was clear and long predated the presidency of George W. Bush. Vice President Cheney and his right-hand man, David Addington, were devout advocates of presidential power for years before the 2000 election. Cheney opposed the investigation of the CIA by the Church and Pike committees. As a member of Congress, he labored to quash opposition to President Reagan's attack on Libya in 1986. He and Addington concocted the minority report opposing any condemnation of the Iran-Contra operation of Oliver North. Cheney advised James Baker to end the War Powers Resolution. Addington said he would strangle the FISA court. The two men backed neoconservative recommendations for the overthrow of Saddam Hussein during the Clinton administration. They brought neoconservatives into the second Bush administration—notably Douglas Feith and Paul Wolfowitz, who were backed by intellectual lobbyists for the cause such as Irving and William Kristol, Richard Perle, Norman Podhoretz, Midge Decter, and Gertrude Himmelfarb. Aside from this personal surge toward presidential prerogative, there was a long institutional buildup based on the National Security State constructed after World War II. The Meese doctrines of a unitary executive and presidential signing statements joined this drumroll of executive enactments.

Despite this crescendo of presidential arrogance, George W. Bush was, for a time, an unlikely man to bring executive usurpations to their climax. Admittedly, his father had said in his Princeton address that he had the right to go against Congress where foreign policy was concerned. But Bush II was at least partly disposed to go against the track record of Bush I. He had campaigned with a call for humility in America's dealings with other nations, and had opposed the idea of "nation building" abroad. He sounded some old themes of Republican semi-isolationism. It might have been hard for Cheney to prod him out of this inward turning if the attacks of September 2001 had not occurred. Once they did, Bush II gladly embraced the role of "war President." It is always an appealing role for a man who has the chance to play it. Bill Clinton often lamented the fact that only war Presidents achieve historic greatness.

Creating new intelligence procedures, Vice President Cheney's office and Donald Rumsfeld's Department of Defense "stovepiped" information past the CIA and NSA apparatus, directly channeling raw intelligence from sources like Ahmed Chalabi and "Curveball" and Richard Perle. This provided the false information about yellowcake, mobile bioweaponry labs, and centrifuge tubes—presented with scary vividness—that let the administration call a halt to Hans Blix's UN inspection of Iraq for nuclear weapons. (Saddam Hussein could not have used his weapons, if he'd had any, while Blix was on the ground looking for them.)

Just as important for the panicky reaction to terror as this false information were the faulty legal justifications for military tribunals, suspended habeas corpus, extraordinary rendition, secret prisons around the world, warrantless surveillance of citizens at home, abrogation of the Geneva Conventions, unilateral dispensation from treaties, and enhanced interrogation methods like waterboarding. In a stunning series of secret memoranda, the Justice Department claimed the legal right to all these and other actions. The point of origin for these claims was the little known but extremely powerful Office of Legal Counsel (OLC) in the Justice Department. This is where the executive branch gives itself legal permission to do what it wants to do. Since Ed Meese's time as Attorney General, this has been an office stocked with young conservative lawyers, often members of the Federalist Society and/or former clerks to conservative judges and justices like Rehnquist, Scalia, Thomas, and Bork. Scalia himself had earlier been a lawyer in the OLC, as were John Roberts and Samuel Alito.

As fate would have it, the head of the OLC at the time of the 9/11 attacks was a relatively passive man, Jay Bybee, with a hyperactive and prodigiously productive assistant named John Yoo, who would write legal opinions sometimes signed by Bybee, sometimes by White House Counsel Alberto Gonzales, sometimes by Yoo himself. Yoo, whose hero was David Addington, had clerked for Justice Clarence Thomas. He became a member of the tight little White House circle known as the War Council. It had only four other members: Gonzales, Addington, Timothy Flanigan (in the White House Counsel's office), and William J. "Jim" Haynes (Addington's man in the Pentagon).[1]

It was Yoo's job to invent the legal rationales for actions universally seen as illegal before 9/11. Yoo came to the task with preformed certitudes about the limitless extent of presidential prerogative. He considered himself a beneficiary of President Truman's right to wage undeclared war in Korea, from which Yoo's parents brought him as a child to America. Yoo had a visceral hatred for communism which he easily shifted to terrorism in 2001. He declared that America was a literal battleground in this new war, with wartime discipline justified in the treatment of citizens as well as foreigners, since the distinction between foreign and domestic action was erased by terrorists. His President is "the sovereign," and sovereignty is by definition free of external control.[2] Yoo cites a 1937 Supreme Court case against depriving the sovereign of his prerogatives. Since questioning prisoners of war is a President's right, he cannot be deprived of it. But the 1937 case, like all American law, means by "the sovereign" the Republic, the national entity, not the President. Even in England, the sovereign was "the king in Parliament." Yoo would make the President more powerful than the monarch we renounced in 1776.

We have already noted the way modern Presidents unconstitutionally claim that the office of Commander in Chief gives them power *over civilians*. Yoo's memoranda deepened that claim, giving a war power over domestic surveillance, in defiance of the FISA court. Since interrogation is a war measure, the President can authorize "enhanced" interrogation methods, in defiance of the Geneva Conventions and the anti-torture laws. President Bush frequently said that "the United States does not torture." But at the beginning of February 2008, CIA Director Michael Hayden admitted in congressional testimony that the CIA had used waterboarding (simulated drowning) on al Qaeda suspects, and a day later White House spokesman Tony Fratto, in a press briefing, confirmed that the President had authorized such methods.[3] How could they claim then that the United States does not torture?

They were relying on an eighty-page "torture memo" by John Yoo, which defines torture in such a way that it is almost impossible to commit. As Hayden said in his testimony: "We don't maim. . . . We don't mutilate. We don't sodomize. These are things that are always bad. . . . [I]ntellectually, there has got to be a difference between waterboarding and the others." Yoo tortures meaning to allow the CIA to torture men. He takes the anti-torture law enacted to comply with the international Convention Against Torture (18 USC 2340) and notes that it says the torture must be "specifically intended to inflict severe physical or mental pain or suffering." To him that means "the infliction of such pain must be the defendant's precise objective" (pp. 36–37). If the aim is not to inflict pain but to get information, and the pain is an undesired necessity for that aim, then "even if the defendant knows that severe pain will result from his actions, if causing such harm is not his objective, he lacks the requisite intent" to be held guilty. And if a CIA interrogator inflicts something Yoo tells him is not torture, he cannot be breaking the law.

Yoo does his familiar philological hocus-pocus with the term "severe harm." For him severe harm "must rise to the level of death, organ failure or the *permanent* impairment of a *significant* body function" (p. 38; emphasis added). Nonpermanent impairment, or impairment of an "insignificant" body function, does not meet Yoo's test. So with "prolonged mental harm." Short mental harm is okay, and if the harm lasts longer than the interrogator calculated, that was not his "specific intent" (p. 42). The same with mind-altering drugs. They, too, must have a *severe* effect.

> By requiring that the procedures and the drugs create a profound disruption, the statute requires more than that the acts "forcibly separate" or "rend" the senses or personality. Those acts must penetrate to the core of an individual's ability to perceive the world around him,

substantially interfering with his cognitive abilities, or fundamentally alter his personality. (p. 43)

The most savage acts can be justified by Yoo's arguments for the President's sovereign rights. In a 2005 debate between Yoo and Notre Dame law professor Douglas Cassel, this exchange occurred:

> CASSEL: If the president deems that he's got to torture somebody, including by crushing the testicles of the person's child, there is no law that can stop him?
> YOO: No treaty.
> CASSEL: Also no law by Congress—that is what you wrote in the August 2002 memo.
> YOO: I think it depends on why the president thinks he needs to do that.[4]

When Jay Bybee left as the head of the OLC to take up an appointment as an appeals court judge, the White House wanted to appoint Yoo to take his place, but Attorney General John Ashcroft, who had pushed back on some White House efforts to boss him around, did not trust Yoo. When Yoo was not made the formal head of the OLC, he returned to teach law at the University of California at Berkeley. Once freed to speak in public, Yoo took his views on tour. Comparing himself to Alexander Hamilton defending George Washington, he said he was making the public case for George Bush, since Bush's other appointees were not very good at that:

> I decided to take Hamilton as my role model. I wrote and spoke constantly to defend the policies in the war on terrorism, even if the Bush administration would not. Since leaving government, I have [by 2006] written almost twenty opinion pieces in newspapers such as the *Wall Street Journal* and the *Los Angeles Times* discussing terrorism policy, and

have spoken at more than seventy panels, workshops, forums, and debates on the subject.[5]

Yoo quickly produced a book defending all of President Bush's
initiatives—pre-emptive war, assassinations, warrantless surveillance,
torture (defined as nontorture), military commissions, and abrogat-
ing the Geneva Conventions. He was freer now to do things like attack
the Supreme Court's declaration that the Bush military commissions
are unconstitutional, in *Hamdan v. Rumsfeld*. Salim Hamdan, a driver
for Osama bin Laden, was captured in Afghanistan, held without
charges in the prison at Guantánamo, then accused of conspiring to
commit terrorist acts (an accusation later dropped), then convicted by
a military commission of giving material support to terrorists (the
chauffeuring).

Congress under the Constitution has the sole right to establish federal court systems. It sets up district and appeals courts, and also courts
martial. It establishes (and has changed) the number of justices on the
Supreme Court. Yet President Bush, on his sole authority, set up a third
entity that recognized none of the legitimate court systems (state and
federal courts, and courts martial) and defied the Geneva Conventions
on the treatment of war prisoners. The Bush system had no justification in constitutional or international law.

Yoo maintains that the Supreme Court is wasting the President's
valuable time when it rules on crimes committed by the executive
branch:

> Two years ago, the same [Supreme Court] justices declared they would
> review the military's detention of terrorists at Guantanamo Bay.
> Congress and the President expended time and energy to overrule
> them. *Hamdan* will force our elected leaders to go through the same
> exercise again, effort better spent preventing the next terrorist
> attack.[6]

Yoo's decisions in a whole string of memoranda were so flawed that his own former teacher and fellow Korean-American, Dean of the Yale Law School Harold Koh, told Congress, "In my professional opinion, the August 1, 2002, OLC memorandum is perhaps the most clearly erroneous legal opinion I have ever read."[7] Yet this and the other "torture memos" were accepted by President Bush, Vice President Cheney, and Counsel David Addington, to give the CIA its marching orders for things like waterboarding, intimidation with dogs, freezing isolation in the nude, sleep deprivation, and slamming into walls. Mark Twain once wrote that America was becoming "the United States of Lyncherdom." Guided by John Yoo and his sponsors in the White House, we became in the world's eyes "the United States of Torturedom."

With both Bybee and Yoo gone from the OLC in the Justice Department, the office of Vice President Cheney needed a reliable underling there to continue endorsing torture and other executive usurpations. A safe-looking candidate was another conservative young lawyer, Jack Goldsmith. Not only was he a Republican, a member of the Federalist Society, and a supporter of the war in Iraq and of the Bush administration more generally, he had even collaborated with his friend John Yoo on a 2001 article saying that the President has the right to abrogate the ABM treaty without congressional authority. But Goldsmith was also a good legal thinker, and he soon realized, to his horror, that the legal thinking of the Yoo memos was inexcusably shabby—"legally flawed, tendentious in substance and tone, and overbroad"—the same judgment Professor Koh had reached. He later wrote:

> "*Any* effort by Congress to regulate the interrogation of battlefield detainees would violate the Constitution's sole vesting of the Commander-in-Chief authority in the President," the August 2002 memo concluded. This extreme conclusion has no foundation in prior OLC opinion, or in judicial decisions, or in any other source of law.

And the conclusion's significance sweeps far beyond the interrogation opinion or the torture statute. It implies that many other federal
laws that limit interrogation—anti-assault laws, the 1996 War Crimes
Act, and the Uniform Code of Military Justice—are also unconstitutional, a conclusion that would have surprised the many prior presidents who signed or ratified those laws, or complied with them during
wartime.[8]

Goldsmith sympathized with the aims of the administration, and he
surely did not underestimate the danger of further terrorist attacks.
What struck him was the unnecessary exclusion of all parties but
the executive—Congress, the courts, the American populace, allied
governments—at a time when they were all anxious to cooperate with
efforts against al Qaeda. The FISA court, for instance, was prompt to
issue warrants to surveil terrorist suspects. Addington and Cheney did
not want to recognize that it had any role in what the executive wanted
to do. Congress would have set up emergency courts in a constitutional
way. Cheney said the Constitution was irrelevant to executive power.
There were more trustworthy interrogation techniques than the ones
improvised by largely untrained interrogators (many of them hired con-
tractors with no interrogation experience). International cooperation
with allies was more important than secretly kidnapping people in their
jurisdiction by "extraordinary rendition." The Bush people were as concerned with creating an unchecked and omnicompetent executive as
with hunting for terrorists. The tight little circle around Cheney and
Addington wanted to keep the Office of Legal Counsel memos from
any who might oppose them—including National Security Adviser
Condoleezza Rice and Secretary of State Colin Powell.[9]

Goldsmith concluded that he had to do something unparalleled—
reverse a legal opinion of his own office by canceling Yoo's torture
memo. He braced himself for the biting personal unpleasantness
encountered by all who crossed David Addington. The Addington

treatment was famous. Alberto Gonzales, when he was White House Counsel, said: "David is just permanently stuck on LOUD."[10] When Deputy Assistant Secretary of Defense Matthew Waxman gathered the objections of military officers to any suspension of the Geneva Conventions, he was summoned to the Vice President's office to meet with Addington and Scooter Libby: "The two men handed Waxman his head, Libby cool and polite about it and Addington not much of either. . . . Addington called Waxman's directive 'an abomination,' dumbest proposal he had ever heard, and a direct affront to a decision the president had already made [to suspend the Geneva Conventions]."[11]

So Goldsmith knew how Addington would react to his canceling of the torture memos. He was not surprised when Addington shouted at him, "If you rule that way, the blood of the hundred thousand people who die in the next attack will be on your hands."[12] That was the kind of talk with which Addington had cowed and bullied all who opposed him. But Goldsmith stood his ground. Yoo would later accuse Goldsmith of playing politics with people's lives:

> In the summer of 2004, as the Abu Ghraib controversy hit the front pages, the Justice Department bowed to administration critics and withdrew the leaked 2002 opinion. I thought this a terrible precedent. It showed that Justice Department judgments on the law had become just one more political target open to partisan attack and political negotiation. The implication was that if one put enough pressure on the Justice Department it, like any other part of the government, would bend. It also suggested that the leadership of the Justice Department that had replaced the team there on 9/11 was too worried about the public perceptions of its work.[13]

We have seen this line of argument (if that is what it is) before. Henry Kissinger, you may recall, said that William Colby was not following the Constitution when he honored congressional oversight of the CIA—he was just surrendering to demonstrators in the street. Actually, of course, Yoo was the one who yielded to pressure from Cheney and Addington. Goldsmith resisted such pressure, at some personal cost. "Goldsmith's decision to stand up to the White House had come at a price. There was no chance that he would ever be made a federal appeals court judge, the reward the Bush-Cheney White House had paid to his 'team player' predecessor at the Office of Legal Counsel, Jay Bybee."[14] Law professor Peter Shane lists some of the people whose government careers were stalled, sidetracked, or ended when they argued with Addington—Goldsmith, Alberto Mora, James Comey, Patrick Philbin—in a reign where "dissent was not merely discouraged, but punished."[15]

The canceling of Yoo's memos was a rare setback for the Bush executive, but its ability to rebound would be proved in the case of Senator John McCain's anti-torture legislation. McCain, who had been tortured himself and who said that torture does not yield reliable information, joined with Senator John Warner of Virginia to add an anti-torture amendment to a military budget bill. It was a moderate measure that simply restricted questioning methods to those that had long stood in the Army Field Manual—they had been formed to follow treaty requirements of the Geneva Conventions. Vice President Cheney rushed to the Hill to have Bill Frist, the Republican Majority Leader, block a vote by withdrawing the budget bill. Over the next six months Cheney worked energetically to prevent passage of McCain's measure, but McCain lined up more than two dozen retired generals (including Colin Powell) to say that observing the Geneva Conventions was necessary to ensure proper treatment of our own military personnel when they are taken prisoner. President Bush's press secretary, Scott McClellan, said that the President would veto the bill if it included the McCain measure (Bush had to this point not used his veto pen even once). But when the bill passed in the Senate by 90 votes to

9 (including 46 of the 55 Republicans), Bush knew any veto would easily be overridden.

Cheney had still not given up. He urged that the bill make an exemption for CIA agents, to allow them (if no one else) to torture. The House had been stalling, giving Cheney more time to influence people; but it finally voted, too—308 to 107 in favor of McCain. The *New York Times* wrote that the bill's passage was a "particularly significant setback for Vice President Dick Cheney, who since July has led the administration's fight to defeat the amendment or at least exempt the Central Intelligence Agency from its provisions."[16] Cheney's daughter Elizabeth would later say that voting for McCain as President would be "bad for the country."[17] In her eyes, a President who will not torture is betraying her father's gift to the nation.

But then, as so often happened with Bush, the law was undone with a signing statement. Appended to McCain's anti-torture law in the *Federal Register* were these words:

> The executive branch shall construe [it] . . . in a manner consistent with the constitutional authority of the President to supervise the unitary executive branch and as Commander in Chief, and consistent with the constitutional limitations on the judicial power, which will assist in achieving the shared objective of the Congress and the President . . . of protecting the American people from further terrorist attacks.[18]

Needless to say, this reading of the Constitution was that of John Yoo and David Addington (who wrote the signing statement), and it followed the canceled torture memo. What the executive's new Legal Counsel said meant as little to President Bush as had an overwhelming vote in both houses of Congress.

The claims for an American monarch became, after eight years of the Bush presidency, too much for the public to support. A consensus was forming in the periodic surveys done by American historians that

Bush was the worst President in American history, the patron of unnecessary pre-emptive war, of unilateral abrogation of treaties, of ignoring allies, of torture, of imprisonment without charges or representation, of illegal surveillance, of unaccountability to Congress, of economic mismanagement, of incompetence and cronyism and corruption (as in the politicizing of the Justice Department), and on and on.[19] As strong a claim could be made for Dick Cheney as the worst Vice President and Alberto Gonzales as the worst Attorney General. Even members of the Bush administration became disillusioned with it and accusers of it—Colin Powell, Lawrence Wilkerson, Paul O'Neill, Scott McClellan, and others. By the summer of 2008 Bush had record low approval ratings in public polls—23 percent in the *New York Times/ Bloomberg* survey.

At one point, the whole top echelon of the Justice Department was ready to resign in protest at Bush's illegal activities. This occurred when Attorney General John Ashcroft was just out of surgery and the White House wanted to circumvent the acting Attorney General, James Comey, and the Legal Counsel, Jack Goldsmith, to reimpose warrantless surveillance. Mrs. Ashcroft had said her husband was too weak to receive visitors, but President Bush called her and asked that she admit White House Counsel Alberto Gonzales to the hospital room—he was being sent to get Ashcroft's signature on the warrantless plan. Ashcroft from his hospital not only refused to sign, but told Gonzales that he (Ashcroft) should not have approved the plan at an earlier stage: "You drew the circle so tight I couldn't get the advice I needed" (he was referring to the War Council's use of John Yoo).[20] As Gonzales left the hotel room, Janet Ashcroft stuck her tongue out at his back.

Andrew Card, the White House Chief of Staff, who had accompanied Gonzales to the hospital, summoned Comey and Goldsmith to the White House, to inform them that the President would go ahead with warrantless surveillance despite the Justice Department's declaration that it was illegal. Comey and Goldsmith returned to their offices to start drafting letters of resignation. Others in the Justice Department, including FBI Director Robert Mueller, were lining up to do the same. So was Valerie Caproni, the FBI's General Counsel, and Assistant Attorney General Christopher Wray. Even over at the CIA, General Counsel Scott Muller wanted to join the exodus. Two dozen or so of the top echelon of Justice Department lawyers were poised to resign.

None of this mattered to David Addington. He drafted a statement that the President, by his inherent power, had the right to surveil whomever he wanted, whenever he wanted. Lacking a Justice Department signature he could append, Addington added that of the White House Counsel at the time, Alberto Gonzales, though Gonzales was telling Bush that he had misgivings over the measure. The President signed Addington's statement, not aware that the Justice Department lawyers were packing to leave. "For the first time, a president claimed in writing that he alone could say what the law was."[21]

Gonzales and Card gave the President a warning that there could be trouble in the Justice Department, and Bush, at the regular meeting with his security team, asked Comey to stay behind and talk with him. Bush said the matter could be worked out; Comey said he did not agree, and let him know that Mueller at the FBI, a favorite of Bush's, was preparing his resignation. Bush said it was not proper to bring this up at the last moment—he had just heard of any difficulty. Comey answered: "Mr. President, if you've been told that, you have been very poorly served by your advisors. We have been telling them for months we have a huge problem here that we can't get past."[22]

Bush sent a Secret Service man out to stop Mueller before he left the White House, and confirmed from him what had been going on in the Cheney-Addington parallel government. Bush backed off the statement he had signed just one day earlier, a rare yielding on this President's part. Even he knew that massive resignations by his own appointed lawyers was something he could not survive. That would point to an obvious and immediately impeachable offense—something far more serious than the political break-in of Watergate or the sexual hanky-panky of Monicagate, the grounds for recent impeachments. Cheney and Addington had let Bush stumble, unaware, into the trap of his presidency's potential destruction. And they were still unyielding. Addington sent an angry memo to the Justice Department, saying it had invaded the President's constitutional prerogative. Andrew Card later told a journalist he had no right even to know what had gone on in the Ashcroft hospital room, since "You're not Article Two" (on presidential power).[23] The President as monarch had narrowly escaped regicide.

AFTERWORD

George W. Bush left the White House unpopular and disgraced. His successor promised change, and it was clear where change was needed. Illegal acts should cease—torture and indefinite detention, denial of habeas corpus and legal representation, unilateral canceling of treaties, defiance of Congress and the Constitution, nullification of law by signing statements. Powers given the President under the unitary executive theory should not be exercised. Judges should not be confirmed who are willing to give the President any power he asks for. But the momentum of accumulating powers in the executive is not easily reversed, checked, or even slowed. It was not created by the Bush administration. The whole history of America since World War II caused an inertial rolling of power toward the executive branch. The monopoly on use of nuclear weaponry, the cult of the Commander in Chief, the worldwide web of military bases to maintain nuclear alert and supremacy, the secret intelligence agencies, the whole National Security State, the classification and clearance systems, the expansion of state secrets, the withholding of evidence and information, the permanent emergency that has melded World War II with the Cold War

and the Cold War with the war on terror—all these make a vast
and intricate structure that may not yield to efforts at dismantling it.
Sixty-eight straight years of war emergency powers (1941–2009) have
made the abnormal normal, and constitutional diminishment the settled order.

The truth of this was borne out in the early days of Barack Obama's
presidency. At his confirmation hearing to be head of the CIA, Leon
Panetta said that "extraordinary rendition" was a tool he meant to
retain.[1] Obama's nominee for Solicitor General, Elena Kagan, told
Congress she agreed with John Yoo's claim that a terrorist captured
anywhere should be subject to "battlefield law."[2] On the first opportunity to abort trial proceedings by invoking "state secrets"—that policy
based on the faulty *Reynolds* case—Obama's Attorney General, Eric
Holder, did so.[3] Obama refused to release photographs of "enhanced
interrogation."[4] The CIA had earlier (illegally) destroyed taped
depictions of such interrogation—and Obama refused to release documents describing the tapes.[5] The President said that past official crimes
would not be investigated—certainly not for prosecution, and not even
in terms of an impartial "truth commission" just trying to establish a
record. He said, on the contrary, that detainees might be tried in Bush's
unconstitutional "military tribunals."[6] When the British government,
trying a terrorist suspect, decided to use some American documents
shared with the British government, Obama's Attorney General pressured them not to do it.[7] Most important, perhaps, was the new
President's desire to end the nation building in Iraq with a long-term
nation-building effort in Afghanistan, a drug-culture government not
susceptible to our remolding.

Even in areas outside national security, the Obama government
quickly came to resemble Bush's administration. Gay military personnel, including those with valuable Arabic language skills, were being
dismissed at the same rate as before.[8] Even more egregiously, the Obama
administration continued the defiance of the Constitution's "full faith

and credit" clause, which requires states to recognize laws passed by other states, when it defended the Defense of Marriage Act, which lets states refuse to recognize gay marriages legally obtained in another state.[9] In another area, Dick Cheney would not name energy executives who came to the White House, though Hillary Clinton, as First Lady, had been forced to reveal what health advisers had visited her— yet the Obama team, in June of 2009, refused to release logs of those who had come to the White House.[10] It later reversed itself, under threat of a lawsuit.

Some were dismayed to see how quickly the Obama people grabbed at the powers, the secrecy, the unaccountability, that had led Bush into such straits. Leon Panetta at the CIA especially puzzled those who had known him. A former CIA official told the *Washington Post*, "Leon Panetta has been captured by the people who were the ideological drivers for the interrogation program in the first place."[11] A White House official told Jane Mayer of the *New Yorker*, "It's like *Invasion of the Body Snatchers*."[12]

Perhaps it should come as no surprise that turning around the huge secret empire built by the National Security State is a hard, perhaps impossible, task. I noted earlier that after most of the wars in U.S. history there was a return to the constitutional condition of the prewar world. But after those wars there was no lasting institutional security apparatus of the sort that was laboriously assembled in the 1940s and 1950s. After World War I, for instance, there was no CIA, no NSA, no mountain of secret documents to be guarded from unauthorized readers; there was no atomic bomb to guard, develop, deploy, and maintain in readiness on land, in the air, and on (or in) the sea. Now a President quickly becomes aware of the vast empire that is largely invisible to the citizenry. The United States maintains an estimated one thousand military bases in other countries. I say "estimated" because the exact number, location, and size of the bases are either partly or entirely cloaked in secrecy, among other things to protect nuclear installations.[13]

The secrecy involved is such that during the Cuban missile crisis, President Kennedy did not even know, at first, that we had nuclear missiles stationed in Turkey.

An example of this imperial system is the Indian Ocean island of Diego Garcia. In the 1960s, to secure a military outpost without fear of any interference from indigenous peoples, the two thousand Chagossian inhabitants were forcibly expelled, deprived of their native land, and sent a thousand miles away. (It is the same ploy we had used in removing native peoples from the Bikini and Enewetak atolls and Lib Island, so we could conduct our sixty-eight atomic and hydrogen bomb tests there.)[14] Though technically Diego Garcia is leased from the British, it is entirely run by the United States. It was the United States that expelled the Chagossians and confiscated their property. Diego Garcia has become a vast armory, storage and staging area, harbor and launch site, from which supplies and air strikes are fanned out over the Middle East, heavily used in the Gulf and Afghanistan and Iraq wars. No journalists are allowed to visit it. It was funded on a vast scale by various deceptions of Congress. Even the leasing terms with Great Britain were kept secret, to avoid congressional oversight.[15]

That is just one of the hundreds of holdings in the empire created by the National Security State. A President is greatly pressured to keep all the empire's secrets. He feels he must avoid embarrassing the hordes of agents, military personnel, and diplomatic instruments whose loyalty he must command. Keeping up morale in this vast shady enterprise is something impressed on him by all manner of commitments. He becomes the prisoner of his own power. As President Truman could not *not* use the Bomb, a modern President cannot *not* use his huge power base. It has all been given him as the legacy of Bomb Power, the thing that makes him not only Commander in Chief but Leader of the Free World. He is a self-entangling giant.

On January 25, 2002, White House Counsel Alberto Gonzales signed a memo written by David Addington that called the Geneva

Conventions "quaint" and "obsolete."[16] Perhaps, in the nuclear era, the Constitution has become quaint and obsolete. Few people even consider, anymore, Madison's lapidary pronouncement, "In republican government the legislative authority, necessarily, predominates" (*The Federalist* 51). Instead, we are all, as citizens, asked to salute *our* Commander in Chief. Any President, wanting leverage to áccomplish his goals, must find it hard to give up the aura of war chief, the mystery and majesty that have accrued to him with control of the Bomb, the awesome proximity to "the football," to "the button."

Nonetheless, some of us entertain a fondness for the quaint old Constitution. It may be too late to return to its ideals, but the effort should be made. As Cyrano said, "One fights not only in the hope of winning" (*Mais on ne se bat pas dans l'espoir du succès*).

NOTES

INTRODUCTION: WAR IN PEACE

1. Daniel Patrick Moynihan, *Secrecy: The American Experience* (Yale University Press, 1998), p. 154.

CHAPTER 1: FATAL MIRACLE

1. Robert McMahon, *The Cold War* (Oxford University Press, 2003), pp. 6–9.
2. Catton had an insider's knowledge of war contracts, since he had served as Director of Information at the War Production Board.
3. Of course, stupid management can make government efficient in producing disaster, as in the Soviet destruction of agriculture. But in America, government is normally inefficient only if the market interferes with it, lobbyists distorting the outcome (for instance, in health policy).
4. David McCullough, *Truman* (Simon & Schuster, 1992), pp. 289–90.
5. Robert Jay Lifton and Greg Mitchell, *Hiroshima in America: Fifty Years of Denial* (G. P. Putnam's Sons, 1995), p. 128.
6. Kai Bird and Martin J. Sherwin, *American Prometheus: The Triumph and Tragedy of J. Robert Oppenheimer* (Alfred A. Knopf, 2005), pp. 181–83.
7. Richard P. Feynman, *"Surely You're Joking, Mr. Feynman": Adventures of a Curious Character* (W. W. Norton, 1985), p. 110.
8. Jennet Conant, *109 East Palace: Robert Oppenheimer and the Secret City of Los Alamos* (Simon & Schuster, 2005), p. 258.
9. Robert S. Norris, *Racing for the Bomb: General Leslie R. Groves, the Manhattan Project's Indispensable Man* (Steerforth Press, 2002), pp. 198–200.

10. Ibid., p. 221.

11. Ibid., p. 202.

12. Bird and Sherwin, op. cit., p. 210.

13. Conant, op. cit., p. 216.

14. Rabi had scruples about working directly on the Bomb himself, but he visited his close friend Oppenheimer at Los Alamos, giving advice and support.

15. Emilio Segrè, *Mind Always in Motion* (University of California Press, 1992), p. 182.

16. Feynman, op. cit., pp. 114–19.

17. Conant, op. cit., pp. 260–61.

18. Richard Rhodes, *The Making of the Atomic Bomb* (Simon & Schuster, 1986), p. 566.

19. Bird and Sherwin, op. cit., pp. 256–57.

20. Conant, op. cit., p. 182; Bird and Sherwin, op. cit., p. 263.

21. Norris, op. cit., p. 265.

22. Conant, op. cit., p. 4.

23. Bird and Sherwin, op. cit., p. 260.

24. One of the many absurd things in *Fat Man and Little Boy,* the movie made about Los Alamos, was the inept casting—short and trim Paul Newman to play large and lumpy Groves, slack and everyday Dwight Schultz for intense and charismatic Oppenheimer. The burning blue eyes were present in the movie, but on the wrong person, on Newman's Groves, not on Schultz's Oppenheimer.

25. Conant, op. cit., p. 54.

26. Rhodes, op. cit., pp. 149, 60.

27. After the war, a congressional chairman used Groves's slow promotion rate to suggest that his qualifications were negligible.

28. I. I. Rabi et al., *Oppenheimer* (Charles Scribner's Sons, 1969), p. 7.

29. Richard Rhodes, *Dark Sun: The Making of the Hydrogen Bomb* (Simon & Schuster, 1995), p. 537.

30. Ibid., p. 8.

31. Lifton and Mitchell, op. cit., p. 15.

32. Ibid., p. 169.

33. Conant, op. cit., p. 316.

34. Ibid., p. 325.

35. Clark Clifford advised against this change to the seal. Clifford, *Counsel to the President* (Random House, 1991), p. 62.

36. Nuel Pharr Davis, *Lawrence and Oppenheimer* (Simon & Schuster, 1968), p. 260.

37. McMahon, op. cit., p. 25.

CHAPTER 2: ATOMIC POLITICS

1. Robert S. Norris, *Racing for the Bomb: General Leslie R. Groves, the Manhattan Project's Indispensable Man* (Steerforth Press, 2002), pp. 291–92.

2. Ibid., pp. 296–306.

3. Len Giovannitti and Fred Freed, *The Decision to Drop the Bomb* (Coward-McCann, 1965), p. 107.

4. Alice Kimball Smith, *A Peril and a Hope: The Scientists' Movement in America, 1945–47* (MIT Press, 1971), pp. 52–53.

5. Groves's favorite target was Kyoto, but Stimson, who had visited the city and revered its historical and religious associations, struck it off the list. Groves tried repeatedly to reinstate it, perhaps a dozen times, but Stimson was unbudgeable. Norris, op. cit., pp. 386ff.

6. Robert Jay Lifton and Greg Mitchell, *Hiroshima in America: Fifty Years of Denial* (G. P. Putnam's Sons, 1995), p. 133.

7. Richard Rhodes, *The Making of the Atomic Bomb* (Simon & Schuster, 1986), p. 642.

8. Norris, op. cit., p. 392.

9. David McCullough, *Truman* (Simon & Schuster, 1992), p. 441.

10. These are the 1946 figures of the United States Strategic Bombing Survey (pp. 22–23), and they do not take into account later deaths from injury and radiation. Oppenheimer had predicted a death toll from the first drop of twenty thousand. McCullough, ibid., p. 456.

11. "Operation Crossroads," Naval Historical Center home page. A second bomb at Bikini was exploded underwater, and it contaminated the whole fleet with a degree of radioactivity shocking to the conductors of the experiment: Barton C. Hacker, *Elements of Controversy: The Atomic Energy Commission and Radiation Safety in Nuclear Weapons Testing, 1947–1974* (University of California Press, 1994), p. 4.

12. Eisenhower voiced his objection at Potsdam. Michael Korda, *Ike: An American Hero* (Harper, 2007), pp. 596–97.

13. United States Strategic Bombing Survey: Summary Report, July 1, 1946, p. 21.

14. Ibid., p. 26.

15. Lifton and Mitchell, op. cit., p. 4.

16. Norris, op. cit., p. 378.

17. Lifton and Mitchell, op. cit., p. 125.

18. Ibid., p. 17.

19. Richard Rhodes, *Dark Sun: The Making of the Hydrogen Bomb* (Simon & Schuster, 1995), pp. 155–56.

20. Norris, op. cit., pp. 455–56.

21. Rhodes, *Making of the Atomic Bomb*, p. 231.

22. Ibid., p. 212.

23. Dean Acheson, *Present at the Creation: My Years in the State Department* (W. W. Norton, 1969), p. 153.

24. Ibid., p. 154.

25. Kai Bird and Martin J. Sherwin, *American Prometheus: The Triumph and Tragedy of J. Robert Oppenheimer* (Alfred A. Knopf, 2005), pp. 343–44.

26. Rhodes, *Dark Sun,* p. 240.

27. Ibid., p. 209.

28. Ibid., p. 381.

29. Ibid., pp. 401–2.

30. Thomas Powers, "An American Tragedy," *New York Review of Books,* November 11, 2005.

31. Priscilla J. McMillan, *The Ruin of J. Robert Oppenheimer and the Birth of the Modern Arms Race* (Viking, 2005), p. 59.

32. Richard Rhodes, *Arsenals of Folly: The Making of the Nuclear Arms Race* (Alfred A. Knopf, 2007), pp. 76–77.

33. Acheson, op. cit., p. 347.

34. Bird and Sherwin, op. cit., p. 332.

35. Rhodes, *Dark Sun,* p. 407.

36. Ibid., pp. 532–33.

37. Ibid., p. 491.

38. McMillan, op. cit., pp. 95–99.

39. Ibid., pp. 171–72.

40. Ibid., pp. 177–81.

41. Eisenhower's loyalty standard became known as the Caesar's wife rule, since Julius Caesar dismissed his wife for suspicion of infidelity. Allegedly he said, "I consider that my wife should be beyond the reach of rumor" (*mede hyponoethenai,* Plutarch's *Caesar* 10).

CHAPTER 3: THE CARE AND KEEPING OF THE BOMB

1. Richard Rhodes, *Arsenals of Folly: The Making of the Nuclear Arms Race* (Alfred A. Knopf, 2007), p. 79.

2. Ibid., p. 101.

3. Robert S. Norris, *Racing for the Bomb: General Leslie R. Groves, the Manhattan Project's Indispensable Man* (Steerforth Press, 2002), pp. 313–24.

4. Rhodes, op. cit., p. 85.

5. Ibid., p. 412.

6. Ibid.

7. David Alan Rosenberg, "The Origins of Overkill," *International Security* 7 (1983), p. 22.

8. Public Law 585, 79th Congress, Section 6.

9. Daniel Ford, *The Button: The Pentagon's Strategic Command and Control System* (Simon & Schuster, 1985), pp. 27, 91.

10. Barry Sussman, *The Great Coverup: Nixon and the Scandal of Watergate* (Crowell, 1974), p. 261.

11. *Journals of the Continental Congress,* 2.89.

12. Ibid., 2.92.

13. Dutchess County court ruling, July 25, 1950, cited in Lester S. Jayson, *The Constitution of the United States: Analysis and Interpretation* (Library of Congress, 1973), p. 467.

14. The act has been amended according to the addition of cabinet members or changes in their titles.

15. Bruce G. Blair, *The Logic of Accidental Nuclear War* (Brookings Institution, 1993), pp. 46–52.

16. Ibid., p. 47.

17. James Mann found three participants in these exercises who were willing to be interviewed about them early in the twenty-first century: Mann, *Rise of the Vulcans: The History of Bush's War Cabinet* (Penguin Books, 2004), pp. 138–45.

18. National Commission on Terrorist Attacks Upon the United States (Government Printing Office, 2004), p. 41. For a good analysis of the commission findings on the phone contacts between the President and the Vice President, see Charlie Savage, *Takeover: The Return of the Imperial Presidency and the Subversion of American Democracy* (Little, Brown, 2007), pp. 3–7.

19. Savage, ibid., p. 43.

20. Ibid.

CHAPTER 4: BEGINNINGS (1945–1946)

1. Michael J. Hogan, *A Cross of Iron: Harry S Truman and the Origins of the National Security State* (Cambridge University Press, 1998), p. 41.

2. Bradley F. Smith, *The Shadow Warriors: OSS and the Origins of the CIA* (Basic Books,

1963), p. 39. For Stimson's comment, see Walter Isaacson and Evan Thomas, *The Wise Men: Six Friends and the World They Made* (Simon & Schuster, 1986), p. 181.

3. Tim Weiner, *Legacy of Ashes: The History of the CIA* (Doubleday, 2007), pp. 3–10; Anthony Cave Brown, *The Last Hero: Wild Bill Donovan* (Times Books, 1982), pp. 792–93.

4. Michael Warner, "Salvage and Liquidation: The Creation of the Central Intelligence Group," *Studies in Intelligence* (CIA), vol. 39, no. 5 (1996), pp. 116–17.

5. Truman, Letter to Wayne Morse, March 14, 1963, cited in Sallie Pisani, *The CIA and the Marshall Plan* (University Press of Kansas, 1991), p. 128.

6. Weiner, op. cit., pp. 17–18.

7. George Kennan, *Memoirs, 1925–1950* (Little, Brown, 1967), pp. 292–93. Kennan says the telegram was 8,000 words long, and it has entered fame at that number, but better counters bring it closer to 5,400 words.

8. Ibid., p. 295.

9. Ibid.

10. Ibid., p. 294.

11. Arthur Krock, *Memoirs: Sixty Years on the Firing Line* (Funk & Wagnalls, 1968), pp. 419–22. I cite the memorandum from Krock's pagination.

12. Isaacson and Thomas, op. cit., p. 376.

13. Kennan to Clifford, in Elsey Papers, Box 63, Harry S Truman Library.

14. David Mayers, "Soviet War Aims and the Grand Alliance: George Kennan's Views, 1944–1946," *Journal of Contemporary History* 21 (January 1986), p. 75.

15. David Mayers, "Containment and the Primacy of Diplomacy: George Kennan's Views, 1947–1948," *International Security* 11 (Summer 1986), pp. 124–62.

16. Ibid., pp. 128–33.

17. In his *Memoirs* (pp. 354–55), Kennan omits his first response to Willett and Forrestal's request for a rewrite.

CHAPTER 5: *ANNUS MIRABILIS* (1947)

1. Kennan's CFR speech quoted in Anders Stephanson, *Kennan and the Art of Foreign Policy* (Harvard University Press, 1989), pp. 65–74.

2. George Kennan, *Memoirs, 1925–1950* (Little, Brown, 1967), p. 294.

3. Ibid., p. 355.

4. Ibid., p. 356.

5. David McCullough, *Truman* (Simon & Schuster, 1992), p. 548.

6. Ibid., p. 549.

7. Kennan, op. cit., pp. 319–20.

8. George Kennan, Policy Planning Staff 1, cited in Thomas H. Etzold and John Lewis Gaddis, eds., *Containment: Documents on American Policy and Strategy, 1945–1950* (Columbia University Press, 1978), pp. 106–7. Other declassified security documents cited in these chapters are taken from this volume.

9. Robert J. McMahon, *The Cold War* (Oxford University Press, 2003), pp. 28–29.

10. Carl Bernstein, *Loyalties: A Son's Memoir* (Simon & Schuster, 1989), pp. 195–98.

11. Tim Weiner, *A Legacy of Ashes: The History of the CIA* (Doubleday, 2007), pp. 25–31.

12. Walter Millis, ed., *The Forrestal Diaries* (Viking, 1951), p. 328 (October 31, 1947).

13. Joseph M. Jones, *The Fifteen Weeks (February 21–June 5, 1947)* (Viking, 1955). Kennan's praise of the book is in *Memoirs*, p. 314. Acheson's is in *Present at the Creation: My Years in the State Department* (W. W. Norton, 1969), p. 230.

14. Acheson, op. cit., pp. 220, 227, and Robert L. Beisner, *Dean Acheson: A Life in the Cold War* (Oxford University Press, 2006), pp. 56, 71.

15. Acheson, op. cit., p. 230.

16. Sallie Pisani, *The CIA and the Marshall Plan* (University Press of Kansas, 1991), p. 73.

17. NSC 20 (August 18, 1948).

18. David Mayers, "Containment and the Primacy of Diplomacy: George Kennan's Views, 1947–1948," *International Security* 11 (Summer 1986), p. 135.

19. Edward Gibbon, *The Decline and Fall of the Roman Empire*, ed. J. B. Bury (Methuen, 1911), vol. 5, pp. 401–2. Kennan does not say that Gibbon was talking about the delusions of Muhammad when he brings up the Socrates comparison.

20. Walter Lippmann, *The Cold War: A Study in U.S. Foreign Policy* (Harper & Brothers, 1947).

21. Kennan, op. cit., p. 356.

22. Ibid., p. 360.

23. Mayers, op. cit., pp. 144–45.

24. Pisani, op. cit., p. 58.

CHAPTER 6: COMPLETING THE APPARATUS (1948–1952)

1. Thomas H. Etzold and John Lewis Gaddis, eds., *Containment: Documents on American Policy and Strategy, 1945–1950* (Columbia University Press, 1978), pp. 1164–69.

2. Kennan to Marshall, *Foreign Relations of the United States, 1948* (Government Printing Office), pp. 848–49.

3. Sallie Pisani, *The CIA and the Marshall Plan* (University Press of Kansas, 1991), pp. 67–69.

4. Tim Weiner, *Legacy of Ashes: The History of the CIA* (Doubleday, 2007), p. 28.

5. Etzold and Gaddis, op. cit., p. 127.

6. Burton Hersh, *The Old Boys: The American Elite and the Origins of the CIA* (Charles Scribner's Sons, 1992), pp. 439–48; John Prados, *Safe for Democracy: The Secret Wars of the CIA* (Ivan R. Dee, 2006), pp. 50, 62.

7. Prados, op. cit., p. 41.

8. Weiner, op. cit., pp. 47–48.

9. Etzold and Gaddis, op. cit., pp. 172–203.

10. Ibid., pp. 203–11.

11. Ibid., p. 154 (PPS 41, November 23, 1948).

12. Ibid., pp. 211–23.

13. Dean Acheson, *Present at the Creation: My Years in the State Department* (W. W. Norton, 1969), p. 374.

14. Ibid., p. 375.

15. Ibid., p. 364.

16. Ibid., p. 377.

17. Etzold and Gaddis, op. cit., p. 386 (NSC 68)—pages cited in the text will refer to this document.

18. See John Prados, *The Soviet Estimate: U.S. Intelligence Analysis and Soviet Strategic Forces* (Princeton University Press, 1982).

19. Pisani, op. cit., pp. 129–30.

20. Hayden quoted by Eric Lichtblau, James Risen, and Scott Shane in the *New York Times,* December 15, 2007, and by Dana Priest in the *Washington Post,* December 30, 2005.

21. Arthur M. Schlesinger, Jr., *The Imperial Presidency* (Houghton Mifflin, 1973), p. 164.

22. *The Constitution of the United States of America, Analysis and Interpretation,* prepared by the Congressional Research Service (Government Printing Office, 1973).

23. Ibid., p. 376.

CHAPTER 7: KOREA

1. Robert L. Beisner, *Dean Acheson: A Life in the Cold War* (Oxford University Press, 2006), p. 341.

2. Dean Acheson, *Present at the Creation: My Years in the State Department* (W. W. Norton, 1969), p. 405; Beisner, ibid., p. 333.

3. Harry S Truman, *Memoirs,* vol. 2, *Years of Trial and Hope* (Doubleday, 1956), p. 335.

4. Acheson, op. cit., p. 415.

5. Francis H. Heller, *The Truman White House: The Administration of the Presidency, 1945–1951* (University Press of Kansas, 1980), p. 13.

6. Acheson, op. cit., p. 415.

7. Cited in Arthur M. Schlesinger, Jr., *The Imperial Presidency* (Houghton Mifflin, 1973), p. 135. It should be noted that in the time of the Constitution's ratifying debates, "prerogative" and "prerogative men" were roundly denounced.

8. Acheson, op. cit., p. 410.

9. Ibid., p. 414.

10. Schlesinger, op. cit., p. 133.

11. Jefferson, First Annual Address, in *Writings*, ed. Merrill D. Peterson (Library of America, 1984), p. 502.

12. Louis Fisher, *Presidential War Power,* 2nd ed., rev. (University Press of Kansas, 2004), p. 103.

13. Acheson, op. cit., p. 408.

14. Glenn D. Paige, *The Korean Decision: June 24–30, 1950* (Free Press, 1968), pp. 92–93.

15. Ibid., p. 103.

16. Ibid., p. 117.

17. Ibid., pp. 204–5.

18. Ibid., p. 132.

19. Robert Bork, "Comments on the Articles of the Legality of the United States Action in Cambodia," *American Journal of International Law,* vol. 65 (1971), p. 81.

20. Paige, op. cit., p. 188.

21. David McCullough, *Truman* (Simon & Schuster, 1992), p. 782.

22. Fisher, op. cit., p. 93.

23. Ibid., pp. 94–95.

24. Ibid., p. 82.

25. Woodrow Wilson, *Constitutional Government in the United States* (Columbia University Press, 1917), pp. 70, 78.

26. Beisner, op. cit., p. 410. MacArthur had assured Truman at their meeting on Wake Island that the Chinese had only 100,000 to 125,000 troops to deploy near the Yalu River, not enough to prevent his success in North Korea. McCullough, op. cit., pp. 804, 815.

27. Acheson, op. cit., p. 478.

28. Ibid., p. 489.

29. James Chace, *Acheson: The Secretary of State Who Created the American World* (Simon & Schuster, 1998), pp. 311–12.

30. Ibid., pp. 306–7, 321–22.

31. Truman, op. cit., pp. 395–96; Acheson, op. cit., pp. 478–79; Beisner, op. cit., p. 412; McCullough, op. cit., pp. 821–22.

32. Acheson, op. cit., p. 479.

33. Ibid., pp. 481–83.

34. Truman, op. cit., pp. 410–11; Acheson, op. cit., p. 478; Beisner, op. cit., pp. 420–21.

35. Beisner, op. cit., pp. 420–21.

36. Acheson, op. cit., p. 484.

37. Richard F. Haynes, *The Awesome Power: Harry S Truman as Commander in Chief* (Louisiana State University Press, 1973), p. 222.

38. Acheson, op. cit., p. 514.

39. Ibid.

40. Ibid.

41. Ibid., p. 517.

42. Ibid., p. 519.

43. McCullough, op. cit., p. 837.

44. Acheson, op. cit., p. 524.

45. Ibid., p. 537.

46. Truman, op. cit., p. 460.

47. Bert Cochran, *Harry Truman and the Crisis Presidency* (Funk & Wagnalls, 1973), p. 348.

48. Ibid.

49. Acheson, op. cit., p. 652.

CHAPTER 8: PERMANENT EMERGENCY

1. Dean Acheson, *Present at the Creation: My Years in the State Department* (W. W. Norton, 1969), p. 485.

2. Richard F. Haynes, *The Awesome Power: Harry S Truman as Commander in Chief* (Louisiana State University Press, 1973), pp. 80–87.

3. Bert Cochran, *Harry Truman and the Crisis Presidency* (Funk & Wagnalls, 1973), pp. 204–5.

4. David McCullough, *Truman* (Simon & Schuster, 1992), pp. 500–501.

5. Ibid., p. 501.

6. Clark Clifford, *Counsel to the President* (Random House, 1991), pp. 88–90.

7. Ibid., p. 91.

8. Cochran, op. cit., pp. 207–8.

9. Harry S Truman, *Memoirs* (Doubleday, 1956), p. 471.

10. McCullough, op. cit., p. 897. A panel of sixty-five legal scholars, rating the first one hundred Supreme Court judges, found only eight "Failures," and Vinson was the only one of these who was a Chief Justice. Albert P. Blaustein and Roy M. Mersky, *The First One Hundred Justices: Statistical Studies on the Supreme Court of the United States* (Archon Books, 1978), p. 40.

11. In the experts' ranking of Justices mentioned in the last note, Minton joins Vinson as one of the eight "Failures," while Reed is classified as merely "Average."

12. Of the six in the majority, two (Black and Frankfurter) are in the experts' list of twelve "Greats." Two more (Douglas and Jackson) are among the "Near Greats." One (Tom Clark) is merely "Average," and one (Burton) is among the "Failures."

13. Truman, op. cit., p. 426.

14. Actually, Congress made its view of the seizure clear just after it occurred—it cut off funding for the steel mills under government operation. Then after the Court's decision, it rejected Truman's appeal for Congress to force the mills to operate. Truman, op. cit., pp. 473, 477.

15. Max Farrand, ed., *The Records of the Federal Convention of 1787* (Yale University Press, 1911), vol. 1, p. 254.

16. Kenneth R. Mayer, *With the Stroke of a Pen: Executive Orders and Presidential Power* (Princeton University Press, 2001), pp. 51–52.

17. Ibid., p. 79.

18. *Ex Parte Milligan* (April 3, 1866). The legitimacy of martial rule in regained Confederate land was affirmed in *U.S. v. Diekleman* (1875). Cf. James G. Randall, *Constitutional Problems Under Lincoln* (A. Appleton, 1926), pp. 225–28.

19. *Ex Parte Merryman* (May 27, 1861).

20. Abraham Lincoln, "Proclamation," in *Speeches and Writings,* ed. Merrill D. Peterson (Library of America, 1989), vol. 2, p. 371.

21. Randall, op. cit., pp. 59–65.

22. Lincoln, op. cit., p. 424.

23. Ibid., p. 497 (Lincoln to James Conklin, August 25, 1863).

24. Ibid., p. 501 (Lincoln to Salmon Chase, September 2, 1863).

25. Randall, op. cit., pp. 371–85. And see Brian McGinty, *Lincoln and the Court* (Harvard University Press, 2008), pp. 111, 314–16.

26. Richard H. Dana, *New York Tribune,* April 13, 1865.

27. Jon DiIulio, *Esquire,* October 2002.

28. William G. Howell, *Power Without Persuasion: The Politics of Direct Presidential Action* (Princeton University Press, 2003), p. 6.

29. Mayer, op. cit., p. 3.

30. Louis Fisher, "Laws Congress Never Made," *Constitution* (Fall 1993), p. 60.

31. Mayer, op. cit., p. 3.

32. Ibid., p. 25.

33. Ibid., pp. 29–31.

CHAPTER 9: SECRECY AS EMBARRASSMENT COVER

1. Daniel Patrick Moynihan, *Secrecy: The American Experience* (Yale University Press, 1998), p. 160.

2. Kenneth R. Mayer, *With the Stroke of a Pen: Executive Orders and Presidential Power* (Princeton University Press, 2001), p. 142.

3. Max Weber, "Bureaucracy," in *Essays in Sociology,* trans. H. H. Gerth and C. Wright Mills (Oxford University Press, 1946), pp. 233–34.

4. Moynihan, op. cit., p. 75.

5. *Information Security Oversight Office of the National Archives, Report to the President* 13 (2006).

6. Mayer, op. cit., p. 145: "In the 1950s, the Army War College prepared an annual guide to the U.S. government consisting of basic information on the separation of power, the Constitution, and the organization of the executive branch. It quoted extensively from the Constitution. In July 1953 the College asked the White House to check the accuracy of revisions to a new edition of the book, the pages of which were classified 'Restricted.' Evidently the Army considered the Constitution and the U.S. Government Manual military secrets."

7. Lynne Duke, "How to Bury a Secret," *Washington Post,* January 16, 2007.

8. Peter M. Shane, *Madison's Nightmare: How Executive Power Threatens American Democracy* (University of Chicago Press, 2009), p. 122.

9. Mayer, op. cit., p. 145.

10. Erwin Griswold, "Secrets Not Worth Keeping," *Washington Post,* February 15, 1989.

11. Barry Siegel, *Claim of Privilege: A Mysterious Plane Crash, a Landmark Supreme Court Case, and the Rise of State Secrets* (Harper, 2008), pp. 185, 297, 361.

12. Louis Fisher, *In the Name of National Security: Unchecked Presidential Power and the Reynolds Case* (University Press of Kansas, 2006), pp. 44–46.

13. Siegel, op. cit., p. 133.

14. Fisher, op. cit., p. 218.

15. Siegel, op. cit., p. 117.

16. Albert P. Blaustein and Roy M. Mersky, *The First One Hundred Justices: Statistical Studies on the Supreme Court of the United States* (Archon Books, 1978), pp. 37–40.

17. Chief Justice Fred Vinson, *United States v. Reynold et al.,* 345 U.S. 1 (1953).

18. Ibid.

19. Siegel, op. cit., p. 41.

20. Fisher, op. cit., pp. 171–75.

21. Siegel, op. cit., p. 249.

22. Ibid., pp. 195–97.

23. Ibid., pp. 261–62.

24. Ibid., p. 263.

CHAPTER 10: SECRECY AS CONGRESS DECEIVER

1. National Security Act, 503 b1.

2. *Iran-Contra Affair: Report of the Congressional Committees Investigating the Iran-Contra Affair* (Government Printing Office, 1988), vol. 1, p. 208.

3. *Testimony at Joint Hearing Before the House Select Committee to Investigate Covert Arms Transaction with Iran and the Senate Select Committee on Secret Military Assistance to Iran and the Nicaraguan Opposition* (Government Printing Office, 1987), vol. 3, p. 267.

4. Theodore Draper, *A Very Thin Line: The Iran-Contra Affairs* (Hill and Wang, 1997), pp. 185–91.

5. Lou Cannon, *President Reagan: The Role of a Lifetime* (Public Affairs, 2000), p. 581.

6. Colonel North was convicted of using missile sale money for a fence at his home, and Richard Secord and others took over four million dollars of the funds as "commission" (Cannon, op. cit., p. 524).

7. Lawrence E. Walsh, *Firewall: The Iran-Contra Conspiracy and Cover-Up* (W. W. Norton, 1997), p. 346.

8. Ibid., pp. 170–81.

9. Ibid., pp. 454–59.

10. William Shawcross, *Sideshow: Kissinger, Nixon, and the Destruction of Cambodia* (Simon & Schuster, 1979), p. 29.

11. Ibid., pp. 22–24.

12. Tom Wells, *The War Within: America's Battle over Vietnam* (University of California Press, 1994), p. 421.

13. Shawcross, op. cit., p. 140.

14. Ibid., p. 28.

15. Walter Isaacson *Kissinger: A Biography* (Simon & Schuster, 1992), pp. 275–77.

16. Richard Reeves, *Richard Nixon: Alone in the White House* (Simon & Schuster, 2001), p. 216.

17. Wells, op. cit., p. 425.

18. Shawcross, op. cit., p. 214.

19. Arthur M. Schlesinger, Jr., *Robert Kennedy and His Times* (Houghton Mifflin, 1978), pp. 482–85.

20. Tim Weiner, *Legacy of Ashes: The History of the CIA* (Doubleday, 2007), pp. 186–87.

21. Arthur M. Schlesinger, Jr., *The Imperial Presidency,* with new epilogue (Houghton Mifflin, 1989), p. 478.

22. Porter McKeever, *Adlai Stevenson: His Life and Legacy* (William Morrow, 1989), pp. 489–90.

23. Alistair Cooke, "Adlai Stevenson, the Failed Saint," in *Six Men* (Alfred A. Knopf, 1977), pp. 137–38.

24. Schlesinger, op. cit., p. 472.

25. Ibid., p. 476.

26. Ibid., p. 480.

27. Ibid., p. 478.

28. Michael Dobbs, *One Minute to Midnight: Kennedy, Khrushchev, and Castro on the Brink of Nuclear War* (Alfred A. Knopf, 2008), p. 17.

29. Ibid., pp. 178–79.

30. Ibid., pp. 33–34.

31. Daniel Patrick Moynihan, *Secrecy: The American Experience* (Yale University Press, 1998), pp. 16, 54, 144–46.

32. McKeever, op. cit., pp. 531–32. Since Kennedy had leaked to Fritchey his displeasure with Chester Bowles before forcing him out, it was widely thought that Kennedy was signaling a plan to get rid of Stevenson. McKeever, a friend of Stevenson's as well as his biographer, thinks it was a way of "cutting Stevenson down to size" rather than forcing him out.

CHAPTER 11: SECRECY AS POLICY DISABLER

1. *New York Times,* November 29, 1990; *Foreign Affairs,* March–April 1999, p. 47.

2. Arthur M. Schlesinger, Jr., *Robert Kennedy and His Times* (Houghton Mifflin, 1978), p. 44.

3. Theodore C. Sorensen, *Kennedy* (Harper & Row, 1965), p. 305.

4. Daniel Patrick Moynihan, *Secrecy: The American Experience* (Yale University Press, 1998), pp. 222–23.

5. Sorensen, op. cit., p. 295.

6. Arthur M. Schlesinger, Jr., *A Thousand Days: John F. Kennedy in the White House* (Houghton Mifflin, 1965), p. 272.

7. Evan Thomas, *The Very Best Men—Four Who Dared: The Early Years of the CIA* (Simon & Schuster, 1995), p. 249.

8. Ibid., p. 244.

9. Sorensen, op. cit., p. 296.

10. Thomas, op. cit., pp. 247–48.

11. Keeping his campaign promise to "go to Korea" if elected, Eisenhower flew by small "spotter" airplane over the battle terrain and found the enemy entrenchments too hard to take at an acceptable cost. Dwight D. Eisenhower, *Mandate for Change* (Doubleday, 1963), pp. 94–96. As Murray Kempton said of this passage: "All else would be conversation; one look had decided Eisenhower to fold the war." Kempton, "The Underestimation of Dwight D. Eisenhower," in *Rebellions, Perversities, and Main Events* (Times Books, 1994), p. 441.

12. Though some military advisers told Eisenhower he would have to confront rebel forces inland, he confined U.S. troops to the country's harbor capital: "If the Lebanese army were unable to subdue the rebels when we had secured their capital and protected their government, I felt, we were backing up a government with so little popular support that we probably should not be there." Dwight D. Eisenhower, *Waging Peace, 1956–1961* (Doubleday, 1965), p. 275.

13. Ibid., p. 631.

14. Ibid., pp. 613–14.

15. Kempton, op. cit., p. 445.

16. Sorensen, op. cit., pp. 304, 307.

17. *The Eisenhower Diaries*, ed. Robert H. Farrell (W. W. Norton, 1981), p. 390.

18. Stephen Ambrose, *Eisenhower, Soldier and President* (Simon & Schuster, 1990), p. 553.

19. Ibid., p. 554.

20. Thomas, op. cit., p. 347.

21. Ibid., p. 296.

22. Ibid., p. 297.

23. Sorensen, op. cit., p. 298.

24. Ibid., p. 302.

25. Schlesinger, *A Thousand Days,* p. 260.

26. Ibid., p. 261.

27. Thomas, op. cit., p. 242.

28. Sorensen, op. cit., p. 302.

29. Schlesinger, *A Thousand Days,* p. 262.

30. John Prados and Margaret Pratt Porter, *Inside the Pentagon Papers* (University Press of Kansas, 2004), p. 119.

31. Executive Order 10501 (1953).

32. David Rudenstine, *The Day the Presses Stopped: A History of the Pentagon Papers Case* (University of California Press, 1996), p. 36.

33. Tom Wells, *Wild Man: The Life and Times of Daniel Ellsberg* (St. Martin's Press, 2001), p. 165.

34. Rudenstine, op. cit., pp. 31–41. There were fifteen copies of the Papers, locked in various safes, including five in the Pentagon, one in Henry Kissinger's National Security Council safe, two at the State Department, two in the Washington office of RAND. These last two were in the custody of Leslie Gelb, Morton Halperin, and Paul Warnke. The first two men gave Ellsberg access to the Papers, without suspecting that he would copy and leak them.

35. Prados and Porter, op. cit., pp. 75–77.

36. Ibid., pp. 6, 86.

37. Walter Isaacson, *Kissinger: A Biography* (Simon & Schuster, 1992), p. 329.

38. John Ehrlichman, *Witness to Power* (Pocket Books, 1982), pp. 275–76.

39. Henry Kissinger, *Years of Renewal* (Simon & Schuster, 1999), pp. 53–54.

40. William Safire, *Before the Fall: An Inside View of the Pre-Watergate White House* (Doubleday, 1975), pp. 296–97.

41. Prados and Porter, op. cit., pp. 80–81.

42. Wells, op. cit., pp. 492–501.

43. Rudenstine, op. cit., pp. 346–47.

44. Ibid., p. 267.

45. Prados and Porter, op. cit., pp. 125–26.

46. Rudenstine, op. cit., pp. 266–67.

47. *New York Times Co. v. U.S.* (1971). The majority was made up of Hugo Black, William O. Douglas, William Brennan, Potter Stewart, Byron White, and Thurgood Marshall. The dissenters were Warren Burger, John Marshall Harlan, and Harry Blackmun.

48. Prados and Porter, op. cit., pp. 147–82.

49. Erwin N. Griswold, "Secrets Not Worth Keeping," *Washington Post,* February 15, 1989.

CHAPTER 12: SECRECY AS CRIME CONCEALER

1. For the 1967 explosion of an Air India plane on which Zhou Enlai was supposed to be flying, see Brian Urquhart, *Hammarskjold* (Harper & Row, 1971), p. 121; Arthur M. Schlesinger, Jr., *Robert Kennedy and His Times* (Houghton Mifflin, 1978), p. 481; Peter Grose, *Gentleman Spy: The Life of Allen Dulles* (Houghton Mifflin, 1994), pp. 411, 501, 505. CIA Director William Colby called complicity in the Diem murders America's "worst mistake of the Vietnam War"—Stephen Kinzer, *Overthrow: America's Century of Regime Change from Hawaii to Iraq* (Henry Holt, 2006), p. 207.

2. The United States Army School of the Americas, run at Fort Benning in Georgia, was based on a simple premise: Cheaper than training and financing insurgents in Latin America to overthrow left-wing governments is the training of right-wing military leaders to put down revolutionaries. In this way, the school trained people who turned out to be violators of human rights like Manuel Noriega. See Lesley Gill, *The School of the Americas: Military Training and Political Violence in the Americas* (Duke University Press, 2004)—pp. 80–81 on Noriega; p. 237 summarizing SOA graduates in "the impunity-backed state terror that fractured countries such as Guatemala, El Salvador, Chile, and Argentina." In 2001, the school was renamed the Western Hemisphere Institute for Security Cooperation.

3. Kinzer, op. cit., pp. 1–6.

4. Tim Weiner, *Legacy of Ashes: The History of the CIA* (Doubleday, 2007), p. 53.

5. Kinzer, op. cit., p. 122.

6. James A. Bill, *The Eagle and the Lion: The Tragedy of American-Iranian Relations* (Yale University Press, 1988), p. 63.

7. Kinzer, op. cit., pp. 75–76.

8. Stephen Ambrose, *Eisenhower, Soldier and President* (Simon & Schuster, 1990), p. 354.

9. Stephen Kinzer, *All the Shah's Men: An American Coup and the Roots of Middle East Terror* (John Wiley & Sons, 2008), p. 159.

10. Bill, op. cit., p. 87.

11. Kermit Roosevelt, *Countercoup: The Struggle for the Control of Iran* (McGraw-Hill, 1979).

12. Thomas Powers, *Intelligence Wars: America's Secret History from Hitler to al-Qaeda*, rev. ed. (New York Review Books, 2004), p. 160.

13. Kinzer, *All the Shah's Men*, pp. 129–30.

14. Nick Cullather, *Secret History: The CIA's Classified Account of Its Operations in Guatemala, 1952–1954* (Stanford University Press, 1999), p. 21.

15. Grose, op. cit., pp. 377–81.

16. Ibid., p. 382.

17. Weiner, op. cit., pp. 583–84; John Prados, *Lost Crusader: The Secret Wars of CIA Director William Colby* (Oxford University Press, 2003), p. 320: "Frederick Baron, the single Church committee staffer allowed access to the cable traffic on the case of the death of African nationalist Patrice Lumumba, came away with what he recalled as 'the clearest evidence that a president [Eisenhower] had ordered an assassination attempt.' Baron, a lawyer from the 'Show Me' state of Missouri and formerly aide to the director of the National Legal Aid and Defender Association, would not have come to that conclusion lightly."

18. Prados, op. cit., pp. 320–21.

19. Powers, op. cit., p. 52.

20. Weiner, op. cit., pp. 138–40.

21. Powers, op. cit., p. 167.

22. Weiner, op. cit., p. 308.

23. Walter Isaacson, *Kissinger: A Biography* (Simon & Schuster, 1992), p. 290.

24. Weiner, op. cit., p. 309.

25. Ibid., pp. 210–12; Isaacson, op. cit., pp. 303–11.

26. Kinzer, *Overthrow,* p. 238.

27. Ibid., pp. 1–6.

CHAPTER 13: "WAR POWERS"

1. James Madison, "Helvidius," No. 1, August 14, 1791, in Thomas A. Mason et al., *The Papers of James Madison* (University Press of Virginia, 1985), vol. 15, pp. 69–71. Compare Madison's letter to Jefferson, April 2, 1798: "The Constitution supposes, what the history of all governments demonstrates, that the Executive is the branch of power most interested in war and most prone to it. It has accordingly with studied care vested the question of war in the Legislature." James Morton Smith, ed., *The Republic of Letters: The Correspondence Between Thomas Jefferson and James Madison, 1776–1826* (W. W. Norton, 1995), vol. 2, p. 1032.

2. John Yoo, *The Powers of War and Peace: The Constitution and Foreign Affairs After 9/11* (University of Chicago Press, 2005), p. 145.

3. Peter Irons, *War Powers: How the Imperial Presidency Hijacked the Constitution* (Henry Holt, 2005), p. 196.

4. Ibid., p. 199.

5. Ibid., p. 201.

6. Congressman Dick Cheney, on *The MacNeil/Lehrer News Hour,* PBS, April 11, 1986.

7. Louis Fisher, *Presidential War Power,* 2nd ed., rev. (University Press of Kansas, 2004), p. 164. President Reagan's air strikes hit Tripoli and Benghazi, killing Qaddafi's daughter, wounding his two sons, and killing many civilians, to the outrage of many in the international community—cf. Lou Cannon, *President Reagan: The Role of a Lifetime* (Public Affairs, 1991), p. 580.

8. Bob Woodward, *The Commanders* (Simon & Schuster, 1991), p. 346.

9. Charles Tiefer, *The Semi-Sovereign Presidency: The Bush Administration's Strategy for Governing Without Congress* (Westview Press, 1994), p. 128.

10. Ibid., p. 126.

11. Fisher, op. cit., p. 174.

12. Barton Gellman, *Angler: The Cheney Vice Presidency* (Penguin, 2008), p. 101.

13. Yoo, op. cit., p. 145.

14. *Oxford English Dictionary,* "declare" 5 c, "to declare war": "1552 Huloet, 'Declare warre, *arma canere, bellum judicare.*'"

15. Max Farrand, ed., *The Records of the Federal Convention of 1787* (Yale University Press, 1911), vol. 2, p. 319.

CHAPTER 14: CHALLENGING SECRECY

1. Henry Kissinger, *Years of Renewal* (Simon & Schuster, 1999), p. 324.

2. Thomas Powers, *The Man Who Kept the Secrets: Richard Helms and the CIA* (Alfred A. Knopf, 1979), p. 297.

3. John Prados, *Lost Crusader: The Secret Wars of CIA Director William Colby* (Oxford University Press, 2003), pp. 266–68.

4. William Colby, *Honorable Men: My Life in the CIA* (Simon & Schuster, 1978), pp. 414–16.

5. James Mann, *Rise of the Vulcans: The History of Bush's War Cabinet* (Penguin Books, 2004), p. 61.

6. Charlie Savage, *Takeover: The Return of the Imperial Presidency and the Subversion of American Democracy* (Little, Brown, 2007), p. 35.

7. Prados, op. cit., p. 299.

8. Ibid., pp. 300–301. Cf. Tim Weiner, *Legacy of Ashes: The History of the CIA* (Doubleday, 2007), pp. 338–39; Colby, op. cit., p. 409.

9. Powers, op. cit., p. 291.

10. Ibid., p. 293.

11. Colby, op. cit., p. 400.

12. Powers, op. cit., p. 272.

13. Prados, op. cit., p. 309.

14. Colby, op. cit., pp. 395–96.

15. Ibid., pp. 337–38.

16. Ibid., pp. 338–40; Prados, op. cit., p. 260; Kissinger, op. cit., p. 312.

17. Prados, op. cit., p. 310.

18. Kissinger, op. cit., p. 326.

19. Prados, op. cit., p. 324.

20. Ibid., p. 307. Colby had met Knox in England, where they were both training to parachute behind enemy lines during World War II (Colby, op. cit., p. 36). Kissinger, when castigating Colby's timorous behavior with Congress, had to admit that he had (with Knox) been an exceptionally courageous fighter in the underground resistance of World War II (Kissinger, op. cit., p. 325), which makes rather despicable Kissinger's suggestion that Colby was selling out his country in 1975.

21. Prados, op. cit., p. 310.

22. Powers, op. cit., p. 300.

23. Thomas Powers, *Intelligence Wars: America's Secret History from Hitler to al-Qaeda*, rev. ed. (New York Review Books, 2004), pp. 279–80.

24. Colby, op. cit., p. 433.

25. Richard Helms with William Hood, *A Look over My Shoulder: A Life in the Central Intelligence Agency* (Random House, 2003), p. 433.

26. Colby, op. cit., pp. 383–87.

27. Powers, *The Man Who Kept the Secrets,* pp. 298–305.

28. Kissinger, op. cit., p. 343.

29. Powers, *The Man Who Kept the Secrets,* p. 298.

30. Kissinger, op. cit., p. 340.

31. Prados, op. cit., p. 314.

CHAPTER 15: THE UNITARY EXECUTIVE

1. Edwin Meese III, *With Reagan: The Inside Story* (Regnery, 1992), p. 322.

2. Thomas Friedman, *Hot, Flat, and Crowded: Why We Need a Green Revolution and How It Can Renew America* (Farrar, Straus & Giroux, 2008), p. 14.

3. Lou Cannon, *President Reagan: The Role of a Lifetime* (Public Affairs, 2000), p. 740.

4. Max Farrand, ed., *The Records of the Federal Convention of 1787* (Yale University Press, 1911), vol. 2, p. 537.

5. For Hamilton's monarchizing President see ibid., vol. 1, p. 289.

6. Steven G. Calabresi and Christopher S. Yoo, *The Unitary Executive: Presidential*

Power from Washington to Bush (Yale University Press, 2008), pp. 10–12, 19, 402–4.

7. Ibid., pp. 20–21, 429.

8. Henry Kissinger, *Years of Renewal* (Simon & Schuster, 1999), p. 323.

9. Edwin Meese III, "The Law of the Constitution," *Tulane Law Review* 61 (1987), p. 985.

10. *The Lincoln-Douglas Debates,* ed. Rodney O. Davis and Douglas L. Wilson (University of Illinois Press, 2008), pp. 222–23.

11. *La Abra Silver Mining Co. v. United States* (1899), 175 U.S. 423.

12. Christopher S. Kelley, "The Significance of Presidential Signing Statements," in Kelley, *Executing the Constitution: Putting the President Back into the Constitution* (State University of New York Press, 2006), pp. 75–76.

13. Ibid., p. 74.

14. Edwin Meese III, Address to the National Press Club, February 25, 1986.

15. Ralph Tarr, OLC memo, October 28, 1985, cited in Charlie Savage, *Takeover: The Return of the Imperial Presidency and the Subversion of American Democracy* (Little, Brown, 2007), p. 233.

16. Ibid., pp. 233–34 (Alito, LSWG memo, February 6, 1986).

17. Phillip J. Cooper, "George W. Bush, Edgar Allan Poe, and the Use and Abuse of Presidential Signing Statements," *Presidential Studies Quarterly* 35 (2005), p. 519.

18. Ibid., pp. 519, 527.

19. Neil Kinkopf and Peter M. Shane, "Signed Under Protest," a Database of Presidential Signing Statements (2007). President Clinton raised objections to 105 sections of the laws he signed in his eight years as President.

20. Cooper, op. cit., p. 521.

21. Savage, op. cit., p. 230.

22. *Presidential Signing Statements: Constitutional and Institutional Implications* (Congressional Research Service, 2007), Summary. This report concluded: "It appears that recent administrations, as made apparent by the voluminous challenges lodged by President George W. Bush, have employed these instruments in an attempt to leverage power and control away from Congress by establishing these broad assertions of authority as a constitutional norm."

23. Charles Tiefer, *The Semi-Sovereign President: The Bush Administration's Strategy for Governing Without Congress* (Westview Press, 1994), p. 58.

24. Savage, op. cit., p. 240.

25. *Task Force on Presidential Signing Statements and the Separation of Powers Doctrine* (American Bar Association, 2006), pp. 13–14.

CHAPTER 16: AMERICAN MONARCH

1. Jane Mayer, *The Dark Side: The Inside Story of How the War on Terror Turned into a War on American Ideals* (Doubleday, 2008), p. 66.

2. John Yoo, Memorandum to General Counsel at the Pentagon, William Haynes, March 14, 2003.

3. Greg Miller, "Waterboarding Is Legal, White House Says," *Los Angeles Times,* February 7, 2008.

4. John Yoo and Douglas Cassel Debate, Chicago Council on Foreign Relations, December 1, 2005.

5. John Yoo, *War by Other Means: An Insider's Account of the War on Terror* (Atlantic Monthly Press, 2006), p. xii.

6. Ibid., p. x.

7. Charlie Savage, *Takeover: The Return of the Imperial Presidency and the Subversion of American Democracy* (Little, Brown, 2007), p. 211.

8. Jack Goldsmith, *The Terror Presidency: Law and Judgment Inside the Bush Administration* (W. W. Norton, 2007), pp. 148–49.

9. Tim Golden, "Administration Officials Split over Stalled Military Tribunals," *New York Times,* October 25, 2004.

10. Barton Gellman, *Angler: The Cheney Vice Presidency* (Penguin, 2008), p. 346.

11. Ibid., p. 352.

12. Goldsmith, op. cit., p. 171.

13. Yoo, *War by Other Means,* p. 182.

14. Savage, op. cit., p. 191.

15. Peter M. Shane, *Madison's Nightmare: How Executive Power Threatens American Democracy* (University of Chicago Press, 2009), pp. 106–8.

16. Eric Schmitt, "President Backs McCain Measure on Inmate Abuse," *New York Times,* December 16, 2005.

17. Gellman, op. cit., p. 388.

18. Savage, op. cit., p. 225.

19. An interim report two years before the end of Bush's term was Sean Wilentz, "The Worst President in History?" *Rolling Stone,* April 21, 2006.

20. The words were reported by James Comey, in the best treatment of this whole sequence of events, Gellman, op. cit., pp. 299–323.

21. Ibid., p. 324.

22. Ibid., p. 318.

23. Ibid., p. 323.

AFTERWORD

1. Jane Mayer, "The Secret History," *New Yorker,* June 22, 2008.

2. Charlie Savage, "Obama's War on Terror May Resemble Bush's in Some Areas," *New York Times,* February 18, 2009.

3. John Schwartz, "Obama Backs Off a Reversal on Secrets," *New York Times,* February 8, 2009; Chris Herder, "Obama and State Secrets? Shhh . . .," *Columbia Journalism Review,* April 10, 2009.

4. Nancy Youseff, "Why'd Obama Switch on Detainee Photos?" McClatchy News Service, June 1, 2009.

5. Evan Perez and Siobhan Gorman, "Obama Tilts to CIA on Memos," *Wall Street Journal,* April 16, 2009; R. Jeffrey Smith and Joby Warrick, "CIA Fights Full Release of Detainee Report," *Washington Post,* June 7, 2009.

6. Savage, op. cit.

7. Mayer, op. cit.

8. Matthew Yglesias, "Obama's 'Don't Ask, Don't Tell' Hypocrisy," *Daily Beast,* May 11, 2009.

9. "A Bad Call on Gay Rights," editorial, *New York Times,* June 15, 2009.

10. Bill Dedman, "Obama Blocks Access to White House Visitor List," MSNBC, June 16, 2009.

11. Smith and Warrick, op. cit.

12. Mayer, op. cit.

13. David Vine, *Island of Shame: The Secret History of the U.S. Military Base on Diego Garcia* (Princeton University Press, 2009), pp. 41–55.

14. Ibid., pp. 63–64.

15. Ibid., pp. 87–88.

16. Jane Mayer, *The Dark Side: The Inside Story of How the War on Terror Turned into a War on American Ideals* (Doubleday, 2008), p. 124.

INDEX